FIRE HALL COOKING

with JEFF the CHEF

FIRE HALL COOKING

with

JEFF the CHEF

SUREFIRE RECIPES TO FEED YOUR CREW

JEFF DERRAUGH

VICTORIA · VANCOUVER · CALGARY

TouchWood Editions	TouchWood Editions
#108–17665 66A Avenue	PO Box 468
Surrey, BC V3S 2A7	Custer, WA
www.touchwoodeditions.com	98240-0468

LIBRARY AND ARCHIVES CANADA CATALOGUING IN PUBLICATION

Derraugh, Jeff, 1959–
    Fire hall cooking with Jeff the Chef: surefire recipes to feed your crew / Jeff Derraugh.

Includes index.

ISBN 978-1-894898-56-0

    1. Cookery. 2. Fire stations—Anecdotes. 3. Fire fighters—Anecdotes.
I. Title.

TX714.D46 2007   641.5   C2007-902323-1

LIBRARY OF CONGRESS CONTROL NUMBER: 2006940549

Edited by Marlyn Horsdal
Proofread by Marial Shea
Book design and layout by Jacqui Thomas
Cover photographs by Lee Harrison. Pictured on front are Glen Godri (left), Jeff Derraugh (centre) and Mike Dowhayko (right).

Printed in Canada by Friesens

TouchWood Editions acknowledges the financial support for its publishing program from the Government of Canada through the Book Publishing Industry Development Program (BPIDP), Canada Council for the Arts, and the province of British Columbia through the British Columbia Arts Council and the Book Publishing Tax Credit.

PRIMARY SEARCH

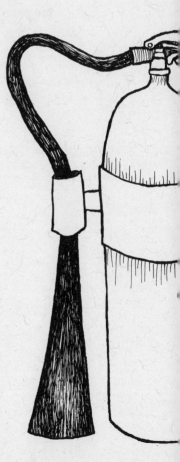

For my brother firefighters, Captain Tom Nichols and Captain Harold Lessard,

two courageous leaders who made the ultimate sacrifice while

serving the citizens of Winnipeg, on February 4, 2007.

May your guiding spirits forever live on.

THE PART NO ONE READS

Hey, what are you doing? I thought you'd skip by the intro and get right into the recipes, and I could just fill this space with meaningless drivel. Great—now I have to make something up here. Some friend you are, putting me on the spot before I even get going.

(Pssst ... Introduce yourself and tell them why you wrote the book.)

Oh sure, good idea. I'm Jeff Derraugh, also known by my fire hall nickname, Jeff the Chef. How did I get to be the go-to food guy in the hall? Like most firehouse chefs, I simply volunteered to pick up groceries. I had some humble beginnings, believe me, but my crewmates stuck with me and through their reinforcement, both positive and negative, I've come to be under the delusion that I've actually figured this gig out.

I should admit that I'm not a trained cook, at least not in the traditional sense. I trained with my comrades in the fire hall, picking up secrets, getting ideas, trying new recipes and experimenting with bold new food combinations. I love food, and you probably won't find a group of people as into food as firefighters. The first question before the next shift is, "What are we having tomorrow?" The anticipation of sharing a great meal together is one of the reasons we look forward to coming to work.

In Winnipeg we work two 10-hour day shifts followed by two 14-hour nights, so unlike departments that work 24-hour shifts, we only have to worry about serving one meal per shift. On days we'll serve lunch Monday through Friday, with brunch on weekends, and on each night shift we serve dinner. At some halls firefighters take turns cooking, while in others they rely on one or more chefs—rank, seniority or sex mattering not— to come through with a meal, and it better be good because firefighters' appetites are incredible and demand to be satisfied. As seasoned veteran Doug Miller told me when I contemplated cooking my rookie meal back in 1990, "Jeff, the firefighters' triangle has three requirements, and each one must be met for a successful fire hall meal. The big three are delicious flavour, ample quantities and reasonable price. If you fail to meet any of these, in any way, well, you're in for one loooooooong night!"

Cooking in the firehouse has its advantages. It can get you out of daily cleaning duties and cut short your participation in practice drill sessions. Also, firefighters may spare you the wrath of their practical jokes because they know that since you cook their food, you have the ultimate power. As it is often said, "Don't mess with the fire hall chef."

This book came about when I decided that my recipes were too disorganized. Some were written on scrap paper, some were cut out of magazines while others were in books, defaced by notes that I'd jotted down to remind myself of the modifications I'd made. Then came the big motivator: losing my handwritten recipe book at the fire hall. I knew that it was time to get my act together, and assemble those favourite recipes in one accessible place. Enter the personal computer!

Once I started writing this book I thought, "You know, this would make a nice gift. Friends do favours and rarely want money in return, so I'll pass along my recipe collection as a thank you." Plans changed when fellow firefighters found out about the cookbook and wanted copies. Requests grew exponentially as friends, and friends of friends, heard the word. The response has been not only humbling but also valuable, as reader feedback has led to numerous enhancements and revisions. So go ahead and take a shot; I welcome any constructive criticism you may have. Believe me, as a firefighter working in a hall full of critics, pests and practical jokers, I've developed thick skin.

The recipes in this book were inspired by a number of sources, and to give credit where credit is due, I've tried to acknowledge them. You'll notice many contributions from friends and fellow firefighters. They've cooked these recipes for me, and I've in turn prepared them for family, friends and firefighters alike. Other culinary creations were prompted by restaurant dishes that I loved and felt compelled to clone or by my Pavlov's-dog-like reaction to recipes that I've spotted in books, magazines or on the Internet.

Call it a human failing if you will, but I just can't help but tinker with a good thing. So I'll personalize the basic recipe idea, modify it, play around with it and even blend elements from two, three or more recipes together in an attempt to make it even better. I hope that you do the same with these recipes.

Hey, you could even host a firehouse-theme dinner party! Just remember to invite guests who can eat twice what mere mortals can, and hope that the alarm gong doesn't ring as soon as you sit down to eat.

So let's get cooking. It's time for food, folks and firehouse fun!

Omissions, omissions

I know what you'll be thinking after you've read a few of my recipes: "Why doesn't this jerk include pertinent information such as prep time and nutritional breakdown in his recipes?"

Glad you asked. I'd be happy to address your concerns.

Preparation Time: Let's face it, some cooks just work faster than others; some can only mono-task, while other "octopus chefs" simultaneously chop, sauté and barbecue, as pots of pasta and sauce boil away on the range. Factor in phone calls, people popping by for a visit unannounced, or, in the case of the firehouse, the alarm gong ringing, and that estimated prep time is right out the window anyway. I refuse to be held responsible for such intangibles.

Nutritional Info: As I've mentioned, I'm no trained chef and I'm definitely no dietician. So why waste time and money having food analyzed by a lab when you're only going to sabotage the calorie count by powering back slices of white Texas Toast slathered with butter before supper? Then, an hour or two after dining, you'll be tying into a bucket of Rocky Road ice cream topped with mounds of double-double, ooey-gooey chocolate sauce, and I'll be the one held accountable for your weight gain. "He misled me. He said that his meals average only 400 calories per serving. I'm going to sue!" Sorry, my friend, but you're not going to suck me into your little game that easily.

Also, nutritional breakdowns feature details such as "Contains 2 grams of dietary fibre" or "a good source of iron and calcium." Ask a firefighter, "Would you like to have meal A, or meal B, which is a good source of calcium?" His answer will invariably be, "Which one's cheaper?" Nutritional analysis is of no concern to firefighters; they eat so much of every food group that their diet couldn't possibly be deficient in any area.

Besides, you could be reading this book 10 years from now, and by that time the Whale Blubber Diet could be in vogue. So really, why pick apart a perfectly delicious meal by breaking it down into fat, protein, carbohydrates, calories, etc. It takes all the fun out of eating.

The bottom line is, all this information is only going to lead to worry and stress. That can't be healthy. I want you rubbing your tummy with glee, not clutching your chest with pain! Ignorance is bliss, so laugh, smile and, above all, savour the flavour and enjoy the food. Life is good!

WHAT'S FOR BREKKIE? Breakfast, Breads and Brunch

AAAHHH!! WHAT'S FOR BREKKIE?

THE FIREHOUSE BAKESHOP

AAAHHH!! WHAT'S FOR BREKKIE?

The standard response you'll get at many fire halls is bacon, sausages, eggs, hash browns and orange juice. Oh, and we're talking copious quantities of each. I remember years ago working for another firefighter at a cross-town firehouse. When the breakfast call was made, we descended upon the kitchen like hungry wolves, and as we served ourselves at the buffet-style spread, one of the guys asked, "How many bacon each?"

The response from the cook was, "Nine."

I couldn't believe my ears. "Nine?" I asked, "Nine pieces of bacon? You've got to be kidding!"

Well, the guys all looked at me as if I'd said, "What do you say we toss this crap out and get some of that tasty tofu going?"

Undaunted by the peer pressure, I exercised restraint and had three or four pieces of bacon, which cued the opportunistic captain to ask me, "If that's all you're having, Jeff, can I have yours?"

The man had 14 pieces of bacon. That's why our fire trucks now carry defibrillators, so that we can jump-start each other after we send that breakfast barge of cholesterol to our hearts.

Each weekend day shift at the fire hall is a traditional brunch day, but I grew tired of bacon and eggs alternating with sausages and eggs and started looking for alternatives. Omelettes, crepes, waffles, eggs Benny, frittatas, homemade fruit cocktail instead of orange juice—why, I've even served the **Outrageous Egg Foo Yung** recipe (page 145) for a fire hall breakfast, in my quest for something different.

But I'm not the only firefighter who thinks outside the cereal box. Michael—how's this for a firefighter's name?—Sparks makes a great **Breakfast Pizza** (page 12). Yes, fresh warm pizza from the oven, not stale cold pizza from the fridge. The recipe is in this book and it's fabulous!

Or try my pre-workout mix of steaming-hot oat bran cereal, combined with 3 tablespoons of ground flax. It's like a Roto-Rooter for your veins! You get dietary fibre, cholesterol-lowering and disease-fighting Omega 3 oils and ... man, am I getting old, or what!

So break free of the ordinary and try something different. Then, when your family, or family of firefighters, asks, "What's for brekkie?" you can fire off a menu item they weren't expecting to hear.

Grandma's Famous
BUTTERMILK PANCAKES

Well, they're famous in our family. On Fridays, when we were growing up, my grandmother would drop by to make them for lunch, which often led to a pancake-eating contest among my three brothers and me. My brother Mark always won, eating up to 10 or 12 of these size-large cakes. Yes, the boy should have become a firefighter. I've modified Grandma's original recipe by adding more eggs and whole-wheat flour to boost the protein count.

BATTER UP!

- 4 eggs—or as many as 6 for high protein
- ¼ cup white sugar
- 2 tablespoons vegetable oil
- 1 cup unbleached white flour
- 1 cup whole-wheat flour or another cup of white—your choice
- 1 teaspoon salt
- 1 teaspoon baking powder
- 1 teaspoon baking soda
- 2 cups buttermilk

THE BASES ARE LOADED, IT'S ALL UP TO YOU!

Heat the griddle to 275–300 degrees. A low temperature makes for golden-brown pancakes. If it's too high, the cakes will darken before the centre is cooked, and that's just not acceptable!

Combine the eggs, sugar and oil until creamed. Not creamed as in smeared, creamed as in creamy!

In a separate bowl, combine the flours, salt, baking powder and baking soda. Add the dries to the creamed along with the buttermilk, and fold with a wooden spoon until just combined—in other words, still a bit lumpy. For a thinner batter, simply add more buttermilk.

Grandma once broke a wooden spoon on my butt. Deservedly? Yes.

Place the batter on the griddle—not all at once—a ladleful at a time! When bubbles form on the top, flip them and cook until the cakes are cooked through. Remember, it's that handsome, golden-brown look you're after.

Serve them with maple syrup or go for gold and mix up some **Apple-Cinnamon** or **Berry Berry syrup**. Recipes for both are on page 4.

Blueberry Pancake Option: Toss blueberries in flour—to minimize bleeding—and add them to the batter just before cooking.

Incredible Homemade
PANCAKE SYRUPS

The fire hall kitty's running low on syrup? Not to worry, these from-scratch, "may- contain"-free syrups kick the storebought brands' butts around the block. The best thing is, they're no big fuss. The sauces go great over pancakes, waffles, French toast and even crepes!

FOR BOTH YOU'LL NEED

- 2 tablespoons butter
- ½ cup brown sugar
- ¼ cup water

LET'S GET IT TOGETHER

Melt the butter in a large frying pan over medium heat. Introduce the brown sugar, and meld the two together for about 3 minutes.

Add the water to the meld slowly, as it will start to sizzle and bubble.

FOR THE APPLE-CINNAMON SYRUP

Toss in ½ teaspoon cinnamon and about 3 large apples—sliced into thin wedges.

Cook until the apples are just tender, about 8 minutes.

If the syrup needs thickening, add 1 tablespoon each water and cornstarch mixed together. Pour in a little at a time. Or simply add a few tablespoons of apricot, strawberry or apple jam.

FOR THE BERRY BERRY SYRUP

Add a selection of your favourite berries to the basic syrup. I like a combination of blueberries, strawberries and cranberries. Try about ½ cup of each.

Cook over medium–low heat until the berries are softened.

Try adding a few tablespoons of your favourite jam—strawberry, blueberry, saskatoon berry. Go for it; try them all! The jam will both thicken and flavour the syrup.

So you went too nuts on the berries? Well, if you need more syrup, better get down on your knees and apologize to the bottled syrup and hope that its feelings aren't irreversibly hurt.

Better
BUTTERMILK WAFFLES

They're light, tasty and, with that whole-wheat flour blend, nutritious to boot. So don't waffle; set your mind to making these for breakfast today.

YOU'LL NEED A WAFFLE IRON AND ...

- 1 cup each whole-wheat and all-purpose flour
- 1 teaspoon baking soda
- ½ teaspoon salt
- ½ teaspoon cinnamon
- 2 tablespoons brown sugar
- 2 eggs, separated—no need to bring in a lawyer to draw up the divorce papers, that's only going to delay breakfast indefinitely!
- ⅓ cup melted butter
- 2 cups buttermilk

HERE'S HOW TO MAKE THEM LIGHT AND TASTY

In a bowl blend the flours, baking soda, salt, cinnamon and brown sugar with a whisk.

Separate the eggs. Place the whites in a second bowl and the yolks in a third, smaller bowl.

Add the melted butter and buttermilk to the yolks, and combine.

With a few strokes of a wooden spoon, add the wets to the dries.

Whip the whites with an electric mixer until they are just stiff but not so stiff that they become dry.

Now fold in the egg whites until they're just combined.

Scoop out ⅓ cup of batter for each waffle, or whatever amount your waffle iron calls for. Cook as per your waffle iron's instructions.

OH, FOR
CREPE'S SAKE!

They're easy, and you'll knock your company out with the presentation and flavour. Be creative with fillings and toppings, as just about anything goes!

THE MATERIALS

- 1 cup unbleached all-purpose flour
- 2 teaspoons sugar
- ¼ teaspoon salt
- 4 eggs
- 1¼ cups buttermilk, plus
  2 tablespoons water
- 5 tablespoons vegetable oil
- 1 19-ounce can pie filling—for example, peach, apple or blueberry
- Spray can of whipped cream—some people actually use it for cooking
- Icing sugar

THE CONSTRUCTION PLANS

In a bowl whisk together the flour, sugar and salt.

In a separate bowl scramble the eggs. Add the buttermilk—or milk if you wish—and water and blend them together.

Bring the dry ingredients into the egg/buttermilk mix while whipping the batter into a wild frenzy with a whisk.

Now add the vegetable oil slowly, whisking continually until smooth. Your batter should be thin, much thinner than pancake batter. If it appears too thick, just thin it out with more water.

Heat a 9-inch non-stick frying pan to medium low, give it a shot of vegetable spray, and pour in just enough batter to make a thin crepe. Tilt the pan to the side to make sure the batter makes it to the edges.

When the bottom is light brown, carefully flip it over and brown the other side.

Remove crepe from pan. Allow it to cool.

Place 3 healthy tablespoons of pie filling across each crepe. Roll up the crepe, top with a zigzag of whipping cream from one end of the crepe to the other and dust lightly with icing sugar.

Push this one over the top by topping them with one of the **Incredible Homemade Pancake Syrups** (page 4). Then do the whipped cream–icing sugar thing. Now we're talking decadence!

HAM-AND-ASPARAGUS
OMELETTE

Don't knock this one till you try it. You know how great Eggs Benedict are! Sure, they clog your arteries, but that's why man developed angioplasties. Make these for company and they'll ooohh and aaahh!

ROUND UP PER OMELETTE

- 2 large eggs
- **Hall-a-Blaze** (page 206) or packaged hollandaise sauce
- 3–4 stalks of asparagus—snap off the woody ends
- Kosher salt and pepper
- 2–3 thin slices of ham— try honey ham or Black Forest
- 1 tablespoon olive oil
- 1 or 2 teaspoons fresh parsley —chopped fine
- Dash of cayenne pepper

AND MAKE IT HAPPEN

Whisk the eggs together in a bowl with a dash of salt till scrambled.

Prepare the hollandaise sauce. You can use packaged hollandaise for convenience or, if you're making it for several people, try the homemade **Hall-a-Blaze Sauce**.

In a frying pan, melt a little butter over medium heat and add the asparagus. Add a dash of salt and a few grinds of pepper. Stir-fry until they just start to soften. Remove and set aside.

Heat the ham until just warmed in the microwave.

All of the elements are ready, so let's do it! Warm a non-stick frying pan over medium–low heat. Add a tablespoon of olive oil. Swish it around. Add the eggs and swirl them to cover the bottom of the pan. Cover and lower the heat to simmer. Cook until the eggs are completely set.

Place the ham open-faced in the centre of the omelette and place the asparagus across the middle. With a spatula, fold one side of the omelette over the ham and asparagus—you may have to hold it there for a second for it to stay. Now bring the other side over top. Heat through and remove to a plate.

Drizzle a generous amount of hollandaise over top. Sprinkle with cayenne pepper and parsley. Oh man, does that ever look good!

Overnight
OVEN OMELETTE

No, you don't throw it in the oven overnight and then wake to the sound of your alarm system blaring and firefighters breaking your door down with an axe! Rather, you prepare it the night before and pop it into the oven when you wake up. Have a shower, pour a coffee, and it's breakfast time!

LET'S SEE HERE, WE NEED

- About ¾ pound of bacon or ham or a combo of both
- 1 cup red onion—diced
- ½ green and ½ red pepper—diced
- 1 pound fresh mushrooms—sliced
- 1 dozen eggs
- 1½ cups milk
- 2 teaspoons each of seasoning salt and Italian seasoning
- 1 teaspoon dry mustard
- ¼ cup sherry—what is this, a hangover-remedy omelette?
- 4 cups of shredded cheese—I like a mix of mozzarella and cheddar

OH, SO WE CAN DO THIS THE NIGHT BEFORE?

Fry the bacon on medium heat until good and crisp. Remove the bacon to a paper-towel-lined plate to make it healthy—he giggled.

Add the onions and peppers to the bacon drippings. Hey, there's a lot of flavour to be had here! Okay, you can skip the drips if your pacemaker is starting to balk at simply the thought of it.

Add ½ teaspoon of seasoning salt and 1 teaspoon Italian seasoning to the veggies. Cook till soft. Toss in the mushrooms, frying briefly.

Beat the eggs, milk, 1½ teaspoon of seasoning salt, 1 teaspoon each Italian seasoning and dry mustard. Now let's bring in the bacon to the mix—and/or ham if you prefer— and, oh yeah, who could neglect the sherry, and of course 3 cups of shredded cheese.

Pour the mix into 2 greased 8- x 8-inch baking pans. Cover. Into the fridge it goes until tomorrow morning. Or, if you failed to pre-plan, send your breakfast special off to the oven right away.

The next morning, bake, uncovered, at 350 degrees for 40 minutes. Sprinkle the remaining cup of cheese on top, and bake 5 more minutes or until done. Let stand 15 minutes so that it can set up before serving.

Fired-Up
FRITTATAS

Okay, so it's nothing more than a spicy omelette with some salsa wrapped in a flour tortilla, but you don't have to tell your company how easy it is.

GO TO THE STORE, SEÑOR OR SEÑORITA

- 2 chorizo or Italian sausages
- 1 8- to 10-inch soft flour tortilla per frittata
- 2 eggs per frittata
- Dash of milk
- Chili powder
- Green onions—diced
- 1 red or green pepper—diced fine
- Chopped fresh cilantro
- Cheddar, marble or Monterey Jack cheese—shredded
- Salsa and sour cream for garnish

HEY, THERE'S NO TIME FOR A SIESTA! WE'RE HUNGRY HERE!

Take the sausages out of their casings, and place them in a preheated frying pan. Break up the sausages and cook 'em until they're no longer pink. Drain, place on paper towels, and set aside.

For each frittata, break up 2 eggs in a bowl, and whisk in a dash of milk and chili powder. Add the green onion, pepper and cilantro.

Spray an 8- or 9-inch non-stick frying pan with non-stick coating. Heat 'er up over medium–low heat. Add 1 tablespoon of vegetable oil. Tilt the frying pan so that the oil has made contact with the entire bottom.

Add the egg mixture, cover the pan, and cook until set.

Remove the omelette to a greased baking pan. Sprinkle the top with sausage meat and cheese. Broil until light brown.

Remove omelette from oven and cut in half. Cover half of the tortilla with half of the omelette. Toss in some salsa and sour cream. Fold the other side overtop. Cut the remaining omelette in half again—making two quarters.

Place one quarter omelette over one quarter of the tortilla—hey, salsa and sour cream, get in there—and fold the tortilla overtop once more. Open wide!!

All right, Jeff, now what do I do with the remaining quarter omelette? Well, if you're making a few frittatas, do the math. For every 3 frittatas you make, you'll have 3 extra quarters or 1 more frittata. Or if you're really hungry, just jam that baby in before you make the final fold.

In Search of the
PERFECT FRIED EGG

Sure they're simple, yet many cooks—even in restaurants—goof them up. Why? Mainly because the cooking surface is too hot when they hit the grill, resulting in an ugly, greasy crust on the egg. It doesn't have to be that way.

SO HERE'S HOW WE'LL DO IT

Warm a non-stick frying pan over medium–low heat.

Drop in a pat of butter—just enough to lightly coat the bottom. The pan should be warm enough to melt the butter slowly. Easy does it for this over easy.

Carefully add the eggs, making sure to not overcrowd the pan.

Allow the eggs to set briefly, and slowly pour about 3 tablespoons of warm water around the outside of the eggs.

Sprinkle the eggs lightly with seasoning salt.

Cover the pan and cook until the eggs are just the way you like them.

If you're an over-easy fan, give them a flip to finish.

Eggs
BENNY

This is a personal fave. I know it's not the lightest, but oh, it's such a treat!

THE INGREDIENTS

- Hollandaise or **Hall-a-Blaze Sauce** (page 206)—warmed up

- 2 eggs—poached

- 2 slices of ham or back bacon—warmed in a microwave

- 2 English muffins—toasted

- Cayenne pepper—hot, hot, hot, man that's hot!

THE INSTRUCTIONS

Get the hollandaise sauce going. You can prepare packaged hollandaise or try your hand at making the **Hall-a-Blaze Sauce**.

Bring 2 inches of water to a slow boil in a frying pan. Drop in a couple tablespoons of vinegar, as this will help keep the eggs together.

Add the eggs to the water carefully, and cook for about 4–5 minutes.

Remove eggs and drain. Top a toasted English muffin, open-faced, with warmed ham, 1 egg, hollandaise sauce and a sprinkle of cayenne!

Fire this recipe up by topping each creation with sautéed asparagus!

Breakfast
Pizza

Oh sure, you can cook up a big batch of the eclectic pizzas (pages 156–158), place the leftovers in the fridge and, when you wake in the morning, simply revisit your dinner. Or you could get busy in the kitchen and tailor-make an early-riser pizza with bacon, sausage, veggies, hollandaise sauce and eggs. I say, get off your butt and go for the Breakfast Pizza!

BEFORE YOU HIT THE HAY MAKE SURE YOU HAVE

- 2 large store-bought pizza shells, or even better . . .
- **Bread-Maker Pizza Dough** (page 155)
- 1 package prepared hollandaise sauce or **Hall-a-Blaze Sauce** (page 206)
- 10 large eggs
- ½ pound bacon
- 6 hot Italian or chorizo sausages
- 1 small red pepper—diced
- 1 bunch green onions—diced
- ¼ pound or so mushrooms —sliced into Ts
- Mozzarella cheese—about 1 pound

DOUGH DE DOUGH!

Spread out the dough on cooking stones or pizza pans.

The "heart-attack helper" hollandaise needs some attention, so make it up as per directions, except that I want you to use only half the butter it calls for, because I care about you. I do! I know you could make up the **Hall-a-Blaze Sauce**, but I'm a reasonable man. It's first thing in the morning and I can only expect so much from you at this time of day. Go on, grab a coffee!

Scramble the eggs, fry up the bacon, and set both aside.

Parboil the sausages to rid them of excess fat—I told you, I care. Slice them into pieces, like slices of pepperoni, and brown in a frying pan. Set aside.

Preheat the oven to 400 degrees.

It's time to go to town. Spread a thin layer of hollandaise on the dough, followed by the eggs, bacon, sausage, pepper, onions and 'shrooms.

Finally, top your creation with a thin layer of mozzarella cheese.

Off to the oven for 15–20 minutes, long enough to brown the crust and melt the cheese, and it's Breakfast Pizza Up!

Fire Hall
HASH BROWNS

Rarely does a Saturday or Sunday morning pass at your local fire station when they don't serve up these hash browns—or a reasonable facsimile thereof. If you're in a hurry, or it's a lazy Sunday and you can't be bothered, simply use frozen hash browns as a cheat to speed up your feed.

YOU NEED

- 5 pounds russet potatoes —Yukon Golds are also excellent

- Spices—seasoning salt, garlic powder, onion powder, chili powder, basil and oregano

- 1 jumbo onion—diced

- 1 green or red pepper—diced

- ½ pound mushrooms—sliced

- Garlic butter

- ½ pound marble cheese—grated. Optional, but oh so good!

YOU NEED TO

Preheat the oven to 375 degrees.

Cut the potatoes into bite-sized pieces. You can keep the skins on if you're a hash-brown purist.

Toss the potatoes with just enough vegetable oil to coat them lightly, meaning that there should be almost no oil left in the bowl.

Sprinkle the potatoes with seasoning salt, garlic powder, onion powder and chili powder. Don't ask for exact amounts here, I never measure; just keep tossing until the potatoes are richly coloured with spices. Potatoes absorb a lot of spice.

Bake on a baking pan, turning the little critters often till light brown—crusty on the outside, soft on the inside.

Meanwhile, fry the diced onion, green pepper and mushrooms in a pan with a little butter. Spice the veggies with basil and oregano.

You can push this one over the top by tossing the taters in a little melted garlic butter just before serving.

Combine the veggies and the potatoes. If you want to go for the works—as in the "firefighter triple play"—add the grated cheese on top, and bake until cheese is melted and lightly browned.

Heavenly
HASH-BROWN PIE

I watched Emeril make a similar recipe on Food-TV, and it inspired me to come up with my own version. It goes great with a couple of fried eggs!

THE SUPPLIES

- 4 tablespoons vegetable oil
- 3–4 red potatoes—grated
- Garlic powder
- **Fired-Up Santa Fe Spice** (page 200)
- Seasoning salt and pepper
- 6 slices bacon—as Emeril says, "Pork fat rules!"
- 1 medium onion—cut in rings
- 10–12 mushrooms—sliced
- ¼ pound or so grated marble cheese

THE METHODOLOGY
—it's not as difficult as that is to say

Bring a 10-inch non-stick frying pan to temperature over medium heat.

Add 2 tablespoons vegetable oil to the pan, and follow with enough grated potatoes to completely cover the bottom of the pan.

Spice with 4 or 5 shakes each of garlic powder, **Fired-Up Santa Fe Spice** and seasoning salt, and oh, about 4 grinds of pepper.

When the potatoes are browned on the bottom, carefully flip them over—the trick is to have the mixture stay together—and season once more.

In a separate pan, cook the bacon until crisp. Add the onions to the drippings, and sauté until very tender and caramelized.

Toss in the mushrooms and cook for 1 minute. The mushrooms only need to meet the heat briefly. Season the 'shrooms as you go with another little hit of **Fired-Up Santa Fe Spice.**

Place your first disc of hash browns in the bottom of a pie plate.

Preheat the oven to 375 degrees.

Cook a second batch of hash browns.

Place the bacon, onions, mushrooms and cheese on the first potato layer, and cover with the second potato layer.

Bake, uncovered, for 20 to 30 minutes or until completely heated through. Oh, and a little more cheese on top wouldn't hurt. Don't sue me if it actually does end up hurting.

No-Time-To-Eat
BREAKFAST SHAKE

If you have trouble wolfing something down in the morning, here's a great solution: simply "shake it up!" Use this smoothie shake as a meal replacement or even as a protein supplement. Tastes great, less filling!

ASSEMBLE

- A banana
- A pear, nectarine, peach, apple, orange, kiwi or even strawberries
- 1¼ cups of skim milk
- 6 heaping tablespoons of yogurt —I use strawberry, peach or mango
- 1 big scoop of vanilla ice milk or ice cream—optional
- 2 heaping tablespoons of powdered egg whites or packaged protein powder such as powdered whey

THEN FIRE UP THE BLENDER

Place the banana, other fruit, milk, yogurt and ice milk in the blender.

Hit blend—well, that was certainly predictable.

Once the shake is combined, add the powdered egg whites or whey while the machine is still running. Blend the works until smooth.

There's no end of fruit combinations for you to try. Just be sure to keep the banana in the mix, as it adds a lot of body to the shake.

THE FIREHOUSE BAKESHOP

It's a day-shift tradition of mine at the fire hall, making muffins for morning coffee break. Invariably, district chiefs—highly trained in such matters, which is why they're paid so handsomely—pick up on the scent and drop by for a little something to tide them over until lunch. So yes, I have been referred to as the "Muffin Man"—among other names requiring thicker skin—on occasion. Hey, being able to take a good old-fashioned firehouse ribbing is part of the job description.

You'll notice in the recipes that I like to make my baked goods a little healthier by using a 50-50 blend of whole-wheat and all-purpose flours—unbleached if possible. You can use all-purpose exclusively if you wish, with equally good results, but I don't recommend using 100 percent whole-wheat, as you'll find that the muffins are heavy and won't rise as much as you'd like them to.

I also like to use two eggs in my recipes because—as of the writing of this book, though things could have changed three or four times since—eggs are *in* and good again. So let's get that protein count up!

Buttermilk is another ingredient that I just can't bake without. Sure, you can use milk, or do a buttermilk fake by adding one tablespoon of lemon juice to a cup of milk, but buttermilk works best. I'm Irish; it's what I grew up on. I just love the sweet-and-sour flavour that it gives baked goods. If fat is an issue, 1% buttermilk is readily available.

The freshness of ingredients can also affect your results. Using old baking powder or yeast—not to mention that open box of baking soda in the fridge that's sucked up all the bad odours—will only lead to disaster. Always go fresh, because I don't want to see you tossing your clubs "helicopter style" in frustration on the course ... oh sorry, that's golf.

This is one section in which you should hold back on ad-libbing, at first. Give these recipes a go, verbatim, to start, and try any substitutions later. If the delicate balance of ingredients gets out of whack, your baking won't turn out and, well, don't come running to me!

So here's my latest grouping of baked favourites. Better put a pot of coffee on; the chief's out doing his rounds, and if you bake it, he will come!

Good Morning
MUFFINS

Orange juice and a muffin for breakfast, anyone? Or how about an orange juiced in a muffin? These are number one on the muffin-request charts at the firehouse, and personal favourites of mine. Best of all, they require no advanced culinary skills. We're talking fast and easy!

ARE YOU SURE THAT'S IT?

- 1 medium seedless orange
- ½ cup orange juice
- ¼ cup canola oil
- 2 eggs
- 1¾ cup flour—try a 50-50 blend of white and whole-wheat
- ¾ cup white sugar
- 2 teaspoons baking powder
- 1 teaspoon each baking soda and salt
- ¾ cup raisins

SINCE WHEN WERE MUFFINS THIS SIMPLE TO MAKE AND BAKE?

Preheat the oven to 375 degrees.

Cut the orange into several segments—skin and everything!

Place the orange segments, orange juice, oil and eggs in a blender and fire up that noisy bad boy until the mixture is smooth.

In a mixing bowl combine the flours, sugar, baking powder, baking soda and salt. Stir with a spoon until well mixed.

Fold the blended orange mixture into the dry ingredients. If you're using a large, mutant orange, simply add more flour to the mix to avoid having too wet a batter. Think thick batter ... up!

"Excuse me, Mr. Jeff, what's a fold?"

Glad you asked. A fold isn't quite a mix. Rather, it's a large folding movement, done only enough times so that the wet and dry ingredients are just combined. Hey, get your hands out of the batter!!

"Ouch!!"

Where was I here? Oh, don't forget to add the raisins.

Distribute the batter equally in a greased 12-slot muffin pan.

Bake until the muffins are lightly browned—about 20 minutes.

Mrs. Moore's
RAISIN BRAN MUFFINS

When my wife was growing up, her neighbour used to make her famous muffins for those close enough to her to be on her "A" list. The bananas are my addition, and I'm not sure that Mrs. Moore would have approved.

HERE'S WHAT MRS. MOORE USED

- ¼ cup margarine—softened
- ½ cup brown sugar
- ¼ cup molasses
- 2 eggs
- 1 cup buttermilk
- 1½ cups wheat bran
- 2 ripe bananas—optional
- 1 cup unbleached all-purpose flour —or 1¼ cups if using bananas
- 2 teaspoons baking powder
- 1 teaspoon baking soda
- ½ teaspoon salt
- 1 cup raisins or blueberries; walnuts are also a good addition

HERE'S HOW MRS. MOORE MADE THEM

Preheat the oven to 375 degrees.

In a bowl, cream the margarine and sugar with an electric mixer. Do NOT use an eclectic mixer, as the results would be too bizarre and far too surreal to comprehend.

Add the molasses, eggs and buttermilk, and mix until smooth.

Bring the bran to the liquid mixture. If you're using bananas, mash 'em up real good, and invite them to the bran-slurry party as well.

Whisk the flour—remember to add more flour if using bananas—with the baking powder, baking soda and salt.

If you see blueberries in these muffins' future, then toss the berries in a light coating of flour to prevent them from bleeding into the batter.

Toss the berries or raisins with the dry guys before you mix the flour ingredients with the bran ingredients. Fold together until just combined and load the batter into a greased 12-slot muffin pan.

Bake for about 15 to 20 minutes.

Hey, the chief's here—it must be coffee time!

Banana Bread
MUFFINS

Our neighbour Terrie Bell made these for us, and after we tried them we shredded our other banana muffin recipes. These are excellent! Oh, and keep in mind, this batter also makes incredible banana bread.

THE GROCERIES

- 1 cup each all-purpose and whole-wheat flour
- ½ teaspoon salt
- 2 teaspoons baking powder
- 1 teaspoon baking soda
- ⅔ cup margarine—softened
- ¾ cup white sugar
- 2 eggs
- 3 ripe bananas
- 1 teaspoon vanilla
- ⅔ cup buttermilk
- ½ cup raisins—or chocolate chips for a kid's version
- ½ cup walnuts—optional, especially for kids

THE WORK
—a labour of love, really

Fire up the oven to 350 degrees.

In what we could call Bowl A, we'll blend together the dry ingredients —the flour, salt, baking powder and baking soda.

In what we could call Bowl B, we'll mix together the wet ingredients —the margarine, sugar—okay, I know the sugar isn't really wet, but it will be—eggs, bananas, vanilla and buttermilk.

Now let's bring these bowls together in culinary matrimony. Create a well in the middle of Bowl A and pour in the contents of Bowl B. Blend the two with a wooden spoon for a wonderful traditional effect—the grandmother effect we could call it—until just combined.

The fruit and nuts are getting impatient, so let's add them to the mix, and spoon everything into the greased muffin pan. This will make about 15 big muffins, or even more of the little fellas.

Bake in the middle of the oven for 20–25 minutes, or until nicely browned and cooked through.

Tip: Freeze ripe bananas and simply defrost them when you're ready to bake.

Raisin
OATMEAL MUFFINS

Or if you're making them for the chocoholic kids—or women—simply use chocolate chips in the place of raisins. Simple yet succulent.

FIRST UP IT'S

- 1 cup quick-cooking oats
- 1 teaspoon baking soda
- 1 cup buttermilk

Whisk the oats and baking soda together in a bowl and add the buttermilk, allowing it to soak into the oats.

Turn that oven on to 375 degrees.

ON DECK IT'S

- 2 eggs
- ½ teaspoon vanilla
- ½ cup margarine
- 1 cup packed brown sugar

While the oat-sorption process is taking place, cream the eggs, vanilla, margarine and brown sugar together in a separate bowl with an electric mixer or, if you want to develop arms like a Hulk Hogan's, try a whisk.

NOW THAT THE OTHERS ARE ON BASE, COMBINE

- 1½ cups all-purpose flour
- ½ teaspoon salt
- ¾ cup raisins or chocolate chips

IT'S GRAND SLAM TIME

Let's bring the players together in one bowl and fold them together with a good old-fashioned wooden spoon until just combined.

Spoon the batter into a greased muffin tin designed for a dozen.

Bake for approximately 20–25 minutes, or until cooked through.

Banana Oatmeal Muffins, anyone? Add 2 mashed ripe bananas to the wet ingredients and ¼ cup flour to the dry.

Rum-and-Eggnog
MUFFINS

Here's a nice warm Yuletide shot to get your motor started in the morning. Kids, get your fake IDs ready! Moms, set up the mistletoe. Dads, mark a line on that bottle of Caribbean pleasure. Muffin shooters up!

SO GO TO THE PANTRY AND LIQUOR CABINET FOR

- 1 cup each all-purpose and whole-wheat flour
- 1 tablespoon baking powder
- ½ teaspoon nutmeg
- ½ teaspoon salt
- ½ cup crushed walnuts
- ½ cup raisins or better yet, craisins. Craisins cry out Christmas!
- 2 eggs
- ⅔ cup sugar
- ⅓ cup canola oil
- ¾ cup eggnog
- ¼ cup dark rum—yes, really

CAN I HAVE YOUR ATTENTION, PLEASE!

First, get that oven going: 375 degrees please.

Combine the two flours, baking powder, nutmeg and salt with a whisk until well mixed. Shake your Xmas presents for valuable clues.

Add the walnuts and raisins. Mix again. Oh, and speaking of mix ... In a separate bowl combine the eggs, sugar, oil, eggnog and that measured shot of your highly prized bottle of vintage rum.

Make a well in middle of the flour mix. Pour the liquid ingredients —into the flour mix, not your gullet! —and fold in with a wooden spoon until just combined.

If the mixture appears too dry, add a bit more eggnog.

Fill a greased 12-slot muffin tin with the batter, and bake for about 20 minutes, or until light brown on top and cooked through.

Do you smell something burning? BEEP, BEEP, BEEP! Great! Now the smoke alarm is going off. Don't tell me ... Hey, the rum was for the muffins! You forgot about the muffins!

Load a few muffins onto a plate and stand patiently under the mistletoe. Don't worry, the fresh-baked aroma will suck 'em in.

Monkey
BREAD

Bring your neglected, your blackened, your abused bananas, and set out on a quest for delicious banana bread. Remember, the riper the better.

MAKE YOUR LITTLE MONKEYS HAPPY BY ASSEMBLING

- ½ cup margarine—softened
- 1 cup sugar
- 3 eggs
- 1 cup mashed ripe bananas—about 3
- 2 teaspoons vanilla
- 1 tablespoon finely grated orange rind
- 1 cup each whole-wheat and all-purpose flour
- 2 teaspoons baking powder
- 1 teaspoon each baking soda and salt
- 1 teaspoon nutmeg or allspice
- 1½ teaspoon cinnamon
- ½ cup buttermilk
- 1 cup raisins or chopped walnuts—optional

STOP MONKEYING AROUND AND GET BAKING!

You know the drill: preheat that oven to 350 degrees.

Cream the margarine and sugar in a bowl with an electric mixer.

Add the eggs one at a time, and beat well after each addition. Why? I have no idea; I don't carry the Julia Child gene. It just works, okay?

Beat in the bananas, vanilla and orange rind.

Combine the dry ingredients in a bowl. You know, the flour, baking powder, baking soda, salt, nutmeg and cinnamon.

Stir the dry mixture into the wet mixture, alternating with the buttermilk.

Get the raisins or nuts in, or go for gold and add raisins *and* nuts.

Place in a greased Bundt pan and bake for 45–50 minutes.

You can make this loaf into a cake by combining 1½ cups icing sugar, 2 tablespoons yogurt, 1 teaspoon orange rind, and 1 teaspoon orange juice. Spread the frosting over the loaf once it has cooled.

For variety, you can make a banana loaf from the **Banana Bread Muffin** recipe (page 19). Or make them both, and let them fight it out on the counter for Ultimate Banana Bread superiority!

Irish
SODA BREAD

This is a traditional Irish recipe that goes great with a lovely cuppa tea!

YOU PROBABLY HAVE THESE ON HAND

- 3½ cups unbleached all-purpose flour or 1¾ cups each whole-wheat and unbleached all-purpose flour

- 1 tablespoon white sugar—¼ cup for a sweeter bread

- 1½ teaspoons baking powder

- 1 teaspoon baking soda

- ½ teaspoon salt

- ¼ cup margarine—softened

- 1 cup raisins

- 1½ cup buttermilk—well, it's always on hand at my house

- A 4-leaf clover—for luck. Rise, bread, rise!

CUT THE BLARNEY AND GET BAKING

Start up that oven to 350 degrees.

Combine the flour, sugar, baking powder, soda and salt in a bowl with a shillelagh or whisk.

Cut in the margarine and whisk it all together until crumbly.

Stir in the raisins—get that Irish jig thing happening with your feet.

Add the buttermilk and work it all together into a lovely soft dough.

Okay, now that your hands are sticky with wet dough, would you please answer your phone? If you hear a click followed by a pregnant pause, hang up immediately, unless you're desperate to talk to someone—anyone—even if it's a telephone solicitor who only wants to discuss parting you from your hard-earned money.

Turn the dough onto a lightly floured board—notice that's "floured" and not "flowered"—and knead to form a soft ball.

Pat by hand onto a greased baking sheet to a 1¼-inch thickness.

Score the surface with a sharp knife, making a cross over the top of the loaf like a big + sign, and bake for 45 minutes or until golden brown and cooked through.

Clean dough from the receiver with a damp cloth, and consider getting your phone equipped with call display.

Sweeeet
BUTTERMILK BISCUITS

Make them plain, and serve them with stew or soup. Add raisins, blueberries or cranberries and serve them with tea. If this recipe looks familiar, well, actually it's the topping on the **Nectarine Cobbler** *(page 218).*

CHECK YOUR PANTRY AND FRIDGE FOR

- 1¼ cups unbleached all-purpose and 1 cup whole-wheat flour
- 5 tablespoons white sugar
- 1 tablespoon baking powder
- ¾ teaspoon salt
- ½ cup margarine—softened
- 2 eggs
- ¾ cup plus 2 tablespoons buttermilk
- 1 teaspoon vanilla
- Raisins, blueberries or cranberries —optional

MIX UP THE BATTER AND GET 'EM IN THE OVEN

Get the ol' cooker going at 400 degrees.

Combine the flours, sugar, baking powder and salt in a bowl. Whisk 'em all together now.

Here's the greasy-fingers part. Cut the margarine into teaspoon-sized pieces and add them to the flour mix. Does the margarine stick to the spoon? Well then, use your fingers and drop the pieces in. Distribute the margarine the best you can for maximum mixitude.

Beat the flour-margarine mixture in a bowl until the texture resembles coarse meal, like little pebbles.

In a separate bowl, mix the eggs, buttermilk and vanilla.

Fold the wets into the dries with a wooden spoon until you get a nice manageable dough. If you're adding fruit, make it happen now.

Roll out the dough with a rolling pin. Oh, you look so domestic!

Cut into biscuit-sized rounds, about 3 inches in diameter, with the top of a glass.

Place on a baking sheet or, better yet, an air-bake cookie sheet or perforated pizza pan. This will avoid burning the biscuit bottoms.

Bake for 15–20 minutes until lightly browned top and bottom.

Whole-Wheat
BREAD-MAKER BREAD

If you have a bread-maker, you may already have a favourite recipe. I've tried numerous bread recipes, but this is the one that I make almost exclusively. The honey gives it a nice hint of sweetness. This makes a 1½-pound loaf. Oh, just wait until you taste this baby with a generous whack of butter!

HERE ARE THE INGREDIENTS, IN ORDER OF APPEARANCE

- 1¼ cups of slightly warm water—the H2O should feel neither cold nor warm to the touch. If in doubt, use room-temperature water.

- 1½ tablespoons powdered milk

- 1 teaspoon salt

- 3 tablespoons honey—soft or liquid

- 3 tablespoons butter—room temperature or softened in microwave

- 2 cups whole-wheat flour

- 1 cup unbleached all-purpose flour

- 2 teaspoons fast-rising or bread-maker yeast

HERE'S ALL YOU HAVE TO DO TO BAKE FRESH BREAD

Add the above ingredients to the bread pan in the order listed.

Make sure that when you add the flour, it completely covers the liquid ingredients. Then place the yeast on top.

Set your bread-maker to the whole-wheat setting. Depending on your machine, that's about 4 hours or 4 hours, 10 minutes.

Or you can set your bread-maker to bake the bread while you sleep. The manufacturers will tell you that you'll wake up to the smell of freshly baked bread. Wrong! Your sense of smell doesn't work while you sleep and that's why you need a smoke alarm. Sorry, the firefighter in me is coming out again.

Tip: For a more traditional-looking loaf, set your bread machine to the dough setting. When the cycle is complete, remove dough and place it in a large loaf pan. Cover with a tea towel and let rise an inch above the side of the pan—say half an hour. Bake in a preheated 350-degree oven for about 30 minutes.

Here's the hard part. Once the bread is baked, you should let it sit for a while to cool. Despite the temptation, resist eating immediately! Use an electric knife to avoid mangling the bread.

White
BREAD-MAKER BREAD

Try this recipe if you prefer white bread to whole-wheat. I make it for the kids when they insist on it. It's also a great substitute for dinner rolls. This recipe is tailored for a 1½-pound bread-maker. You can do the math to adjust it for a 1- or 2-pound bread-maker.

HERE'S WHAT YOU NEED—
MEASURE CAREFULLY

- 1¼ cups slightly warm water—should feel neither cold nor warm to the touch. Use room-temperature water if in doubt.

- 1 tablespoon powdered milk

- 1 teaspoon salt

- 1½ tablespoons sugar

- 2 tablespoons butter—room temperature or softened in microwave

- 3⅓ cups white flour

- 1 teaspoon fast-rising or bread-maker yeast

IN THEY GO,
PRESS START AND BAKE

Add the above ingredients to the bread pan in the order listed.

Make sure that when you add the flour it completely covers the liquid ingredients.

Place the yeast on top. It needs a safe, "liquid-free" place to rest.

Set your bread-maker to basic setting—about 4 hours.

Let 'er rip! Er, disregard that. I mean hit the start button.

In a few hours your house will be filled with the incredible aroma of—I hope you disregarded the "rip" instruction—fresh bread. I know, it smells fantastic, but try not to eat the entire loaf in one sitting.

For a delicious Raisin Bread option, simply add 1 teaspoon vanilla to the wet ingredients, ½ tablespoon of cinnamon to the flour and, when the bread-maker beeps at the end of its first kneading cycle—meaning, "Bring on the fruit, Baker Boy"— toss in 1 cup of raisins.

Cinnamon and raisins are also fabulous additions to the **Whole-Wheat Bread-Maker Bread** (page 25) recipe.

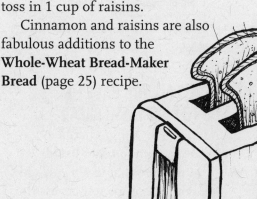

HE HUFFED AND HE PUFFED AND HE ...

At a station downtown, staffed by some 16 to 20 firefighters, the crew had a machine they dubbed "the Lung Tester." The con was to suck co-workers in—literally—by subtly dropping hints that the machine existed, and that only the greatest of firefighters—those with the most impressive lung capacity—could dominate the machine. A small cylinder about the size of a coffee tin, the Lung Tester had a tube sticking out of the side, piped into a wheel that sat atop the unit. The harder you blew into the tube, the faster the wheel spun and the better you were (said to be) suited for firefighting. Well, good old human curiosity—coupled with the eagerness to impress their peers—led many firefighters, especially keen rookies, to plead with the tester's handlers to give it a go.

Once a dupe had been successfully coerced, the boys would assemble to observe the proceedings. The victim would inhale as much air as he possibly could and then blow with all his might into the contraption. Unbeknownst to the victim, who naturally shut his eyes as he blew, the air pressure not only caused the wheel to spin, but also forced a fine mist of soot to shoot out of tiny holes in the side of the machine, covering his face with a fine black powder. Of course, spectators would do their best to keep a straight face, allowing the victim to walk around the hall unaware, never letting him in on the gag until he figured it out for himself.

On one occasion, a firefighter who will go nameless was victimized and, just as he had successfully completed his lung test, the chief approached him and said, "Here's a few bucks. How about you go out and get us all some donuts. I'm buying."

Well, this chief had a reputation for being a tightwad, so his offer should have tipped off the conned firefighter, but he failed to take heed and proceeded to the local donut shop as requested, sporting the blackened complexion of a Cape Breton coal miner. When did he figure out that he'd been had, you ask? When he bent over to scan the variety of donuts in the display window, and spotted his reflection in the glass!

PRANKS IN THE HALL

It's a fundamental part of our job, one steeped in rich firefighting tradition—the good old-fashioned practical joke. When I joined the department, our training officer filled us in on what to expect, recalling many of the classic pranks of yesteryear. He capped his chat off with a warning. "If the guys get you with a gag, just laugh it off. Don't let on that they've got to you, because once they find the button to push, they're going to just keep pushing it until you snap, and then when you do snap, they'll push it even harder and more often."

Once we naïve and impressionable rookies were assigned to our stations, we quickly learned for ourselves how important it was to not only laugh off the pranks, but to keep our heads up for whatever was in store. It seemed that no matter what room we entered, there was some gag lying in wait. It was like tiptoeing through a minefield. Sit down on the throne and just as you placed your buttocks in position, BAANNGG!!! A pressure sensitive firecracker or ketchup packet deftly hidden under the seat went off, not only scaring you to your feet, but making you wonder what the chef put in the chili. Stand to use a toilet, and you'd give your shoes an acid bath due to the invisible film of plastic wrap on the bowl.

Get into the shower, and one of the pranksters would either shut off the hot water supply, or whip the curtain open and toss a bucket of ice water at you. Then, after a pregnant pause they'd ring the gong and announce a fictitious alarm, causing you to panic and stumble out onto the apparatus floor to a chorus of laughs. To add insult to injury, an odd sensation of rapidly building warmth in your nether regions caused you to wonder if your pants were on fire. Yes, some considerate soul had spread Tiger Balm down the inside of your underwear. GOTCHA!

Lie down in the dorm and if someone hadn't replaced your bed's legs with empty coke cans, causing you to crash to the ground, or your sheets weren't floured or baby powdered, then expect ice cubes in a Styrofoam cup hanging precariously over your bed, with a small hole in the bottom to allow melting water to slowly drip onto your forehead.

It's amazing that firefighters haven't died of heart attacks in the dorm, as the alarm gong isn't the only thing that wakes us from our slumber. Firecrackers, spinning metal bowls or weights—why, some have even been awakened by a crewmate starting up a lawn mower or chainsaw right in our sleeping quarters.

Go to get into your vehicle, and you may spot a big puddle of oil underneath the engine. Curious, you pop the hood, check the oil and crawl underneath the car to check for leaks. Meanwhile, the guys back in the hall are peering out the window quietly laughing.

What can I say? Incarcerate a crew of firefighters together for a 10-, 14- or even 24-hour shift, as some departments do, and creative yet devious minds are sure to concoct myriad pranks. But the bottom line is that it's all in the name of fun, and in a job where we truly depend on each other for our lives, practical jokes are in many ways team-building exercises. As the old axiom goes, "They only bug you because they like you." Getting stung by a prank means that you are accepted into the brethren, making you feel like you're part of the team. Besides, practical jokes—like our famous firehouse meals—are yet another reason to look forward to coming to work, at the greatest job in the world.

FROM LUNCHES THAT LADLE TO
LUNCHES THAT CRUNCH Soups, Salads and Lunches

HIGH NOONERS

**Chicken Souvlaki Pitas
with Spicy Tzatziki Sauce** 34
A great Greek lunch

Rockin' Reuben Sandwiches 35
What can I say? This firehouse staple rocks!

King Kong Club Sandwiches 36
We'll politely dub this club tall and full-figured

Buffalo King Kong Club Sandwiches 36
A little hot sauce will fire up that big ape!

Hot Pig Sandwiches 37
My take on the Hard Rock Café classic

Mile-High Denver Sandwiches 38
The air is getting mighty thin up here!

Stacked Steak Sandwiches 39
Steak for lunch? Oh, twist my arm!

Massive Meatloaf Sandwiches 40
We build 'em big at the firehouse

Hot Chicken Caesars 40
A hint of garlic? More like a whack!

Teriyaki Chicken with Asian Mixed Greens 40
It's a Far Eastern barbecue

RABBIT FOOD

Great Greek Salad 44
A touch of sugar sweetens this super salad

Primo Pasta Salad 45
With an option to convert it to a Greek Pasta Salad

Sensational Caesar Salad 46
Garlic, hhhhaaa! The breath of life

Lemon Poppyseed Salad 47
My most-requested salad recipe

Let the Sunshine Salad 48
When you burn out on Lemon Poppyseed

Spinach 'n' Egg Salad 49
With roast beef or a steak, this is the salad

Waldorf Salad 50
The salad of choice when pork is on the menu

Asian Persuasion Coleslaw 51
Funkify your coleslaw with a taste of Asia

Asian Mixed Greens with Sesame Dressing 52
More Far Eastern treats

Awesome Potato Salad 53
Hit a grand slam at your next picnic!

Mighty Caesar Barbecued Potato Salad 54
Garlic and spuds are a team

Nine-Layer Salad for Ten 55
Or do the math and make an 18-layer salad for 20

Warm Mushroom Spinach Salad 56
It's a meal in itself. So, so good!!

A FORK OR A SPOON

HIGH NOONERS

Although lunch at some fire halls can be as simple as "brown bagging" it, many other halls fire up the cooking utensils and make lunch yet another culinary event. Not only does this become a highlight of the day—sharing another good meal with workmates—but it also eliminates Brown Bag Confusion Syndrome. I heard tell of a firefighter who couldn't find the lunch he'd packed in either of the hall's fridges. After scouring the kitchen, he looked at one of the other firefighters seated at the table, spying the food half-eaten in front of him, and exclaimed, "Hey, wait a second. I think you're eating my lunch!"

"Oh, well, ah—I must have gotten it mixed up with mine accidentally," the caught-red-handed lunch crook explained.

"Well, since you've just about finished all of mine," the victim asked, "where's your lunch, so that I can have something to eat?"

"Oh, um, I, uh, didn't bring one," the swiper sheepishly replied.

Yes, another classic tale from the rich annals of Winnipeg's firefighter history!

If you're looking for lunch ideas, you've come to the right place. At Winnipeg fire halls in the winter, soup is on the lunch menu most days. We're talking hearty, thick soups, stew or chili, with a loaf of fresh bread. Hey, try fighting a fire at minus-30 degrees, and you'll know why we serve comfort food during the chilly months. Then, on those hot summer days in the land of temperature extremes, the barbecue gets a workout, and it's burgers, hot dogs, steaks or chicken—the possibilities are endless. Often what I'll do is choose a salad, pair it with a complementary barbecued meat and lunch is on its way!

So don't be bashful about mixing things up; feel free to throw away the rulebook, and fire up a red-hot High-Nooner special today.

Oh, by the way: if you're making your lunch ahead to eat later at work, you may want to seal the top of your brown bag with a mouse trap and label it, "Mine, don't eat!"

CHICKEN SOUVLAKI PITAS
with Spicy Tzatziki Sauce

You could also make this recipe with beef or pork. Makes for a wonderful Greek lunch. Don't forget the all-important sauce!

THE FIRED-UP SPICY TZATZIKI SAUCE

- 1 medium long English cucumber —diced fine
- 2 cups plain yogurt
- 2 tablespoons extra virgin olive oil —What is an extra virgin?
- 2 teaspoons lemon juice
- 1 teaspoon kosher salt
- 2 teaspoons dried dill weed —or even better, 2 tablespoons fresh
- 2 cloves garlic—minced
- 1 teaspoon **Fired-Up Spice** (page 200)

THE PITA AND ITS STUFFING

- Boneless chicken thighs —cut into 1-inch squares
- **Lemon Garlic Marinade** (page 111)
- Wood skewers
- Tomatoes—diced
- Green or yellow pepper—cut into strips
- Red onion—cut in strips as well
- Pita bread

MAKE 'EM THICK AND JUICY!

Make up the tzatziki sauce, preferably the night before.

Marinate the chicken in Lemon Garlic Marinade for 4 hours.

Soak your wood skewers in water for an hour to prevent burning.

Place the veggies on a serving plate.

Skewer the chicken and barbecue until completely cooked through.

Place the chicken in or on the pita bread and toss in the veggies.

Now for the finishing touch; lay on the tzatziki sauce, bring the pita to your salivating mouth and enjoy the show.

If the tzatziki sauce is oozing out the sides of the pita with every bite, splashing on your plate, dripping down your chin and landing on your shirt and lap, then you'll know you've added just the right amount.

Rockin'
REUBEN SANDWICHES

This is a firehouse staple at lunchtime. When in doubt, make up a batch of Reubens. Rest assured, they'll work every time.

REUB'S ANATOMY

- Sauerkraut—for its wonderful, smooth digestive properties

- Corned beef or pastrami— let's just say lots, ¼ pound each!

- Pumpernickel bread—you can also use rye

- Russian dressing—I know Thousand Island is traditional, but try Russian. Trust me, it'll make Reub even happier!

- Sliced Swiss cheese—not that awful processed stuff

- Tomato slices—this is a non-traditional addition, but hey, it's my cookbook and if you don't like it, go out and write your own. Wait—come back—I was only kidding! Sorry!

THE BUILDING OF OUR FRIEND REUBEN

Drain the juice from an appropriate amount of sauerkraut for the number of Reubens you're making. Fry the kraut up over medium heat to warm it through. Drain off any more liquid before serving.

Place a very small coating of oil on a non-stick frying pan, and heat up the corned beef, or preheat it in the microwave—this step is optional.

Butter one side of each piece of bread. Place the buttered side down in a frying pan, and grill over medium–low heat as you would for a grilled cheese sandwich.

Spread a coating of Russian dressing on the bread, and top it with corned beef, Swiss cheese, more corned beef, tomatoes if you're so inclined, and the flatulence-inducing sauerkraut.

Spread another small amount of Russian dressing on the other slice of bread, and place it butter side up on top.

When Reub's bottom is lightly toasted, flip him and toast his topside.

To serve piping hot, you can heat Reub in a microwave for 30 seconds just before serving. Reuben, old boy, you're ready to eat!

You can also make Reub in a sandwich press or waffle iron. Really!

Serve with **Awesome Potato Salad** (page 53) or go the tried-and-true fries and coleslaw route.

King Kong
CLUB SANDWICHES

When you cook at the fire hall, you build 'em wide, and you build 'em tall.

THE BUILDING MATERIALS

- 1 boneless chicken breast per sandwich—flatten slightly with a forcible-entry tool, such as a sledgehammer, between two sheets of waxed paper
- **Fired-Up Spice** (page 200)
- 3 slices of bacon per sandwich
- Onion—cut into rings
- Green pepper—cut into small strips
- Garlic butter
- Large Italian bun
- Salad dressing, Ranch dressing or mayonnaise
- Tomatoes—sliced
- Lettuce—ripped, like your abs

IF YOU BUILD IT THEY WILL COME
—make 'em thick and juicy!

Lightly dust the chicken breasts with **Fired-Up Spice**, and barbecue until they're no longer pink inside.

Toss the bacon in a frying pan over medium heat and cook until crisp.

Fry the onions over medium-low heat in a little butter until caramelized. Add the green pepper and cook through.

Spread garlic butter on a bun, and toast it on the grill.

We're ready to go here! Spread salad dressing or mayo on one side of the bun, and pile on the ingredients.

BUFFALO KING KONG CLUB SANDWICHES

Either purchase spicy breaded chicken breasts and cook as directed or barbecue chicken dusted in **Fired-Up Spice** and spread a mixture of 3 parts Louisiana hot sauce to 1 part melted butter and 1 part brown sugar over chicken to finish.

Instead of using commercial salad dressing, tame the fire with Ranch dressing or, if you can handle the stifling aroma, go for blue cheese dressing. Assemble the King Club as above.

Beat your chest madly and insert primal scream here.

Hot Pig
SANDWICHES

To make this lunch special you ideally need leftover **Blazin' Barbecued Pork Roast***. However, any leftover pork or even beef can be substituted. This is my version of one of the Hard Rock Café's most popular dishes. Everyone who tries it goes nuts, and requests that I make it again at the next possible opportunity!*

GO AND LOCATE

- **Ralphie Slaw** (page 58)

- Garlic butter

- Leftover pork roast—or if you're making it for a crowd, barbecue the **Blazin' Barbecued Pork Roast** (page 115) ahead of time to 190 degrees, or well done, and get those forks a-pulling!

- **Just Like Bull's Eye Barbecue Sauce** (page 205)

- Kaiser buns

THEN MAKE SURE TO

Put together a batch of **Ralphie Slaw** at least 4 hours ahead, or even the day before so that the salad can soak up the flavours.

Mix up the garlic butter by combining 3 parts butter or margarine to about 1 part olive oil. Add some minced or pressed garlic and a few generous shakes of Italian seasoning.

Hey, let's pull the pork roast. Take 2 forks and pull the pork apart along the grain of the meat into stringy pieces. If you don't like it pulled-pork style, just slice it up as you would any roast.

Place the pork in a large frying pan, and drench with barbecue sauce. You can even leave it in the sauce to marinate overnight if you wish.

Before you put some heat to it, add a bit of water so that the sauce doesn't get too thick while it cooks.

Cover the pan, place over medium–low heat and heat through.

Meanwhile, spread garlic butter on the Kaiser bun halves, and lightly toast them in another frying pan or under the broiler.

Place the roast on a toasted garlic bun, and top with a good dollop of (drained) coleslaw. I know it's different, but believe me it works!

Serve with **Glen's Non-Fries** (page 177) and a little more of that wonderful **Ralphie Slaw** on the side.

Mile-High
DENVER SANDWICHES

Here's a classic that we'll build to firefighter size. Simple, easy and inexpensive—sounds like the ideal fire hall lunch to me. This makes at least four mega-wiches. You can do the math when you need to feed more.

STICK YOUR HEAD IN THE FRIDGE TO FIND

- 8 large eggs
- Seasoning salt
- ⅔ cup onion—diced
- ⅔ cup green pepper—also diced
- Italian seasoning
- ⅔ cup ham—diced
- 8 large slices of light rye bread
- 1 cup cheddar or Swiss cheese—grated

HURRY UP, WE'RE HUNGRY HERE!

Whisk the eggs in a bowl. Add a dash of seasoning salt.

Sauté the onion and green pepper in a couple of pats of butter in a frying pan over medium heat. Add a few dashes of Italian seasoning.

Remove the veggies and add them, along with the ham, to the eggs.

Heat a 9- or 10-inch non-stick frying pan over medium–low heat. Toss in a tablespoon of vegetable oil to lightly coat the bottom.

Add half of the egg mixture and cook until the bottom is set—you can cover the pan to speed things up. Then cut the eggs with a spatula right down the middle, and flip each side over. Cook until lightly browned. Repeat for the rest of the egg mixture.

Remove the Denver mixture to a plate. Butter one side of each slice of bread. Place 2 slices of bread butter side down on the pan. Add half of 1 Denver. Place grated cheese on top, cover with the other half of 1 Denver, and cover with a slice of bread, butter side up.

Repeat for the other sandwich. Flip both, browning the outside of the sandwiches, and melting the cheese in between—as if you were making a grilled cheese sandwich. Oh, by the way, if the cheese isn't totally melted by now, it's nothing that 20 seconds in the microwave won't cure.

You won't hurt my feelings by dipping your Denver in ketchup!

Stacked
STEAK SANDWICHES

THE BUTCHER, THE BAKER AND THE GROCER

- 1 pound of sirloin steak—marinade optional. I'll tell you more in a sec.

- 1 jumbo onion—sliced into rings

- ½ red or green pepper—cut into strips

- ¼ pound of mushrooms—sliced into Ts

- Butter or margarine, garlic cloves and Italian seasoning—for garlic butter

- Large Italian-style buns

- Your favourite steak sauce—optional

OH, AND THE COOK

You have choices here. You could pick one of the **Three Great Steak Marinades** (page 87)) or the **Teriyaki Marinade** (page 203) and let the steak soak up the flavours overnight.

Or, if time is a factor and famished firefighters are breathing down your neck, simply season the steaks with seasoning salt and pepper.

Let's get the grill going. Heat up the barbecue over medium–high, and cook the steaks to the desired doneness. Remove from the barbecue and cover with foil on a plate to keep warm.

Sauté the onion in a frying pan with a dash or two of salt and pepper over medium–low heat until very soft. Toss the pepper in with the onion and sauté until tender crisp.

Turn up the heat, add the mushrooms and sauté for about 2 minutes, stirring constantly.

Make up a batch of garlic butter. Okay, use margarine since it's softer, add a few cloves of minced garlic and a good sprinkling of one of my favourite spice combinations, Italian seasoning.

Cut the buns open and spread garlic margarine over the inside. Grill face down until lightly browned.

Slice the steak against the grain into strips.

Okay, let's put this big fella together. Bun, steak, onions, peppers and mushrooms. Oh, I almost forgot, let's put a little steak sauce on that top bun as well, and you know what? I think we're there.

Let's go for a platter, and serve with **Ralphie Slaw** (page 58) and **Glen's Non-Fries** (page 177).

Massive MEATLOAF SANDWICHES

Make a 2-pound batch of **Meatloaf Cordon Bleu** (page 90). You don't have to worry about stuffing it with cheese and ham; just good old-fashioned plain meatloaf will do.

Allow the meatloaf to cool for about 10 minutes or so.

Slice up the meatloaf and place it on bread or toast, and top with **Stroganov Sauce** (page 91).

You can also make these with leftover beef or pork roast. Wait a second —leftover roast? Maybe at home, but never in a firehouse!

HOT CHICKEN CAESARS

Grill chicken breasts marinated in **Lemon Garlic Marinade** (page 111).

Allow the chicken to cool 5 minutes and slice into strips.

Make up a batch of **Sensational Caesar Salad** (page 46).

Place a ration of salad on each plate and top with slices of chicken.

If you have a little leftover Caesar dressing, drizzle it over the chicken slices for maximum presentation.

Look, not a vampire to be found on the radar screen!

TERIYAKI CHICKEN with Asian Mixed Greens

Barbecue a batch of chicken marinated in **Teriyaki Marinade** (page 203).

Allow chicken to cool 5 minutes; this helps the meat retain its juice.

Slice the chicken into strips. Wait! Don't throw out the marinade!

Boil the marinade for at least 5 minutes in a saucepan to cleanse it of any questionable uncooked chicken juices.

Let's get a big bowl of those **Asian Mixed Greens with Sesame Dressing** (page 52) happening.

Place a single serving of greens on a plate and arrange slices of chicken on top.

Go for broke, and top chicken with a drizzle of the reserved marinade. Man, does that ever look good on a plate!

The **Asian Mixed Greens** are also excellent when served with **Korean Chicken** legs (page 142) arranged on top.

A FEW THOUGHTS
from the Fire Hall Kitchen

Before we dive back into the recipes here, I'd like to share a few lessons that I've humbly learned over the years.

- Measure twice, cut once ... No, wait, that's a carpentry tip, sorry.

- When cooking, add salt last. Sure, you can add a reasonable amount to get the dish going, but once you've added salt you can't take it away. That's why most recipes end with the final step, salt and pepper to taste. Salt adds flavour while pepper adds bite.

- When roasting, always sear the meat first. (The searing it received from the rancher's branding iron doesn't count.) With a steak or roast you can fry it in butter or vegetable oil to get the outside deeply browned, or crank up the oven and cook your roast or bird uncovered for 15 to 20 minutes at a high heat, before turning it down to the desired roasting temperature. Searing allows the roast to retain its moisture while cooking. A liberally slathered outer coating of Dijon mustard also aids in the juice-retention process.

- Hail garlic, for it is great! When used properly—for goodness instead of evil—it not only adds but also brings out the flavour in dishes.

- When cutting peppers, after slicing them into sections, place the pepper shiny side—outside—down, and cut through the rough inside to avoid slippage. Now, if I could only remember to take the little label off the outside first so that it doesn't show up in the cooked dish.

- Eat pizza incessantly for impressive "6-pack" abdominal development.

- When planning a meal, try to tie the ingredients together. For example, if **Tequila Lime Chicken** (page 169) is the main course, **Mexican Pesto Pasta** (page 168), which also has cilantro and lime juice, will complement the chicken perfectly, and a **Lemon Poppyseed Salad** (page 47), which shares the spinach with the pesto, will go nicely as well.

- In my innocent teenage years I served my younger brothers the can't-miss combination of fish and ravioli. I only remember this failed marriage because they won't let me forget it. I trust that I've managed to improve my food-coupling skills since.

- Masculinity is epitomized by a firefighter armed with a high-powered electric mixer, beating egg whites into a stiff yet deliciously light meringue. Of course, there's a chance I could be wrong.

- When barbecuing, nothing beats a good marinade. There are a number for you to try in each of the meat sections, as well as in the cultural sections. Marinades tenderize and flavour the meat, a definite must!

- Teflon pans and firefighters don't mix. Sooner or later someone is going to use either a metal spatula on the pan in a violent manner while cooking or a metal scrubbing pad on the surface while washing. It never fails. That's why I have my own Teflon pan that I hide in my locker.

- "You are what you eat"—just say no to Fruit Loops and Cream Puffs!

- When buying ingredients for a salad, pasta dish or stir-fry, think colour. A variety of colours, such as red, green, orange, yellow—peppers are great for this—makes for great presentation. Chopped parsley or cilantro sprinkled atop each serving is an inexpensive way to dress up a plate of food as well.

- If the alarm gong rings during dinner at the firehouse, it's considered proper etiquette to curse once before rifling two shovels full of food into one's trap and excusing oneself from the table.

- So you don't have everything you need for a recipe and you don't feel like going to the store for one ingredient? Don't sweat it, substitutions are allowed. Here are a few to keep in mind:

- *Shortening (1 cup):* use 1 cup softened butter or 1 cup margarine minus ½ teaspoon salt from recipe.

- *Buttermilk,* a big favourite of mine (1 cup): 1 cup yogurt OR 1 tablespoon lemon juice or white vinegar plus enough milk to make 1 cup.

- *Eggs (1 whole):* ¼ cup liquid-egg substitute or 3 tablespoons mayonnaise or half a banana mashed with ½ teaspoon baking powder.

- *Baking soda* is a great quick substitute for a fire extinguisher, should things get out of hand. I learned that the hard way; luckily, I got hold of the red devil before it reached the cupboards.

- One more thing. If a meal doesn't turn out, just remember the immortal words of Jack Handey: "It takes a big man to cry—but it takes a bigger man to laugh at that man."

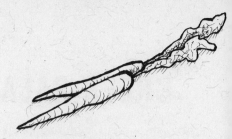

RABBIT FOOD

Salads are becoming more popular in the fire hall as we try to balance our carnivorous ways with a little greenery, especially now that blasphemous diets such as Atkins and South Beach consider such firehouse "fill 'em up" staples as bread and potatoes to be the enemy. I kid a lot about the stereotypical fire hall meal, but we have become more health conscious, most likely due to the aging veterans returning from their yearly physicals with sky-high cholesterol levels.

Caesar salad—at least in my department—is far and away the most popular. Oh, and if you think that we mean restaurant or store-bought dressings, well, that's only the tip of the garlic clove. It's high octane, full-steam-ahead Garlic Appreciation Night at the hall when the Mighty Caesar pops by. Garlic is almost a rite of passage for firefighters in Winnipeg: "I noticed you downed two heads of garlic for breakfast. Congratulations, son, —you've passed your probation test."

One firefighter I know even brings his own garlic press to work and prepares garlic shooters for himself at coffee time. His garlic toast is just that, garlic and toast.

But you can't have Caesar salad every day, unless you're fighting a cold or trying to dissuade a stalker, and that's why I've gone in search of a variety of salads. When choosing a salad, look at the entrée for the evening. For example, **Awesome Potato Salad** (page 53) goes well with a barbecue. If beef is on the menu, try serving **Spinach 'n' Egg Salad** (page 49). If it's pork, nothing goes better than a **Waldorf Salad** (page 50). There are a couple of Asian salads to choose from when you're serving Far Eastern cuisine. And if spicy is on the menu, a good way to balance the bite is with a little sweetness; that's when I suggest the **Lemon Poppyseed Salad** (page 47) or **Let the Sunshine Salad** (page 48).

Another thing to keep in mind about many of these salads is that coupled with barbecued meat, they make a fabulous lunch. Or, in the case of the **Warm Mushroom Spinach**, **Russian Taco** and **Primo Pasta** salads (pages 56, 57 and 45), well, they're basically a meal in themselves.

I love salads, and rarely does a fire hall meal go by when I don't include one. So, unless you feel your manhood threatened by the word "salad," get your garden growing, and fire up the Rabbit Food!

Great
GREEK SALAD

You can make it traditional style without lettuce, or break with tradition and toss in some romaine. Not being an olive fan, I usually exclude them, but hey, if you're into olives, toss 'em in. I think you'll like the subtle sweetness of this Greek dressing—it's good with pasta or **Mike's Lemon Garlic Chicken** *(page 103).*

THE SWEET DRESSING

- ½ cup olive oil
- 3 tablespoons lemon juice— of course fresh is best
- 1½ tablespoons red wine vinegar
- 1 tablespoon sugar— for that touch of sweetness
- 1 tablespoon dried oregano— not the powder
- ¼ teaspoon dry mustard
- Salt and pepper to taste

THE SALAD

- Roma tomatoes—cut in chunks
- 1 red onion—also cut in chunks
- Long English cucumbers—cut in, what else, chunks
- 1 red pepper—cut in—wait for it—chunks
- Olives—whole, or those chunky ones you buy in cans
- Chunky feta cheese—I like the dry flaked feta with herbs myself
- Romaine lettuce—it's optional, but a good way to stretch this salad

THE MIX-IT-ALL-UP-TOGETHER METHOD

Combine the dressing ingredients and refrigerate.

Cut up the salad ingredients as directed. Did I mention that they should be in chunks?

Add the feta cheese. You can toss this salad an hour or so ahead of time—minus the lettuce if you're a non-traditionalist—as the dressing will marinate the vegetables.

If you're using romaine, add it just before serving.

Thanks to my sister-in-law Marg for the great Greek dressing!

Primo
PASTA SALAD

Firefighter Glen Godri made this for us and it was a huge hit. The bacon, tomatoes and cheese give it incredible flavour! Okay, sure, a few more calories, but since when did calories count at a fire hall? This salad borders on the "meal in itself" status, depending on who's dining, and how high their meal expectations are. Better add a meat dish for the firehouse.

THE SALAD

- 10–12 slices bacon
- ½ pound rotini pasta
- ½ cup red onion—chopped small
- Broccoli and cauliflower—
  the tree family, cut into small florets
- 1 red pepper—cut in small cubes
- Tomatoes—cubes again, my friend
- 6 hard-boiled eggs—sliced thin
- 1½ cups marble or cheddar cheese—
  shredded

THE SIMPLE YET SCRUMPTIOUS DRESSING

- ¾ cup salad dressing or mayonnaise
- ⅓ cup sugar
- ¼ cup white vinegar

THE METHOD

—two methods to choose from, actually
Fry the bacon until crisp, and place on paper towels to drain.

Boil the rotini in salted water. Drain, rinse, drain again and cool.

Mix the salad and dressing together and refrigerate until it's time to sit down and eat. That's it! Pass-ta salad, please!

Well, actually that's not it, as you'll probably be spending time afterwards writing out the recipe for friends.

For a little variety, how about making a Greek Pasta Salad? Here are the ins and outs of making the Mediterranean conversion. In: cucumbers, olives, a yellow or orange pepper and feta cheese. Out: cauliflower, broccoli, cheddar, bacon, eggs and leisure suits. Then deep-six the dressing, and import the one from **Great Greek Salad** (page 44).

Sensational
CAESAR SALAD

There's nothing better than having just served Caesar salad at the fire station, and getting a call. When we arrive at the scene someone will invariably say to us, "Have you guys been eating garlic or what?"

THE SALAD

- Croutons—try the directions for homemade
- 1 head romaine lettuce
- Parmesan cheese
- Red onion—sliced thin into strips
- Bacon bits—recommended if your cholesterol count is just too low

THE DRESSING

- ⅓ cup Caesar salad dressing
- ⅓ cup salad dressing or mayonnaise
- ⅓ cup sour cream or plain yogurt
- Juice of half a large lemon— or 2 tablespoons lemon juice
- 4–6 cloves garlic—but why stop there?

ALL RIGHT, LET'S PUT IT TOGETHER

Construct homemade croutons by cutting baguette-style French bread into 1-inch slices. Mix margarine with as much pressed garlic as you like, along with a good shot of Italian seasoning. Butter both sides of the bread, and brown in a frying pan or oven. Allow to cool and cut into cubes.

Combine the Caesar dressing, salad dressing or mayo, sour cream, lemon juice and of course, last but not least, my good buddy garlic.

Wash and break up lettuce. Give it a long ride in the salad spinner.

Sprinkle the lettuce with Parmesan, onions, bacon bits—real are best—and croutons. Bring the dressing into play, toss through and serve.

Make this an entrée by barbecuing chicken marinated in **Lemon Garlic Marinade** (page 111), slice into strips and add to the salad. Why, you'll be able to see your breath in no time!

In a hurry? You can make a Caesar dressing shortcut by adding the lemon juice and garlic to fire up 1 cup of prepared Caesar dressing.

Lemon
POPPYSEED SALAD

Without question this is my most-requested salad recipe. If only I had invented it! Firefighter Bob Bean gets the credit here. Be sure to choose fruit and veggies with a variety of colours for maximum presentation.

THE DRESSING

- ½ cup canola oil—corn oil will also do

- ½ cup sugar—I know that sounds like a lot, but don't worry!

- ¼ cup red wine vinegar or balsamic vinegar. If you're not on a budget, the aged-for-20-years stuff from Italy—yeah, right, Jeff!

- 2 tablespoons lemon juice

- ½ teaspoon salt

- 2 teaspoons poppy seeds

THE SALAD

- 2 cans mandarin oranges—or try a 14-ounce can of mixed mandarins and peaches

- ½ pint strawberries—if unavailable, or just too darn expensive, simply substitute 2 kiwis and 2 green apples

- 1 red pepper—cut in strips

- ½ red onion—also cut in strips

- ½ cup slivered almonds and ¼ cup sunflower seeds

- Butter

- Brown sugar

- 1 small, ½-pound bag fresh spinach or romaine lettuce

THE KNOW HOW

Toss the dressing together and put it in the fridge. If you're using the exotic sweet balsamic vinegar, cut the sugar back to $^{1}/_{3}$ cup.

Slice, dice and organize the fruit and veggies.

Lightly brown the almonds and sunflower seeds in a bit of butter and brown sugar in a skillet over medium–low heat and allow them to cool.

Put the spinach in a bowl, add the fruit, veggies and nuts and toss in the dressing. Work it all through and you've got a great salad.

This recipe can be halved or multiplied successfully, depending on your math skills.

Let the
SUNSHINE SALAD

Here's another terrific, fruit-based salad. It's light and sweet, and a little different. My buddy, firefighter Lee Harrison, gets credit for this super recipe. Depending on the fruit you select, it goes with just about anything.

SO GO OUT AND FIND

- Butter

- Brown sugar

- ½ cup pecans or walnuts—chopped into bits

- 2 heads of butter lettuce or 1 large head of leaf lettuce

- 2 bananas—sliced

- 1 cup of pineapple tidbits—reserve juice for dressing

- 2 cups of red or green grapes—sliced in half

- 2 kiwis—sliced

- 1 pint strawberries—sliced

- Note—You can substitute a tin of mandarin oranges for any of the above. Actually, any combination of your favourite fruits will work.

- 3 sliced nectarines or canned peaches

OH, AND FOR THE DRESSING YOU'LL NEED

- ½ cup canola oil or another lightly flavoured vegetable oil, such as corn

- ¼ cup frozen orange juice concentrate—full strength, high octane

- 2 tablespoons soft or liquid honey

- ½ teaspoon salt

- 1 teaspoon ground ginger

- 1 tablespoon of the reserved pineapple juice

THEN SIMPLY

Warm a sauté pan over medium–low heat, add a couple tablespoons each butter and brown sugar and lightly brown the pecans or walnuts.

As the nuts cool, wash and break up the lettuce. Give it a spin dry.

Combine the dressing ingredients and refrigerate along with the lettuce.

Let's chop up the fruit, shall we? Dinner time is approaching quickly.

We have the fruit; we have the dressing; let's bring them together!

Just before serving, add the lettuce and pecans and toss 'em through.

So easy and so incredibly flavourful! This one is a keeper!

SPINACH 'N' EGG
Salad

How's this for a muscle-building salad? We're talking mega egg protein and the legendary—in cartoons anyway—strength-inducing spinach. This salad, snagged from firefighter Geoff Kyle, goes well with a juicy steak, roast beef or pork dish.

THE SALAD

- 6 eggs
- 1 small, ½-pound bag spinach
- ½ small red onion—sliced into strips

THE DRESSING

- 6 tablespoons light salad dressing or mayonnaise
- 3 tablespoons Dijon mustard
- 2½ tablespoons red wine vinegar
- 1 tablespoon sugar
- Garlic to taste—say 2–3 cloves. I love the stuff!
- Salt and pepper to taste

A FEW QUICK DIRECTIONS BEFORE I GO

Hard-boil the eggs. I find that if I start with the eggs in enough cold water to cover, turn on the heat to high, turn it down to simmer when full boil is reached and cook 10 minutes, they turn out perfectly.

Run eggs under cold water and peel immediately, starting at the top of each egg. I hope they cooperate and shed their shells easily for you. Eggs have been known to conspire, and resist peeling on occasion.

Allow the eggs to cool and slice them up. You can purchase a little egg guillotine at cookware stores that slices eggs thinly without mangling them. That'll teach those peel-resistant eggs to cooperate next time!

Place the spinach and red onions in a bowl and toss. Add the eggs.

Mix up the dressing ingredients, Give the dressing the old taste test, adjust with salt and pepper if necessary and add to the salad.

Push this one over the top by adding real bacon bits! Spinach, eggs and bacon. Now we're talking a fired-up firehouse salad!

WALDORF SALAD

This is my favourite salad to serve with pork. The unique combination of tart apples, sweet grapes, crunchy celery, nuts and a tangy dressing scores big.

SO GO OUT AND FIND

- 1½ cups chopped walnuts or pecans
- Butter
- Brown sugar
- Romaine or butter lettuce
- 1½ cups red seedless grapes—halved
- 1½ cups celery—very thinly sliced
- 4 Granny Smith apples—
  cut into ½-inch cubes

THE DRESSING

- ½ cup light salad dressing or light mayonnaise
- 3 tablespoons light or fat-free sour cream
- 2 tablespoons lemon juice
- 1 teaspoon sugar

OH, YOUR GUESTS ARE GOING TO LOVE THIS

Lightly brown the walnuts or pecans in a frying pan over medium heat with butter and brown sugar. Allow the nuts to cool in the fridge.

Break up the lettuce, wash it and line the bottom of a salad bowl with it.

Bring the mayo, sour cream, lemon juice and sugar together.

Toss the dressing with the veggies—except the lettuce—and walnuts.

Spoon over the lettuce in the salad bowl. Oh, this one is so good!

Asian Persuasion
COLESLAW

Tired of the same old slaw? Here's one that'll liven up the old picnic. It's a little bit sweet, a little bit sour and a little bit crunchy. You'll love it.

THE FUNKY DRESSING

- ½ cup minced onion
- ½ cup peanut oil
- ⅓ cup seasoned rice vinegar
- 2 tablespoons each ketchup and water
- 2 tablespoons freshly minced ginger or ginger paste
- 2 tablespoons minced celery
- 4 teaspoons soy sauce
- 2 teaspoons sugar
- 2 teaspoons lemon juice
- 1½ teaspoons chili-garlic sauce—in your grocer's Asian section
- ½ teaspoon salt
- ¼ teaspoon black pepper

THE SALAD

- 1 small, 1-pound bag ready-cut coleslaw
- ¼ cup each slivered almonds and sunflower seeds
- Butter
- Brown sugar
- 1 package Japanese noodle-soup mix—any flavour
- Bunch of green onions and 3 stalks of diced celery—optional

GET OUT THAT HANDY KITCHEN APPLIANCE

Throw the dressing ingredients into a blender, and blend away till smooth—about 30 seconds should do it.

Add the dressing to the coleslaw mix, toss and refrigerate 1–2 hours.

Brown the almonds and sunflower seeds in butter and brown sugar in a skillet over medium–low heat. Keep an eye on them now, they tend to burn easily.

Bring on the crumbled dry soup-mix noodles. Toss the salad.

Get the cooled nuts, onions and celery in there, and give this baby a final toss. Excellent as a funky alternative to plain old coleslaw.

ASIAN MIXED GREENS
with Sesame Dressing

This is very good served with a barbecued teriyaki steak, or just about any Asian barbecued meat. It's easy, low cal and extremely addictive. Thanks go to firefighter Marcel Gauthier for inspiring this wonderful recipe.

PLACE YOUR FAVOURITE VEGETABLES IN A SALAD BOWL

- Try a selection of your favourite greens: spinach, leaf lettuce, bok choy, beet tops, red Swedish chard, packaged spring mix, lawn and hedge trimmings, etc. (Hey, why compost?) Imagine a variety of colours to maximize the salad's presentation.

- Chopped green onions, or red onions cut into strips

- Mushrooms—feel free to go exotic, like shiitakes—minus the stems

- Hey, let's lightly toast sunflower seeds and almonds in a sauté pan with a little brown sugar and butter. Allow to cool, and in they go!

THEN ADD THIS DELICIOUS DRESSING TO THE VEGGIES

- ½ cup soy sauce

- ½ cup white or rice vinegar

- ¼ cup vegetable oil—preferably peanut or canola

- 2 tablespoons white sugar

- 4 teaspoons sesame oil

- 2 tablespoons ginger—fresh and finely diced

- 2 teaspoons-plus garlic—minced or pressed

HERE'S HOW TO MAKE THIS SALAD A MEAL IN ITSELF

Marinate steak or chicken breasts in **Teriyaki Marinade** (page 203). About 4 hours in the fridge basking in the flavour bath should do it.

Barbecue the breasts until no longer pink inside, or barbecue the steak until it is medium rare inside. Let stand 5 minutes and slice into strips.

Place a serving of salad on a plate, and top with strategically placed strips of teriyaki beef or chicken. Sprinkle sesame seeds over the top.

Go for broke by boiling the marinade for 5 minutes. Then drizzle it over the beef or chicken.

Awesome
POTATO SALAD

I've spent a lot of time goofing around with potato salad recipes, trying to find one that's out of the ballpark. So, on a whim, I decided to try using the dressing from the **Warm Mushroom Spinach Salad** *(page 56) plus a little mustard.* **Oh, he's going back ... back ... back ... It's out of here—a home run!**

INTRODUCING SPUDS ET AL

- 5 pounds Yukon Gold potatoes—cut into chunks
- 10 hard-boiled eggs (see page 49)—sliced up nicely or hacked up, your choice
- 5 stalks celery—diced
- 1 bunch green onions—sliced
- 1 red pepper—diced
- How about good old radishes—a traditional option

FOR THE HOME-RUN DRESSING

- ½ pound bacon—diced
- 2 tablespoons reserved bacon drippings
- 1 medium-sized red onion—finely diced
- 1 cup light salad dressing or light mayonnaise
- ⅓ cup sugar
- 3 tablespoons cider vinegar
- 3 tablespoons prepared mustard
- 2 tablespoons buttermilk

STEP UP TO THE PLATE AND

Toss the taters into a pot of salted water. Boil until just tender. Do not overcook. Drain the spuds and rinse thoroughly with cold water.

Toss the potatoes with the eggs and the rest of the vegetables.

In a medium frying pan over medium heat, cook the bacon until crisp.

Remove the bacon but hang on to the drippings and toss in the onions. Cook the tearjerkers until they are soft.

Combine the dressing ingredients and pour into the pan, heating briefly.

Bring the dressing, bacon and the salad together, toss thoroughly and place the big bowl of fun in the fridge to cool. (Or serve it warm, if you prefer.) A must-serve during the baseball—I mean, barbecue—season.

Mighty Caesar
BARBECUED POTATO SALAD

Firefighter Chris Blasko recommended that I try this one, and it's a winner! I love it! It's potato salad featuring barbecued baby red potatoes, eggs, bacon and onions with a creamy Caesar dressing. The result is amazing!

CHECK THE PANTRY FOR

- 8–10 slices of bacon
- 4 eggs
- Baby red potatoes with the skins on —I usually go for about 20
- ½ bunch green onions

AND FOR THE MIGHTY CAESAR DRESSING

- ⅓ cup bottled Caesar dressing
- ⅓ cup non- or low-fat sour cream
- ⅓ cup light salad dressing or light mayonnaise
- ⅛ cup lemon juice—that's 2 tablespoons
- 4–6 cloves of garlic—minced

LET'S GET BUSY WITH THE TOOLS

Fry the bacon till crisp, hard-boil the eggs (see page 49) and prepare the dressing.

Prick the potatoes a few times each, and place them on a paper towel in a microwave. Cook on high for approximately 10 minutes. This will save you some time on the barbecue. Check them part way through the cooking cycle. Don't overcook the spuds. They should still be firm before you ...

Roll the potatoes in olive oil to coat and toss them on the barbecue on medium–high heat, rotating until each shows lovely grill marks and is just cooked. We're at the slightly firm stage now.

Allow the potatoes to cool for 10 minutes and cut them into quarters or eighths depending on their size.

Bring the team together in the dressing room. Toss the spuds with enough Mighty Caesar Dressing to coat and introduce them to the bacon, eggs and onions.

I prefer this salad served slightly warm or at room temperature.

Nine-Layer
SALAD FOR TEN

This is firefighter Ralph Okrainec's specialty. Perfect for a crowd. If you're going to a party or the fire hall tonight, take this salad along for everyone!

THE SALAD—in order of appearance, from the bottom to the top

- 1 head iceberg lettuce—broken up, washed and spun dry
- 1 medium purple onion—slivered
- 1 long English cucumber—sliced
- 4 ribs of celery—diced
- 2 cups uncooked peas—thaw if frozen
- 1 pound bacon—fried, cooled and diced
- 4–5 tomatoes—sliced
- 6–8 hard-boiled eggs (see page 49) —sliced thin
- 2 cups grated marble cheese

THE DRESSING, ANOTHER SIMPLE YET SUCCULENT ONE

- 1½ cups light salad dressing or light mayonnaise
- ½ cup sugar
- ½ cup white vinegar

THE LAYERING METHOD

In a 9- x 13-inch lasagna dish or roaster, in order of appearance, lay down the cast of characters—lettuce, onion, cucumber, celery and peas.

Top with about ⅔ of the dressing, and allow the salad to sit for 2 hours or more in the fridge. It's not essential, but it is ideal. Come on now, exercise a little patience; you can do it with some pre-planning.

If leaving salad in a firehouse fridge, better affix the sign "Don't Eat" on it. If firefighters are hungry, they'll be browsing in the fridge and they'll eat anything not nailed down, even a semi-prepared salad.

Assemble the remaining layers of bacon, tomatoes, eggs and cheese.

Sprinkle the salad with the rest of the dressing before serving.

Hey, if you have any ingredients you'd like to add, go for it. Be brave! Make it a 10-, 11- or even 36-layer salad.

Warm
MUSHROOM SPINACH SALAD

Whenever I serve this one at the fire hall someone invariably says, "I'd have been happy with just the salad. It's a meal in itself!" Remember, this is coming from staunch meat-and-potato advocates. Consider this decadent! Thanks to firefighter Mike Dowhayko for this incredible recipe.

CHECK THE PANTRY FOR

- 4 cups of spinach—about 1 small, ½-pound bag
- 4-6 slices of bacon—diced
- 4 hard-boiled eggs (see page 49)—sliced
- 4 green onions—diced
- 1½ cups mushrooms—sliced thin
- 1½ cups mozzarella cheese—grated

THE DRESSING
—the only warm part, actually

- 2 tablespoons reserved bacon drippings
- 1 medium-sized red onion—finely diced
- 1 cup light salad dressing or light mayonnaise
- ⅓ cup sugar
- 3 tablespoons cider vinegar
- 2 tablespoons buttermilk

THE METHOD

Toss the salad ingredients together, ensuring that the cheese is spread out evenly and not clumped together. Keep it happy in the fridge.

Fry the bacon in a saucepan until crisp. Pour out all but 2 tablespoons of the drippings. "Mm, bacon drippings! Can I get an IV bacon drip?" asked the carnivorous, cholesterol-and-diet-be-damned firefighter.

Fry the onion in the bacon drippings until soft.

Combine the remaining dressing ingredients and add them to the pan.

Whisk the dressing together until the sugar is dissolved and the dressing is smooth. Well, except for the bits of onion it's smooth. Oh, come on, you know what I mean.

Pour the amazing dressing over the salad and serve immediately. I'm telling you, you won't believe the flavour!

Russian
TACO SALAD

It's terrific as a side dish with any Mexican entree or fantastic on its own for lunch or supper. Or why not have this while the kids have tacos?

THE GROCERIES

- 1 pound lean ground beef
- 1 package taco seasoning
- 1 head iceberg lettuce—shredded
- 5 Roma tomatoes—cubed
- 1 green or red pepper—cut into strips
- 1 19-ounce can kidney beans —washed and drained
- 1 bunch green onions—chopped
- ⅓ pound marble cheese—grated
- 1 small bottle Russian dressing. *Don't you mean Mexican dressing, Jeff?* No I don't, I mean Russian dressing. Give it a chance—it's great!
- 2 cups broken-up nacho or tortilla chips

THE EASY-TO-FOLLOW INSTRUCTIONS

Brown the meat in a frying pan and drain the fat.

Add the taco seasoning to the browned meat and follow the package directions, cooking until the beef is completely dry.

Once your meat is Mexicanized, place it in a bowl and allow it to thoroughly cool off in the fridge.

Okay, let's bring the veggies together in a salad bowl.

Add the Mexi-burger, and spread the shredded cheese over it.

Toss the Russian dressing through the salad.

Just before you serve it up, toss in the munched-up chips.

Assemble a dozen or so full-sized nacho chips around the perimeter of the salad bowl for presentation. Why? Because presentation is important. Oh sure, the kids could care less, but the adults will surely oohh and aahh!

Two Super
SALAD DRESSINGS—all you supply is the veggies

STRAWBERRY-YOGURT SALAD DRESSING

- 4 large strawberries
- ½ cup plain, or even better, vanilla, yogurt
- ¼ cup red wine vinegar
- ⅓ cup sugar
- ½ teaspoon salt

Simply mulch and purée the above in a blender. Goes great over a spinach strawberry salad, like the **Lemon Poppyseed** or **Let the Sunshine Salad** (pages 47 and 48).

DIJON VINAIGRETTE

- ½ cup extra-virgin olive oil
- ¼ cup red wine vinegar
- 1 tablespoon each Dijon mustard and sugar
- 1 teaspoon each dried basil and tarragon
- ½ teaspoon salt

Simply whisk the ingredients together. Serve with your favourite mixed green salad.

Ralphie
SLAW DRESSING

Use this dressing with your favourite coleslaw mix, and add a little celery, grated apple and green onions. Thanks go to firefighter-type buddy Ralph Okrainec.

- ½ cup canola oil
- ⅓ cup sugar
- ¼ cup white vinegar
- ¼ cup lemon juice
- 1 tablespoon salad dressing or mayonnaise—or more for a creamier version
- Salt, pepper and celery seed to taste

THAT DOESN'T SOUND GOOD

The first place we firefighters learn to suspect tampering is in our lockers. Open your locker and, if a firefighter hidden inside doesn't leap out to scare you, an elaborate system of strings and pulleys will be set up to dump a pail of water on you. Garlic, Parmesan cheese, anchovies—if it stinks it'll find its way into a firefighter's locker. Some lockers have even been filled to the brim with popcorn to surprise their proprietors.

Yes, some pranks hit immediately, while others take a little more time to work. I love the subtlety of this one. A firefighter opened his locker to change his attire for work and spotted a label-less tin can on the top shelf. "Where did that come from?" he wondered as he pulled the can off the shelf to examine it. As he looked it over, he heard an odd "glop" sound, and watched helplessly as a blob of grey matter succumbed to gravity and worked its way loose, dropping from the can and landing with an awful *splat* on the brand-new leather jacket that lay on the gym bag at his feet. Upon examination he discovered that it was a tin of cream of mushroom soup, the label removed to raise curiosity, the bottom carefully cut off to allow for "the slow-mo glop-drop."

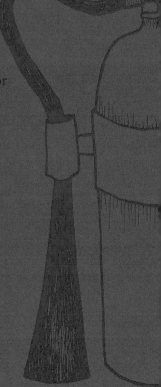

A FORK OR A SPOON

When I started as a firefighter, my idea of making soup was opening a can and heating it up. Oh, how times have changed! Today I wouldn't thank you for a bowl of canned soup; I'm a certified Soup Snob. How did this happen? Well, I've worked with some amazing soup chefs over the years. At first, I found their creations intimidating, and was afraid to try making soup for the critical masses in the fire hall. But I was keen to watch and learn, and before long, I was experimenting at home and ready for the boys at work.

I had the good fortune of working with Glen Godri; he can literally take whatever leftovers he can find in the fridge and make an incredible soup out of them. He never measures anything; he just has the knack of knowing what the soup needs when he tastes it.

Really, what soup boils down to is stew. No, what soup boils down to is stock, meat (optional for some) and veggies. You can make soup stock yourself by simmering chicken, pork or beef bones for several hours, or you can do a cheat by using prepared soup stock. But that will mean visiting the soup aisle at the supermarket—incognito, of course, as you don't want your neighbours to think that you actually eat prepared soup.

You'll notice in the following recipes that soup stock may also be—or include—clamato or tomato juice, milk, cream, sherry or even coconut milk. Hey, the options are endless. Soup really isn't that complicated; it takes a little time, but the results are more than worth it.

The best bit of advice I can give you about cooking soup is to season as you go. Add a bit of salt and spice, let it cook for a while, taste, and decide if it needs more. I always have a bowl beside the soup pot that I pour a taster of soup into as it melds. Remember, you can always add spice, but it's almost impossible to take something away once it's in there.

Here are my favourites. Learn as I did, from Soup Nazis like Glen Godri and Mike Dowhayko, and before long you just may become a certified Soup Snob too!

One more tip: make lots, because soup is always better the next day.

Chicken
CORN CHOWDER

Imagine the flavour of a roast chicken dinner with potatoes, veggies and gravy, all combined in one soup; it's creamy and delicious! Firefighter Keith Kauk gets credit for sharing this recipe with us.

LET ME SEE, WHAT DO I NEED?

- 2 cups cubed chicken—chicken thighs are best, boneless are easiest. You can also use leftover roast chicken.

- 6 slices bacon

- 1 medium onion—diced

- 3 stalks celery with leaves—chopped

- 3 carrots—sliced, or 1 large carrot—grated

- 3 tablespoons flour

- 3 cups chicken broth

- 4 new red potatoes—diced

- 1½ teaspoons dried sage leaves

- ¼ teaspoon—or more to taste—pepper

- 2 cups milk—at least 2%

- 1 19-ounce can kernel corn

OKAY, NOW WHAT DO I DO?

Dice up the chicken into bite-sized pieces. If the chicken is uncooked, then stir-fry it until it's browned and cooked through.

Fry the bacon in a medium-sized pan till crisp. Remove the bacon to a paper-towel-lined plate. Wait! Don't pour away the bacon drippings!

Toss the onion, celery and carrots into the flavourful drippings, and stir-fry the lot until slightly softened.

Bring in the flour and mix through the veggies with a spoon.

Pour the chicken broth in slowly, stirring as you go, to build your base.

Now let's add the diced potatoes, sage and pepper. Cover and cook over medium heat until the potatoes are tender.

Invite the chicken, bacon, milk and corn to the soup party. Continue cooking until heated through but not boiling.

As usual, add the old standbys, salt and pepper to taste.

Fresh chopped parsley over each serving makes for a great garnish!

CHICK 'N' NOODLE
Soup

Here's the classic soup for what ails you. I once made some for a new neighbour, who thanked me later for the chicken stew! Once again in the firefighter tradition, we make them thick and hearty here at the fire hall!

IT'S A GREAT WAY TO SPEND A LEFTOVER ROAST CHICKEN

- Carcass of a 5- to 6-pound roast chicken with some meat still on it, or a 3-pound whole uncooked chicken, or even chicken legs and thighs

- 5 cooking onions—diced

- 6 stalks of celery and 6 carrots—sliced

- 1 tablespoon each dill and basil or Italian seasoning

- 6 cloves garlic—minced or run through the press

- 1 cup frozen corn

- ¼ pound mushrooms—sliced into Ts

- 3 chicken bouillon cubes or 3 teaspoons powdered bouillon

- ⅓ pound broad egg noodles

IF YOU DON'T MIND SPENDING A LITTLE TIME

Boil the chicken carcass in enough water to cover for about 45 minutes. Remove chicken from the water, strip off the meat and set aside. Return the bones to the boiling water for another hour or so.

Skim the fat from surface or, if you have the time, you can refrigerate it overnight. Refrigeration makes it easy to skim off the congealed fat.

Stir-fry the onions, celery and carrots until just tender crisp. Toss in the herbs, garlic and veggies. Boil them until tender.

Re-add the chicken and bring the corn and mushrooms to the mix.

Add the chicken bouillon, one (or 1 teaspoon) at a time, tasting after each addition. This adds flavour and salt, so add it to taste.

Boil the pasta separately. If you don't, it will suck up a lot of the soup stock and you'll end up with chicken casserole. Hey, we want our soup thick, but not to the point where the soup spoon stands in it!

Where was I here? Oh yeah, add the pasta to the soup.

Turn the soup off and let it stand 10 minutes before serving.

A final seasoning of salt and pepper, and a little comfort—and perhaps even a cure for what ails you—is on its way.

Ukrainian
ONION SOUP —as it's affectionately known

Well, that's what we called it when my buddy Ralph Okrainec made it for us at a fire station located in Winnipeg's French quarter of St. Boniface. I mean, what kind of French name is Okrainec? Sure, the recipe looks similar to the French variety, but figure it out—it must be Ukrainian Onion Soup!

QUELS SONT LES INGREDIENTS?

- 2 pounds onions—Sweet Peruvians or Vidalias are excellent

- ⅓ cup butter

- 4 cloves garlic—minced or pressed

- 1 cup dry sherry

- 2 10-ounce cans chicken broth with garlic and herbs

- 2 10-ounce cans beef broth

- 2 teaspoons Dijon (this is French!) mustard

- Toasted French bread or croutons—which is French for "The best-before date has expired on this bread so let's just toss it in a salad."

- 1 cup grated Swiss cheese—hmmm, is this Swiss Onion Soup?

- ½ cup grated Parmesan cheese—or is it Italian Onion Soup?

THE FRENCH AND UKRAINIANS ARE SWIMMING IN THE MELTING POT

Halve the onions. Place the flat—as in cut—side of the onion down on the cutting board, slice the onion thinly and set aside.

Fire up the melting pot, bringing it to medium–low heat.

Add the butter, making sure that the pot isn't so hot that you burn it. Once the butter's melted, add the garlic and cook briefly.

Toss in the onions, and sauté on a simmer for 30 minutes.

Sherry's knocking at the door, so let's bring the alcohol to the party, and let the sherry simmer with the onions for 5 minutes.

Pour the broths into a separate bowl and whisk in the mustard. Get the broths into the soup, cover and simmer for at least 20 minutes.

Locate 4 large soup bowls that can handle the broiling process, pour a portion of soup into each and top with toast. Or try Okrainec's Ukrainian addition, which works great—croutons.

Top with grated Swiss and Parmesan and broil until lightly browned.

Now put aside all the cultural confusion and enjoy this amazing soup!

New England
CLAM CHOWDER

This is probably my most-requested soup. If you are a seafood lover, you've got to give it a go. Makes a great seafaring lunch!

IT'S SEAFOOD AND VEGGIES IN A CREAMY BROTH

- ¼ pound bacon—diced
- 2 medium onions—diced
- 3 stalks celery—sliced
- ¼ pound mushrooms—sliced into Ts
- 2 tablespoons flour
- 2 10-ounce cans baby clams
- 3 large potatoes—diced
- 2 carrots—grated
- 2 teaspoons salt—what kind of salt? Sea salt, of course!
- ½ teaspoon celery seed
- 1 teaspoon fresh ground pepper
- About ¼ bunch fresh parsley— chopped fine
- 2 chicken bouillon cubes or 2 teaspoons bouillon powder
- 3 cups of milk—the creamier the better
- ½ pound scallops
- about ½ pound crab-flavoured pollock— a.k.a. imitation crabmeat

HERE'S HOW YOU BRING IT ALL TOGETHER

Fry the bacon till crisp. Add the onions and celery, frying till opaque.

Toss in the mushrooms, fry 'em up, add the flour and mix through.

Drain the clams and reserve the liquid. Put the clams aside and add enough water to the clam liquid to make 2 cups.

Stir in the clam liquid gradually until slightly thickened.

Add potatoes, carrots, salt, celery seed, pepper, parsley and bouillon.

Cover and cook till the potatoes are tender. The liquid should just about cover the veggies. If not, add a little water or more clam juice.

Bring the clams and milk to the saucepan. Introduce the scallops and imitation-crab pollock. Simmer for about 10 minutes. The seafood cooks very quickly, and it will become tough if it is overcooked.

Let the soup stand off the heat for 15 minutes or so before serving. Adjust the spices if required. You'll probably need more salt and pepper, as potatoes are famous for sucking up the salt. Enjoy!

Manhattan
CLAM CHOWDER

Whenever I say that I'll make clam chowder at the fire hall, I'm asked the same question. Is that the red one or the white one? Well, this is the red one: New England's tomato-based, spicy, New York cousin.

ARRR, ME HEARTIES! YOU'LL BE NEED'N'

- 6 pieces of bacon—diced
- 2½ cups onions—diced
- 1 cup of celery—diced too!
- 2 carrots—diced or grated
- 2 cans of baby clams—you need to reserve the clam juice
- 1 28-ounce can diced tomatoes
- 2 cups spicy clamato juice
- 2 cups potatoes—diced, what else?
- 3 cloves garlic
- 1 bay leaf
- ½ pound baby scallops
- 1½ teaspoons salt— sea salt would be appropriate
- ½ teaspoon each basil, oregano and pepper

ARRR! GET INTO THE GALLEY, LANDLUBBER, AND

Fry the bacon in a stockpot until crisp. Don't dump the drippings!

Toss in the onions and fry until softened in the bacon drippings.

Add the celery and carrots, and fry until tender crisp.

Pour in the clam juice, reserving the clams. On deck, it's the tomatoes, clamato juice, potatoes, garlic and bay leaf. In you go, guys!

Pour in enough water to cover, and bring to a nice slow boil.

Turn the heat down to low and simmer until all of the veggies— especially the potatoes—are fork tender.

Bring on the clams, scallops and any other seafood you happen to like—for example, shrimp, crab-flavoured pollock, pickerel, etc. Toss in the seasonings.

Cook for about 10 minutes on simmer. Don't overcook the seafood though, or it may become tough, and we can't have that.

Remove from heat, garnish with parsley, and let stand for 10 minutes.

There'd best be butter and fresh bread, or you'll walk the plank!

HAM-AND-SPLIT-PEA
Soup

Wondering what to do with the leftover ham? Go with French tradition and make pea soup. But don't just settle for peas and ham; add a variety of vegetables to fire this soup up to the next level!

YOU NEED TO GATHER

- 1½–2 cups split peas—for a thicker pea soup, simply up the pea quotient

- A ham bone—a leftover with plenty of ham still on it will do

- 3 bay leaves

- 5 cloves garlic—minced or pressed

- 6 each carrots and celery stalks—diced and softened slightly by stir-frying in a pan with a little butter. A little salt wouldn't hurt either.

- 1 big bunch green onions

- ½ pound mushrooms

- 1 small bag frozen peas

- 1 tablespoon Italian seasoning

- Get the pepper mill grinding— do it to taste

THEN YOU NEED TO ASSEMBLE YOUR SOUP

Soak the split peas overnight in water—not essential, but preferable.

Place the ham bone in a Dutch oven or good-sized stockpot and add water until just covered—say about 10 to 12 cups.

Boil the ham for 1 hour. Remove it from the water, (now termed broth), skim off any fat or scum and strip the meat from the bone.

Place the bone back in the water, add the split peas, bay leaves and garlic, and get the broth rolling over a slow boil for an additional hour.

Dice up the ham and set it aside. Better put it in the fridge so the mice in the hall—a.k.a. the snackers— don't spot it and wolf it down.

Pull the ham bone and get the carrots, celery and green onions into the soup. Cook on a slow boil until the veggies and peas have softened.

Add the mushrooms, frozen peas and Italian seasoning. Cook through.

Do a final seasoning of salt and pepper to taste, pull the bay leaves out and it's "Soup's up!"

Decadent
HAM-AND-POTATO SOUP

Firefighter Glen Godri made this for us one day, and as I savoured the flavour I told him that if I were served this soup at a five-star restaurant, I'd be blown away. It is absolutely first class!

A BIT OF THIS, A BIT OF THAT

- 8 medium (about 2½ pounds) red potatoes—diced small or grated, as in lots of beaten-up knuckles and handsome bandages

- 1 medium onion—diced

- 5 stalks celery—sliced

- 5 carrots—grated

- 3 tablespoons instant chicken bouillon mix

- 8 cups water

- 4 cups ham—diced

- 4 cups broccoli—cut into florets

- 2 cups mild Italian sausage—fry or parboil first to remove the fat

- 1 cup milk—at least 2% or creamier for high octane

- 2 tablespoons butter

- 2 bay leaves

- ½ tablespoon each dried basil and oregano

- 1½ cups grated marble cheese, or good old orange cheddar

- 2 tablespoons fresh parsley, plus more for garnish—chopped fine

TOSS IN THIS, TOSS IN THAT

Place the potatoes, onion, celery, carrots, chicken bouillon and water in a pot and boil for about 45 minutes until veggies are very soft.

Get out the electric mixer and blend or mash veggies till smooth. Go for a creamy texture here as you establish your soup foundation.

Stir in the ham, broccoli, par-boiled sausage, milk, butter, bay leaves and spices. Simmer for 15 minutes, or until warmed through.

Stir in the cheese. Allow it to melt in the heat, stirring constantly.

Remove the bay leaves, and add, say, 2 tablespoons chopped parsley.

Allow the soup to stand for at least 10 minutes. Oh sure, easy for you to say when the vultures are circling the kitchen.

Here's a line you've heard before: add salt and pepper to taste.

Oh, and what a taste it is! I told you this soup was incredible!

Hearty
HAMBURGER SOUP

I'll gladly pay you Tuesday for a bowl of hamburger (soup) today, as Wimpy in the Popeye cartoons might have said. If time is of the essence, here's one that you can put together in a hurry and it'll taste like it simmered for hours. It's thick and hearty in the rich fire hall tradition.

THE GROCERIES

- 1 pound lean hamburger—no bun required
- 1 envelope onion soup mix—spicy onion if you want to fire it up!
- 3 cups boiling water
- 1 19-ounce can diced tomatoes
- 1 14-ounce can tomato sauce
- 1 tablespoon soy sauce
- ¼ teaspoon each pepper, oregano, basil and seasoning salt
- 2 cloves garlic—minced or pressed
- 1 cup celery—sliced
- 1 cup carrots—sliced
- ¼ pound mushrooms—cut into Ts
- Butter
- 1 cup macaroni, cooked and drained—optional—or ⅓ cup pearl barley—also on the optional list
- Parmesan cheese—but only if you're using pasta instead of barley

THE DIRECTIONS

Brown the hamburger, strain off the fat and keep guarded and warm.

Add the soup mix, water, tomatoes, tomato sauce, soy, spices and garlic to the soup pot. Mix them all together and bring your baby to a boil.

Stir-fry celery, carrots and 'shrooms in butter to establish flavours, and add to the soup. Boil until the veggies are happily fork tender.

Toss in the browned burger. We're rounding the clubhouse turn!

At this point you could add pearl barley if desired. That's Pearl Barley, not Pearl Bailey! It goes great in this soup, but it takes a good half hour to soften, so budget your time accordingly.

If you're not using barley, then add the cooked macaroni. For even more flavour—and a sticky bowl and spoon—you can add Parmesan cheese. Let the soup stand 5 minutes, and make the call, "Lunch up!" Oh, I hear the footsteps of the hungry ... *incoming!!*

Mike's
POPEYE SOUP

This is a terrific deluxe variation on hamburger soup that firefighter Mike Dowhayko passed along to us. Apparently, another firefighter made one of Mike's recipes and claimed that it was his creation. So Mike—a great soup chef in his own right—stole this recipe from him, and renamed it to even the score. Hey, it's an eye for an eye in the fire hall.

SURE, THERE'S A FEW THINGS TO ROUND UP

- 1 48-ounce can spicy clamato juice—for that subtle seafaring touch
- 1 28-ounce can diced tomatoes
- 3 tablespoons instant chicken bouillon powder
- 1 teaspoon each basil and oregano
- ½ teaspoon each garlic powder and paprika
- 2 10-ounce cans consommé
- 4 10-ounce cans water
- 1½ pounds lean hamburger
- 1½ pounds Italian sausage—parboil before frying to de-fat
- 1 medium onion—chopped
- 5 carrots—sliced
- 5 celery stalks—sliced
- 1 medium cabbage—chopped fine
- 3–4 cups coarsely chopped spinach—for Popeye's forearm muscles
- 1 19-ounce can kidney beans—hmm ... beans and cabbage, is that safe?
- 1 19-ounce can white navy beans

BUT DON'T WORRY, IT'LL COME TOGETHER QUICKLY

Mix the clamato juice, tomatoes, bouillon, spices, consommé and water together in—of all things—a soup pot. Let 'em gently boil for 30 minutes.

Brown the burger and sausages. Drain off the fat and set aside.

Sauté the veggies—minus the spinach—until tender crisp, and add them to the soup. Cook the soup on a slow boil for 30 minutes.

Add the meat, spinach and beans. Cook 'em for 20 minutes more.

This soup is thick and hearty as is the firehouse custom. Park a couple of slices of fresh bread beside a bowl and it's a meal in itself.

Freddy's
BORSCHT

I snagged this recipe from my friend, the late Fred Herzberg, who was a chef at several restaurants in Winnipeg. A great character, and a fantastic soup that's oh, so much better the second day.

USE THE EXPRESS LANE BECAUSE ALL YOU NEED IS

- About 4 pounds of meaty pork riblets
- 2 tablespoons kosher salt
- ¼ cup sugar
- 2 jumbo onions
- 1½ pounds fresh beets, peeled
- 5 stalks celery—diced
- 1 28-ounce can pork and beans
- Tomato juice—to taste. You may need as much as 20 ounces.

IT'S BEST TO START THIS ONE A DAY IN ADVANCE

Place the riblets in a soup pot about half full of boiling water.

Add salt, sugar and 1 onion.

Cook the riblets at a slow boil for about 1½ hours.

Remove the big pan from heat, and allow the soup to cool.

Either skim fat from the soup or do it the easy way. Place the soup pot in the refrigerator overnight. Then in the morning skim off that delicious—just kidding!—layer of congealed fat from the soup stock.

Remove the riblets, take the meat from dem bones and cut it up.

Grate half of the beets, and finely chop the onion.

Get the soup stock boiling and toss in the grated beets and onions.

After 30 minutes, add the celery and remaining beets, diced.

When the celery and beets are cooked, add the beans and rib meat.

Pour in the tomato juice and add sugar to taste. Introduce a little sweet at a time, as the flavour should only add to the natural sweetness of the beets, not over-whelm it.

As with all soups we conclude with the following lines: let stand for 10 minutes before serving and add salt and pepper to taste.

Now on to the all-important serving suggestion. It's an option, but a highly recommended one: place a dollop of sour cream in the centre of each freshly poured bowl of borscht, and go to town!

Cream of
MUSHROOM SOUP

What, a soup without meat? **The carnivores at the fire hall are going to kill you, Jeff!** *Well, not if you toss in some cooked chicken or pork, or serve it with a roast beef sandwich or a tuna melt on a bagel. Remember it's a soup, which comes from the Latin term meaning "whatever one can find."*

FIXIN'S

- ¼ pound butter
- ¼ cup red or sweet yellow onion—diced
- 1 pound fresh mushrooms—sliced into Ts
- ¼ cup all-purpose flour
- 4 10-ounce cans of chicken broth—I like garlic and herb chicken broth. Hey, you know me, I need my garlic fix! I really should look into getting a garlic IV drip set up for myself.
- 1 cube beef bouillon or 1 teaspoon powdered bouillon
- ½ cup dry sherry
- 1 cup whipping cream, the thick 'n' rich stuff, or half and half

HOW TO FIX THE FIXIN'S

Melt the butter in a medium-sized saucepan over medium heat.

Cook the onion in the butter for about 2 minutes.

Add the mushrooms and sauté the fungi boys until softened.

Sprinkle the flour over the veggies and stir to combine.

Pour in the chicken broth, a little at a time, stirring madly into a wild frenzy, sloshing broth all over yourself ... On second thought, better stir in a steady, controlled, temperate manner until all the broth is added and the soup in progress is velvety smooth.

Toss in the bouillon and pour in the sherry.

Bring the soup to a slow boil and remove it from the heat.

Slowly—yes, you need to exercise restraint again—stir in the cream and heat through without boiling.

You know the drill by now: freshly ground pepper and salt to taste.

Still ticked off about the lack of meat? Okay then, for a nice touch, why not go deluxe by adding some leftover pork roast or, better yet, **Jamaican Jerk Pork Chops** (page 120). Oh man, now we're talking!

Thai Curried
COCONUT SOUP

Let's wrap up the soup section with an exotic one. C'mon, break free from tradition and have some fun! This soup combines many different flavours, yet it all comes off in a smooth creamy texture with just a bit of bite, a nibble really; well, unless you go for gold with a hot curry paste.

OKAY, SO A FEW INGREDIENTS ARE A LITTLE DIFFERENT

- 2 tablespoons vegetable oil
- 1½ tablespoons curry paste—I like mild, or you could go for the heavy-duty, paint-stripping hot
- 2 large chicken breasts or 6 chicken thighs—cut into small strips
- 1 medium onion—diced
- 1 red pepper—cut into strips
- 1 tablespoon minced fresh ginger
- 1 teaspoon minced garlic
- 3 cups chicken broth—homemade or canned
- 2 400-mL cans unsweetened coconut milk
- ¼ pound shiitake mushrooms—cut off the stems and toss 'em out
- ¼ cup cilantro—finely chopped
- 1 cup bean sprouts—coarsely chopped
- ¼-½ pound fresh shrimp or scallops
- Juice of one freshly squeezed lime

BUT REALLY, IT'S QUITE EASY TO MAKE

Heat a large heavy saucepan to medium high and toss in the oil.

Add the curry paste and stir for about a minute. I love that smell!

Toss in the chicken strips and stir-fry for 2 minutes, stirring often.

Bring in the onion, pepper, ginger and garlic. Fry for 1 minute.

Now pour in the chicken broth. Deglaze the bottom as you go with a spatula to get those flavourful bits off the bottom of the pan.

The coconut milk is ready to go, so let's toss it in there.

Oh, I almost forgot the shiitake heads; they're ready to go in too.

Bring the soup to a very slow boil and simmer for about 15 minutes.

Bring on the cilantro, bean sprouts and seafood, and simmer for about 5 minutes or until the seafood is cooked through.

Add the fresh lime juice and season with salt and pepper to taste.

TURNING UP THE HEAT

A new captain had been promoted to lead us, and on the morning of his first shift he sat us down at the big kitchen table for a chat. He kicked off the discussion by reading us the riot act, a list he had compiled of fire hall dos and don'ts, the big one being, "I don't want to hear or see any evidence of the sideline jobs you guys do here at work. I don't even want the phone ringing about your other jobs. The bottom line is, I don't want you conducting business while you're at work. While you're here in this building, you're a firefighter and that's it!"

The very next day the captain asked, "Has anyone seen Gerry?"

"Yeah, he's out back selling stuff out of the trunk of his car again," Lee matter-of-factly replied, referring to our beloved senior man.

"What?? What did I just tell you guys?" the captain exploded as he stormed out of the kitchen and confronted Gerry at the back of the hall. Truth be known, Gerry wasn't selling anything from his firefighter-clothing line; he was simply talking with an off-duty firefighter. "Gerry, I want you in my office *right* now!" the cap fumed.

Into the office they both stomped, faces red with anger, their blood pressures blasting off the charts. The door slammed behind them, and the yelling from both sides began. Meanwhile Lee sat innocently at the kitchen table, whistling and twiddling his thumbs.

ENTRÉE IF YOU DARE Mains, Sides and Sauces

HAY, WHAT'S MOO?

Dijon Pepper Roast Beef 81
You can't lose cooking roast beef in a fire hall

Mom D's Pot Roast 82
A family favourite that also scores big at the hall

Succulent Slow-Cooker Pot Roast 83
Start it up and just walk away

Beer Steaks with an Ultra-Decadent Sauce 84
Pour your steak a bubbly!

The Ultra-Decadent Steak Sauce 85
Pour those steaks a wine and brandy too!

Steak Neptune 86
There's a seafaring cow in first class

Three Great Steak Marinades 87
Bloody Mary, Key Lime and Dijon Mustard

Easy Beef Tenderloin 88
It's a snap. All you need is a fat wallet

Barbecue-Fired Burgers 89
Is your burger boring? Well, come on, fire it up!

Meatloaf Cordon Bleu 90
Stuff a taste treat into your next loaf

Meatballs Two Ways 91
Try them with **Sweet-and-Sour** or **Stroganov Sauce**

Sizzling Shepherd's Pie 92
Fire up this comfort food with spice and wine

Beef 'n' Banger Stew 94
In a pot, in a crock pot or fire it up with curry

Fred Flintstone Barbecued Beef Ribs 95
For the caveman in you!

Five-Star Whiskey Brisket 96
Cooked low and slow in the oven—easy does it!

HOT CHICKS

Lemon Herb Roasted Chicken 99
Hey, this chick's upside down!

Beer-Can Chicken 100
Get that hot chick dancing on the barbecue

Vampire-Free Chicken 102
Sink your eyeteeth into this, Dracula. Ah, Ah, Ah!

Mike's Lemon Garlic Chicken 103
As good as a stake, right, Count?

Orange Seafood-Sauce Chicken 104
My most-requested recipe. 'Nuff said

Louisiana Chicken 105
Definitely a hot chick, born on the Bayou

Taste-Like-Fried Barbecued Hot Wings 106
Healthy, fired up and tasty!

Derraugh Marinara 107
If I were a Greek man . . . daidle, deedle, daidle . . .

Chicken Cordon Bleu 108
Tell that chick to get stuffed!

Chicken Amandine with Creamy Tarragon Sauce 110
Such presentation!

Two Great Chicken Marinades 111
Choose Beer Chick or Lemon Garlic

PIGS TO THE TROUGH

Pork Roast, A Surefire Winner 114
Always a firehouse favourite

Blazin' Barbecued Pork Roast 115
Fire up the barbecue for a Carolina-style roast

Citrus Honey-Glazed Ham 116
It's a little bit sweet and a little bit fruity

Pork Normandy 117
French cuisine in the firehouse? Well, why not?

Pork Tenderloin with Blueberry Mushroom Sauce 118
Oh, what flavour!

Mom D's Stuffed Pork Tenderloin 119
Pound it, stuff it and tie it up

Jamaican Jerk Pork Chops with Fresh Mango Salsa 120
A tropical treat

Beer-Brined Pork Chops 121
Brining them in beer keeps them juicy on the barbecue

Sweet-and-Sour Pork Steaks 122
Moist and flavourful, plus the price is right

Barbecued Baby Back Ribs 123
When only the best rack will do

Smokin' Side Ribs 124
Just as tasty as backs, but about half the price

SOMETHING'S FISHY

Two Batters for Fire Hall Fish Fry 127
English Style or Crispy Beer, your choice

Cornflake-Battered Fillets 128
There's also an Italian Job option

Sweet-and-Sour Sole 129
It's fired-up Far Eastern sole food

Shrimp Scampi 130
How about some garlic-spiced Italian soul food?

Lee's Salmon Fillet 131
Cue to barbecue and summon the salmon

Killer Crab Cakes 132
Killer good, that is, served solo or on a bun

Pesto Basa 134
Take this succulent Vietnamese fish to Italy or Mexico

Tropical Tilapia 135
Taste how tilapia handles a hearty shot of rum

FROM THE GREAT WALL TO THE TAJ MAFIRE HALL

Chickity China the Chinese Chicken 138
You have a drumstick and . . .

Orange Hoisin Chicken 139
Or try the Plum Sauce Chicken option

Szechwan Peanut Chicken 140
Post the peanut-allergy alert signs!

Lemon Chicken 141
You can deep-fry it, but I have a healthier idea

Korean Chicken 142
From the land of Tae Kwon Do comes a kickin' chick

Beef Tenderloin with Oyster Mushroom Sauce 144
Cost? What cost?

Outrageous Egg Foo Yung 145
For dinner, lunch or even breakfast

What Did You Satay? 146
I SAID IT'S A TASTY THAI MARINADE!

Thai Chicken Curry 147
Fire up your chicken stir-fry with a blast of curry!

Curried Pasta Prima-Derraugh 148
India and Italy have combined forces

Tandoori Chicken 149
The call is in for tasty, fired-up, red-glazed chicken

"Like Butter" Chicken 150
Serve Tums as an accompaniment. FIRE! FIRE!

VIVA ITALIANO!

Lemon Garlic Pesto Chicken 154
Who says pasta sauce needs cooking?

Bread-Maker Pizza Dough 155
I'll be on the treadmill while the dough mixes

Pesto Pizza with Greek Pesto Option 156
Take a break, tomato sauce

Thai Chicken Pizza 157
Thai peanut sauce brings on the heat!

Tex-Mex Pizza 158
The tomato sauce is back, and it brought salsa with it

Pacific Rim Pizza 158
Another funky Far Eastern pizza

Scorchin' Lasagna 159
Salsa plus a pepperoni pizza topping fire it up!

Fettuccine Alfredo 160
I think maybe I'll just stay on the treadmill

Linguine of the Sea 161
Flavourful fish swimming in a sea of white sauce

Red Wine Spaghetti Sauce with Barbecued Meatballs 162
Just do it!

Fired-Up Bolognese Sauce 163
Another great twist on traditional pasta sauce

Mozzasaurus Chicken 164
Meets Godzilla? No, meets your taste buds!

Coq Au Vin Cacciatore 165
Italy and France have come to a compromise

SOUTHERN SIZZLERS

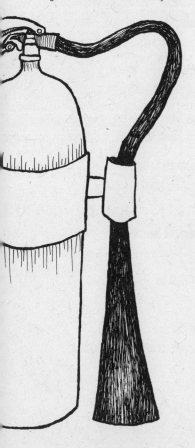

SPUDS AND HIS BUDS

PLAIN WHITE RICE? ARE YOU CRAZY?

Rip Roarin' Risotto 192
Company's coming? Look no further

Mediterranean Rice 193
Won a gold medal at the Athens Olympics

Mexi Rice 194
Go south young (wo)man in search of fired-up flavour

Deluxe Asian Fried Rice 195
A stir-fry isn't a stir-fry without it

Coconut Curried Rice 196
Bland old rice gets an East Indian flavour blast!

Wild Rice Casserole 197
I see fish or chicken by your side

SPICE IT UP, GET SAUCED!

Fired-Up Spice 200
Get your spice rack blazin'

Fired-Up Santa Fe Spice 200
Chili? Bring on the heat!

Simple Tomato Salsa 201
Consider bottled salsa a thing of the past

Scandalous Strawberry-Orange Salsa 201
Taking salsa to the next level

Cheddar Cheese Sauce 202
It's a white sauce, it's a cheese sauce!

Lemon Dill Sauce 203
A great topping for salmon and asparagus

Teriyaki Marinade 203
So easy, so tasty, for beef or chicken

Carolina Mustard Sauce 204
A tangy sauce that I just can't live without

Carolina Tartar Sauce 204
Mix up a batch before the fish hits the pan

Just Like Bull's Eye Barbecue Sauce 205
Hits the target dead centre

Hawaiian Barbecue Sauce 205
No pineapples were harmed making this recipe

Hall-a-Blaze Sauce 206
Get out the blender, it's hollandaise made easy

HAY, WHAT'S MOO?

Firehouse cooking is steeped in the rich, and I mean *rich*, tradition of meat and potatoes. You can't go wrong and almost no one will whine if you put a roast, potatoes, carrots and gravy on the table. In fact, many firefighters insist on this form of gastronomic pairing by name: "It *better* be meat and potatoes, and there better be *lots!*"

Yes, many a firehouse cook has cowered behind the counter, hoping that the ravenous masses will have enough to eat. The rule of thumb is this: buy at least a pound of meat for each firefighter. Yes, one pound, as in 16 ounces. But when it comes to the **Fred Flintstone Barbecued Beef Ribs** (page 95), count on at least two pounds per firefighter or it'll be a scene from the movie *Alive*, and rest assured you won't be one of the diners.

Cook a large roast at the hall—weighing twice what you'd normally need—so that you can serve hot beef sandwich leftovers the following night, and you'd better hide the roast under lock and key or the mice—a.k.a. the late-night nibblers—will throw a wrench into your plans. Oh, and by the way, the mice will be the first to complain if there isn't enough on the second night!

Yes, firefighter appetites are legendary and, over time, often lead to a few unwanted pounds around the middle. In some cases, there comes the realization that it's time to diet. I know of one guy who decided to go the weight-loss milk shake route at work. Another firefighter—with the man's good health clearly in mind—kindly substituted weight-gain powder for the weight-loss powder. The firefighter couldn't understand why he was gaining so he substituted shakes for meals more often, only making matters worse before finally giving up. Yes, that's the great thing about firefighters: we're always there for each other.

Sorry, I wandered off again. Let's get back to the beef. I could play it safe and cook up a roast or steak, and occasionally I do, but often I'll stray from the beaten path and offer new and diverse options. In this section I've included the traditional, the out there, and the out-there versions of the traditional. Whether it's at home or at the hall, here are my favourite beef recipes for you to fire up for firefighters, friends or family.

Dijon Pepper
ROAST BEEF

Here's a great way to cook a lean roast and keep it tender. The Dijon mustard not only adds flavour, it also helps seal in the roast's juices.

THE DIJON DRESSING

- 3 tablespoons Dijon mustard
- 1½ tablespoons lemon juice
- 1 teaspoon Italian seasoning
- 1 tablespoon fresh ground pepper

THE ROAST, GARLIC AND ONIONS

- 4½- to 5-pound baron of beef or sirloin tip roast—with a nice piece of fat from the butcher tied on top
- Garlic powder and onion powder
- 6 cloves garlic—cut into matchsticks
- 2 onions—cut in thick slices
- 1½ cups water

THE BATTLE PLAN

Combine the Dijon dressing ingredients in a bowl.

Flip the roast onto the fat side and spread on the dressing.

Dust the roast with garlic and onion powders. Let the roast sit for 30 minutes to suck up the flavour.

Flip the roast over, fat side up. Insert the matchsticks of garlic and spread the dressing on the top 3 sides, or as much as the force of gravity will allow. Let the roast sit an additional 30 minutes.

Fire up the oven to 500 flaming degrees.

Place the roast on a rack set in a roaster. Surround the roast with onions and add 1½ cups of water to the pan.

Cook at 500 degrees for 30 minutes, uncovered, and then turn down to 250. Don't open the oven to peek! Cook an additional 2–2½ hours.

Check the roast with a meat thermometer. If you haven't reached medium rare, then put the roast back in the oven until you're there.

This method makes the leanest meats almost as tender as prime rib. Oh, and by the way, you can cook prime rib or any premium oven roast this way too! Go for it, big shot, blow the wad!

Mom D's
POT ROAST

Friday was pot-roast dinner night when I was growing up. I love Mom's recipe, not only because of the tremendous flavour but also because cooking the entire meal in one pot makes for easy prep and clean-up. Of course, at the fire hall, who cares about clean-up? The chef doesn't do dishes anyway!

ROAST, VEGGIES AND WINE

- 3½- to 4-pound boneless blade or cross rib roast
- Garlic powder, onion powder, salt and pepper
- Olive oil
- ¼ cup dry red wine
- 1 10-ounce can of consommé
- 3 bay leaves—optional
- 4–5 potatoes—quartered
- 6 carrots—cut into large pieces
- 2–3 parsnips—optional
- 3–4 cooking onions—quartered
- 2 tablespoons flour

LET'S COOK THEM ALL TOGETHER

Rub the pot roast top and bottom with garlic and onion powders, salt and pepper.

Heat 1 tablespoon olive oil in a Dutch oven at medium–high heat. Sear the outside of the roast on all sides. That'll seal in the juices.

Add the red wine to deglaze the pot, scraping the flavour-laden browned bits from the bottom. This should take about a minute.

Toss in the consommé, add the bay leaves and turn down to simmer. Cover the pan and cook for 1½ hours.

Flip the roast over and layer in the veggies. First up it's the potatoes. Drop them in around the roast and sprinkle them with salt. Then in order bring in the carrots and parsnips, and place the onions on top. Cover and simmer an additional 1¼ to 1½ hours.

When the roast appears happy, tender and done, remove the veggies to a bowl and keep them warm. Remove the roast to a carving board, and cover with aluminum foil. Now let's get that gravy happening.

Mix about 2 tablespoons flour with ½ cup water. Add to the drippings slowly, cooking on medium–high heat. Stop adding the flour mixture when the desired consistency is reached. Season with salt and pepper as required. Easy, and oh so good on a cold winter day!

Succulent
SLOW-COOKER POT ROAST

Here's a simple one that you'll find yourself preparing time and time again. What I love about this recipe is that it transforms a tough, low-fat roast, into a tender taste sensation. Before I leave home to work day shift, I leave a roast simmering in the slow cooker in this delicious gravy.

THE PLAYERS

- 5- to 6-pound cross rib, blade, sirloin or round roast
- Salt and pepper
- Vegetable oil
- 1 10-ounce can cream of mushroom and garlic soup
- 1 10-ounce can consommé
- 1 envelope onion soup mix— I like a spicy one
- ¾ cup dry red wine
- Good old salt and pepper to taste

THE BATTING ORDER

Get out a Dutch oven or large frying pan and fire it up to medium heat.

Salt and pepper the roast on all sides. Pour a couple tablespoons of oil in the pan and carefully brown the entire outside of the roast to seal in the flavours. Use a carving fork to move it around.

Place the roast in a large slow cooker.

Combine the soups, soup mix and wine, and pour over the roast. Warning: do not taste this combination as it's quite bitter. However, by the end of the lengthy cooking cycle, you'll find that the gravy is smooth and delicious.

At this point you can cover and refrigerate the roast overnight or, if you're up early enough and have the foresight to start the proceedings in a timely manner, move right along to the next step.

Fire up the crock pot to low, and let the roast cook, covered and unattended, for 8 to 9 hours depending on the size of roast.

Remove the roast from the pan and cover with foil to keep warm.

Depending on the fat content of the roast, you may find that the consistency of the gravy is perfect. If not, transfer to a saucepan, bring gravy to a boil and thicken by slowly adding cornstarch mixed with equal parts water, until it's just right.

Taste test the gravy and add salt and pepper as needed.

BEER STEAKS
with an Ultra-Decadent Sauce

What a great fire hall combo! The boys will go bananas! Even if you don't like beer, this marinade is excellent. Obviously we can't drink at the fire hall, but hey, we can cook with beer, can't we? Sorry, what was that, Chief?

GO TO YOUR FRIENDLY BUTCHER FOR

- 3–5 pounds of your favourite steaks— I'm a sucker for sirloin

FOR THE MARINADE YOU'LL NEED

- 1 12-ounce bottle of beer—pick a favourite. Actually, make it two: one for you, one for the marinade. Days off only, of course.

- ½ cup brown sugar

- 5 tablespoons lime juice

- 3 tablespoons red onion—minced

- 6 cloves garlic—pressed or minced

- 2 tablespoons Worcestershire sauce

- 2 tablespoons grainy Dijon mustard

- 2 tablespoons olive oil

- 1 tablespoon fresh ginger—minced

- 1 teaspoon Louisiana hot sauce

THE COOKING PROCESS

Soak steaks with marinade in plastic bag for 4–24 hours.

Grill the way you like them.

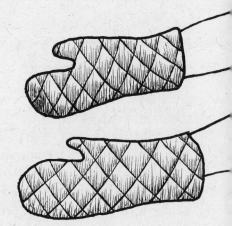

The Ultra-Decadent
STEAK SAUCE

This pushes the **Beer Steaks** *over the top. What? More alcohol?*

WE'RE TALKING WINE AND BRANDY HERE!

- 2 tablespoons butter
- ½ medium onion—diced fine
- 3–4 cloves garlic—minced
- ¼ pound mushrooms—cut into Ts
- ¼ cup each brandy and white wine
- ½ cup beef broth or consommé
- ½ cup whipping cream—the hearty, 35-percent stuff
- 1 teaspoon Dijon mustard
- 1 tablespoon each fresh basil and fresh parsley—chopped

STEAKS ARE ON THE GRILL, SO LET'S MAKE THE SAUCE

Heat the butter in a saucepan over medium heat.

Add the onion and garlic to the pan and stir-fry until softened.

Toss in the mushrooms and cook for 1–2 minutes until just slightly browned. Remove the veggies from the pan.

Bring the brandy to the saucepan to deglaze it.

Let's add the wine and beef broth, and lightly boil the sauce until it's reduced to about half of what you started with.

Whisk in the whipping cream and then the Dijon mustard.

Finally add the basil and the parsley, and warm through until it's cooked down to the desired consistency. Re-add the veggies.

Barbecue the steaks to desired doneness. A little hint of pink is nice.

Slice the steaks against the grain into strips, fan 'em out on individual plates, and top them with the sauce.

Steak
NEPTUNE

Talking about ultra decadent, here's a recipe that's way over the top. Former west coast resident turned Winnipeg firefighter, Marco Cecchetto, suggested this combination, a coming together of a number of recipes, all conveniently located right here in this book.

Marinate steaks as in the recipe for **Beer Steaks** (page 84).

Barbecue to desired level of doneness and set aside tented with foil.

Fire up a batch of **Hall-a-Blaze Sauce** (page 206) or prepare packaged hollandaise sauce.

Meanwhile, don't scrimp, make up the **Shrimp Scampi** (page 130). Try adding scallops to the mix as well for variety and presentation.

Set the scampi aside and do up the **Asparagus Parmesan** (page188).

Cut the steak against the grain and fan out on a plate. Top with the shrimp, then the asparagus and finally the hollandaise. You can place this under the broiler to brown if desired.

Serve with **Twice-Baked Crab Cake Potatoes** (page 181).

Looking for a little variety? Fry veal cutlets battered in Italian bread-crumbs in olive oil, pick up the action at step 3, **Hall-a-Blaze Sauce**, and get into some delicious Veal Neptune.

Three Great
STEAK MARINADES

BLOODY MARY STEAK MARINADE

- 2 cups tomato juice
- ¼ cup Worcestershire sauce
- 2 tablespoons horseradish
- 1½ teaspoons kosher salt
- 3 tablespoons dry sherry
- 2 teaspoons dried basil
- 1 teaspoon dried oregano
- 1 teaspoon fresh ground pepper
- 6 cloves crushed garlic

KEY LIME STEAK MARINADE

- ¼ cup lime juice
- 2 tablespoons each soy sauce and honey
- 2 tablespoons oyster sauce
- 1 tablespoon peanut oil
- 1 teaspoon ground cumin
- ¼ teaspoon cayenne

DIJON MUSTARD STEAK MARINADE

- 3 tablespoons Dijon mustard
- 1 tablespoon each soy sauce and olive oil
- 1 tablespoon fresh ginger—minced or grated
- 3 cloves garlic—minced or pressed
- 1 teaspoon lemon juice
- ½ teaspoon dried thyme
- ½ teaspoon fresh coarsely ground pepper

No matter which one you choose

Marinate steak for 4 hours to overnight in a plastic bag.

Get those babies on the grill over medium–high heat.

Here's a nice touch. Fry up some onions, mushrooms and peppers, and serve them over the steak. It simply has to be done!

Easy
BEEF TENDERLOIN

You can't go wrong with beef tenderloin. Not only is it extremely tender—duh!— but it sure cooks up fast and easy. The meat is so dense that a 6- to 8-ounce portion is plenty. I know, make that 12 to 48 ounces for firefighters.

NOT MUCH TO GATHER

- 1 or more beef tenderloins— say 3–5 pounds

- ¼ cup Dijon mustard—more for a big loin

- 2 teaspoons—about 6–8 cloves— minced garlic

- 2 tablespoons freshly ground peppercorns

- Rosemary or sage—optional

NOT MUCH TO DO EITHER

With a sharp knife carefully remove the silver skin from the loin. Peel it back as you cut under the skin. Not toward your body!

With butchers' string, tie the loin in 3–4 places to keep a consistent, round shape. This will mean folding back the skinny end and tying it together. Or cut that end off, and save it for use in a stir-fry.

Combine the mustard and garlic and spread over the tenderloin. Grind the peppercorns all over the loin as well, then let it sit for an hour at room temperature.

Place loin on a rack in a roasting pan. Crank the oven up to 425 degrees and when the oven's ready, pop that baby in there.

After 10 minutes at 425, turn it down to 350 degrees, and let it cook an additional 25 minutes (for 3 pounds) 35 minutes (for 4 pounds) and about 45 minutes (for 5 pounds). You'll want it medium rare—check it with a meat thermometer—as overcooking a loin will toughen it considerably, due to its low fat content.

If you happen to have some fresh herbs like rosemary or sage, chop and sprinkle them over the roast for the final 15 minutes.

If you really want to impress your guests, serve with **Stroganov Sauce** from **Meatballs Two Ways** (page 91) or **Ultra-Decadent Steak Sauce** (page 85). Toss in some of the drippings from the roast, and oh man, now we're talking richness!

BARBECUE-FIRED BURGERS

Here's a recipe that'll fire up the boring old burger! Give it a shot.

STUFF

- ½ cup quick-cooking—no, not instant—oats
- ¼ cup light salad dressing or light mayonnaise
- 1 large egg
- 4 garlic cloves—minced or pressed
- 1 tablespoon **Carolina Mustard Sauce** (page 204)—regular prepared mustard or Dijon mustard can be substituted
- 1 teaspoon each dried basil and thyme
- 1 teaspoon **Fired-Up Spice** (page 200) or seasoning salt
- ½–¾ teaspoon each pepper and steak spice
- 1 pound each lean ground beef and ground pork—or 2 pounds ground beef

STUFF TO DO

Mix all but the beef and pork together to ensure an even distribution of ingredients. Add the mix to the meat until it is a good consistency.

Dig out the patty stacker from the archives—also available at better garage sales everywhere—or just use those well-washed hands of yours to make the meat into patties.

Cover the burgers with plastic wrap and refrigerate for an hour or more. This helps keep the burgers together and aids in the blissful marriage of ingredients. You know, it makes them taste better.

Get these babies on the grill over medium heat till cooked through.

If desired, do as I do and top both sides with barbecue sauce—try **Just Like Bull's Eye** (page 205)—for the final minutes on the grill.

Why not split open Kaiser buns, spread some garlic butter on them and toast 'em up in a frying pan or on the barbecue?

Then top the big fellas with fried onions, tomatoes and lettuce.

On a diet? Then Atkins-ize these burgers with low-in-killer-carbs bacon and cheese. Still concerned? Instead of a bun, use 2 veal cutlets.

Serve 'em with a healthy batch of **Glen's Non-Fries** (page 177) and a heaping helping of **Ralphie Slaw** (page 58).

MEATLOAF CORDON BLEU

Here's a hybrid recipe. My sister-in-law Marg's meatloaf recipe combined with firefighter Lee Harrison's Cordon Bleu treatment. If you're tired of bland old meatloaf, here's a way to fire it up to a whole new level.

THE MEAT AND ITS LOAF

- 2 pounds lean ground beef—
  or 1 pound each beef and ground pork
- 1 package spicy onion soup mix
- 2 eggs
- ½ cup ketchup
- ½ cup quick-cooking—not instant—oatmeal
- ½ teaspoon dried oregano
- 1 small diced onion—optional
- 1 small diced red pepper—also optional
- ¾–1 cup water
- Several thick slices of Swiss cheese or mozzarella
- ⅓ pound honey or Black Forest ham—sliced thin
- Fresh ground pepper

HOW TO MAKE THE MEAT, WELL, YOU KNOW, LOAF

Preheat your oven to 350 degrees.

Combine all the ingredients except the water, cheese, ham and pepper. Add the water slowly to the meat mixture, until you find that it's slightly wet but still manageable.

Take half of the meat mixture and place it in the bottom of a large greased loaf tin, patting it down into position.

Place the cheese in the middle, leaving about 1 inch of meat around the sides. If you don't, when the cheese melts, it will leak out.

Place the ham on top of the cheese to create the cordon.

Place the rest of the meat mixture over the stuffed centre and pinch the sides to ensure that the stuffed centre remains within the loaf. Sprinkle with ground pepper. Bake, uncovered, for about 1 hour, 10 minutes.

If you're a ketchup lover, place a layer of the red stuff—mixed with some brown sugar—over the loaf halfway through the baking time.

Serve with **Stroganov Sauce** from **Meatballs Two Ways** (page 91).

By the way, this recipe can be doubled, tripled, whatever, with good results. Cooking time, believe it or not, is almost the same.

MEATBALLS TWO WAYS

If you're making meatballs for a crowd, why not make half sweet and sour, and the other half Stroganov style. Come on—let's have some variety here!

HERE'S THE BASIC MEATBALL RECIPE

- 1¼ pounds lean ground beef
- ½ cup fine breadcrumbs
- ½ cup milk
- 1 teaspoon **Fired-Up Spice** (page 200) or seasoning salt
- ¼ teaspoon pepper

Mix the above ingredients together, form it into meatballs and cook in a frying pan, or on a greased baking pan in a 350-degree oven till well browned.

HERE'S THE SWEET-AND-SOUR SAUCE

- 2 cups brown sugar
- 2 tablespoons flour
- ½ cup white or rice vinegar
- ¼ cup water
- 2 tablespoons soy sauce
- 1 tablespoon ketchup
- ½ 14-ounce can of pineapple tidbits—drained

Blend the brown sugar and flour. Add the remaining ingredients. Heat to boiling and pour over the meatballs in a casserole dish. Bake the little guys for 20 minutes at 350 degrees, or until cooked through, and the sauce is happily heated.

HERE'S THE STROGANOV SAUCE

- ½ pound mushrooms
- Butter
- 1 tablespoon flour
- ⅓ cup dry red wine
- 1 10-ounce can consommé
- Sour cream

Brown mushrooms in butter. Sprinkle flour over the fungi and mix to coat evenly.

Add the browned meatballs and red wine. Combine with the mushrooms and allow the wine to reduce slightly.

Let's add the consommé. Heat it through.

Add 2 big dollops of sour cream and whisk the sauce. If need be, add 2 tablespoons water with 1 tablespoon cornstarch to thicken.

Serve as is, or place it all in a casserole and bake for 20 minutes at 350 degrees.

Sizzling
SHEPHERD'S PIE

Why is it called shepherd's pie when they use ground beef instead of lamb? Well, I think it's because the shepherds became too emotionally involved with their flock. It's a great recipe with either beef or lamb.

SO GET YOUR BORDER COLLIE TO ROUND UP

- 1½ pounds lean ground beef—lamb if you're a traditionalist
- **Fired-Up Spice** (page 200)
- Fresh ground pepper
- Butter
- 1 cup onions—chopped
- ¾ cup celery—chopped
- 2 large carrots—chopped fine
- 3 cloves garlic—pressed or minced
- ½ teaspoon each thyme, Italian seasoning, salt and pepper
- ¼ cup all-purpose flour
- ⅔ cup dry red wine
- 1 10-ounce can consommé
- 2 teaspoons Worcestershire sauce
- Cayenne pepper—optional
- ½ cup each frozen corn and frozen peas
- 1 head garlic—yes more garlic. Not a clove either—the whole head!
- 12 medium-sized potatoes—red, russet, or my fave, Yukon Golds

ONCE HOME, PROCEED TO THE COUNTRY KITCHEN

Brown the ground beef in a large, non-stick frying pan. Add a dusting of Fired-Up Spice and a few grinds of the old pepper mill to season the beef. Drain off the fat.

Set the beef aside, add 2 table-spoons of butter to the frying pan and introduce the onions, celery, carrots and 3 cloves of minced garlic.

Season veggies with thyme, Italian seasoning, salt and pepper.

Sauté the veggies until the carrots are tender crisp.

Re-add the beef to the frying pan and sprinkle the flour over top, working it through the meat to coat it.

Pour in that taste-boosting red wine and cook for about 1 minute.

Bring the consommé and Worcestershire sauce—try saying Worcestershire 10 times in a row successfully—into the mix.

Cook over medium–low heat until the liquid is completely reduced. The sauce should be very, very thick.

Check the flavour. This is where I'll often add some salt and even a dash of cayenne to fire it up.

Bring the corn and peas to the party and mix through.

Meanwhile, peel the skins off the remaining garlic and toss them into a pot of boiling salted water with the potatoes. Cook for 20 minutes.

When the spuds and garlic are soft, drain off the water.

Add a couple of dollops of butter and buttermilk or sour cream and smash 'em up. You could even add a little grated cheese, freshly chopped parsley or green onions to the potatoes to fire the spuds over the top!

By the way, due not only to laziness but a desire for smooth results, I prefer to smash my spuds with an electric mixer. For this recipe, the potatoes should be just whipped, not runny.

Test the spuds for flavour and add salt and pepper as required.

All right, it's assembly time. In a large, deep casserole—or two smaller casseroles—place the meat mixture on the bottom.

Completely cover the meat with the smashed potatoes. Each layer should be at least 1 inch thick.

Dust the potatoes with paprika, and bake at 350 degrees for about 45 minutes, or until lightly browned on top.

Why not sprinkle grated cheddar cheese over the potatoes as well, before baking. Look at that calorie counter go!

Looking for a salad to serve? You can't go wrong with the **Spinach 'n' Egg Salad** (page 49) or the **Warm Mushroom Spinach Salad** (page 56).

Sure, there are a few directions involved with making this recipe, but believe me, it's not difficult. Hey if I can make it, anyone can. I'm a lowly Math 301 graduate. It featured such brain-buster questions as, "There were 3 birds on a fence and 1 flew away. How many are left?"

Why am I a fireman and not a businessman? See clue above!

BEEF 'N' BANGER STEW

You have options here—traditional, exotic, even a slow-cooker version.

FROM THE FRIDGE AND PANTRY YOU'LL NEED

- 2 pounds stewing beef
- Seasoning salt and pepper
- 3 tablespoons flour
- 2 tablespoons butter
- ½ cup dry red wine
- 3 bay leaves
- 1 10-ounce can consommé or beef stock
- 3 carrots and 3 stalks of celery—sliced
- 2 medium onions—diced
- ¼ pound mushrooms—optional
- 12 pork or breakfast bangers, a.k.a. sausages—parboiled to de-fat
- Salt, thyme, fresh ground pepper, Worcestershire sauce—optional

OKAY, NOW LET'S MAKE THIS INTO SOMETHING

Cut the stewing beef into 1-inch chunks. Season with seasoning salt and pepper, and roll in flour.

Melt the butter in a medium saucepan and brown the beef.

Deglaze the bottom of the pan by adding the red wine. Scrape up those flavourful browned bits from the bottom.

Re-add the beef, plus bay leaves, soup and an equal amount of water.

Simmer for 2 hours. See what nonsense is happening on the day-time talk shows.

Toss in the vegetables and bring to a boil. Once it's boiling, turn it down and cook over medium–low heat until the veggies are tender.

Toss in the bangers and simmer. If the gravy isn't thick enough for your liking, thicken with 1 table-spoon cornstarch mixed with 2 tablespoons water.

Check for spices. For flavour add salt and 1 teaspoon thyme. For heat add fresh ground pepper and 1 teaspoon Worcestershire.

Let stand 10 minutes before serving over **Rustic Garlic Smashed Potatoes** (page 179).

Curry Option. Instead of the above spices, add 3 tablespoons—or to taste—curry paste or powder and 2 cups plain yogurt, and heat through.

Try it in a slow cooker! Brown the beef first, then add the rest of the ingredients plus 3 potatoes cut in 1-inch squares and another tin of consommé. Eight hours later on low, it's delicious, tender, beef stew!

Fred Flintstone
BARBECUED BEEF RIBS

As you can imagine, the barbaric carnivores at the fire station love this one. Conversely, it's not the recipe to cook for a date that you're trying to impress. Oh, they'll love the flavour, but they won't get that loving feeling, seeing your fingers, face, shirt and pants splattered in barbecue sauce!

ROCKIN' RIBS WITH A CHOICE OF SAUCE

- Beef ribs—2-4 for each person. For this example we'll use 2 racks, or 14 ribs.

- 2 medium onions—sliced in half

- 2 large lemons—also sliced in half

- 1 head garlic—separated into cloves

- 1 10-ounce can consommé or beef broth

- Lots of pepper from the pepper mill

- **Just Like Bull's Eye Barbecue** (page 205) or the **Five-Star Whiskey Brisket** sauce (page 96)

LET'S BOIL 'EM AND BAKE 'EM, MAYBE EVEN BARBECUE 'EM!

Place the ribs in a large Dutch oven. Cover them with water, toss in the onions, lemons, garlic, even some beef broth. Oh, and grind up some pepper in there. These additions to the water will help marinate the meat.

Place this on the stove, bring to a slow boil and simmer for 1 hour.

Remove ribs, place on a cutting board, cut into individual bones, and place in a roasting pan. Coat the ribs in sauce—be verrrrry generous!

At this point you could cover the ribs and toss them in the fridge, then finish cooking them the next day. Lots of great marinating time, which of course means bonus flavour points!

Bake the ribs, covered, in a preheated 425-degree oven for 20 minutes. Then turn these babies down to 300 degrees for about an hour to an hour and a half. Use the longer time if ribs were refrigerated, or if you have tons of ribs.

Turn and toss the ribs once during baking to ensure an even, thick coating of that incredible barbecue sauce.

Okay, the choice is yours. You can uncover the ribs and bake them for another 10–15 minutes, or even better, put them on the barbecue for 5–10 minutes. Baste them in sauce, as you turn them on the barbecue. Go for those aesthetically pleasing grill marks!

Five-Star
WHISKEY BRISKET

Here's another hybrid recipe: firefighter Al Solinske's brisket, combined with my sister-in-law's Whiskey Barbecue Sauce. Put them together and imagine this— beef-rib flavour without all the fat and wasted bone. Fantastic!

IT'S A SMOKY, BOOZY BRISKY ...

- Beef brisket—about 5 or 6 pounds
- Equal parts **Fired-Up Santa Fe Spice** (page 200) and brown sugar
- Liquid smoke—available in your store's barbecue sauce section

... THANKS TO THE FIVE-STAR WHISKEY BRISKET BARBECUE SAUCE

- 3 cups ketchup
- 1 cup rye whiskey—no, it doesn't have to be Five-Star. I just thought that Five-Star made for a catchy title. Besides, the sauce rates Five Stars.
- ½ cup honey
- ⅓ cup brown sugar
- ¼ cup molasses
- 3 teaspoons dried oregano
- 1 teaspoon—or more if you like it hot— dried chili pepper flakes

INTO THE OVEN ON LOW AND SLOW

Mix up a batch of **Fired-Up Santa Fe Spice** and brown sugar, and spread over both sides of the brisket. Allow the brisket to sit for one hour. Place it in a roaster and drizzle liquid smoke over top.

Warm the oven to 200 degrees. Yes, we want a low, slow roast.

Cover the roaster and cook in the oven for approximately 1 hour, 10 minutes per pound. I usually bake a 6-pound brisket for 7 hours before finishing with sauce. The brisket will cook unattended in its own juices.

Blend the sauce ingredients together in a saucepan and keep warm.

Drain about ⅔ of the liquid off the brisket, top it with a healthy helping of sauce and bake a further hour to warm through.

Uncover roaster and broil top of brisket to caramelize the sauce.

Let the brisket cool for 10 minutes. Slice it against the grain, fan out strips of brisket on plate and top with the warmed whiskey sauce.

Oh yeah, this sauce goes great on ribs, chicken or, as I originally tasted it, on meatballs. It's got great zip! And if you managed to restrain everyone, and actually have leftovers, cook them up in the sauce the next day and serve on toasted buns.

WE SHOOT WATER, WE SHOOT PICTURES

At one station, our battalion chief was winding down his last two tours before retirement. At morning coffee he had a camera sitting beside his cup, so Brad asked, "Hey, Chief, I see you've brought along a camera. You know, photography is my life. If you'd allow me to, I'd love to take some candid photographs for you around the hall."

"That would be great, Brad," the chief responded. "Let's get some pictures happening here."

He gathered the captain and lieutenants and struck a pose with them as Brad instructed, "Say cheese!"

"Cheeeese!" they smiled. Brad framed his picture and, unbeknownst to the chief, just before clicking the shutter he quickly lowered the camera, cutting all of their heads out of the picture. This went on all day, pictures of the chief with the chief of the department and the mayor, with his crew of firefighters, standing beside his chief's car—all of them with the heads intentionally cut off. In between posed shots, Brad took candid shots of the grease trap on the grill, a dead mouse caught in a sticky strip, toilets, a full moon or two from obliging crewmates—basically anything and everything offensive.

When we came back to work the next tour the chief was lying in wait. "Very funny. Very, very funny," he sarcastically said as he nodded his head. "I got my pictures back, Brad, and you cut all the heads off. There were all these gross pictures in there too. Very funny indeed."

"Chief, I'm sorry," Brad half-heartedly apologized. "Photography is my life. I was just kidding. I knew you had another tour left to get photos. Please, give me another chance, and you won't be disappointed."

Incredibly, the gullible chief handed Brad the camera, giving him another chance—to repeat what he had done all over again! No kidding. Apparently, there were some things that the chief hadn't learned in his 38 or so years on the job. Oh, we can be a heartless bunch!

The morning of the chief's final (night) shift, we got up early and tied a small chain under the transmission of his car. Yes, we left him with an annoying sound to remember us by, a little rattle to worry him during his tearful ride off into the sunrise.

HOT CHICKS

As legend has it—and I've talked to men who claim to have been in attendance for this gag—firefighters were returning from a call when they passed a chicken producer's warehouse and spotted a chicken crossing the road. Yes, just like in the joke, and oh, what a joke it became. A member of the crew got an idea. Being from the country, he knew that by tucking the head of a chicken under its wing, cradling it in his arms and rocking it, he could put it to sleep. So he gave the chicken the old sleeper hold and took it back to the hall. The prankster sneaked into the dorm, and placed the bird in bed beside one of the sleeping firefighters. The two new buds sawed logs together in harmony until the gong sounded and the firefighter sat up to get dressed for the alarm. The chicken woke up clucking in fright, the firefighter screamed and the chicken rewarded him by dropping something other than eggs on his bed.

Of course, that isn't the only way that chicken finds its way into a fire hall; in fact, the majority of the entrees that I prepare at work feature poultry. I love the way chicken takes on the flavour of the marinade or sauce that it's cooked in. Chicken is a pushover; add another taste and it's an immediate defector.

Lemon and garlic make for great chicken, and you'll spot this combination numerous times in this book. Oh, and try the **Orange Seafood-Sauce Chicken** recipe (page 104); it's number one on the request list at the fire hall. **Derraugh Marinara** (page 107)—a label coined by fellow firefighters—is a unique pasta dish that you should try when you're looking to break free of the spaghetti-and-meat-sauce routine. Promise me you'll take a run at **Beer Can Chicken** (page 100); sure it's trendy, but combine it with the **Beer Chick Marinade** (page 111) and not only will you impress onlookers with your deft culinary abilities, but this smoky, flavourful, juicy chicken just can't be beat.

Chicken can be substituted for the meat in many of the beef, pork and yes, even fish recipes. Also, ground chicken or turkey can replace the trusty (sometimes mad) cow in many of the ground-beef dishes.

So what do you say we line up a hot chick for dinner tonight?

Lemon Herb
ROASTED CHICKEN

Here's a culinary trick for you to try. Firefighter Glen Godri suggested that I utilize his wife's method of cooking a roasting chicken upside down, as the higher fat content in the thighs bastes the breasts, resulting in an evenly cooked, juicy bird. Why, I've been flipping the bird ever since!

CHICKEN, BUTTER, GARLIC AND HERBS

- 5- to 6-pound roasting chicken—or 2 small 3-pound fryers
- Seasoning salt, thyme and sage
- 1 lemon
- 1 medium onion
- ⅓ cup butter—softened
- 5 cloves garlic—minced or pressed—and Italian seasoning
- Seasoning salt, lemon pepper, basil, oregano, tarragon, thyme, sage, paprika, Italian seasoning or any combination of your favourite herbs

STUFFIN', SEASONIN' AND BAKIN': SO LONG, DRY WHITE MEAT

Heat up that oven to 425 degrees.

Rinse the cavity of the bird and pat dry with paper towels. Sprinkle seasoning salt, thyme and sage into the cavity. Cut the lemon and onion in half and stuff both into the cavity.

Mix the butter with the mandatory garlic and Italian seasoning. Make an opening under the skin of each breast with your finger and stuff 2 teaspoons of garlic butter into each pocket. It's like a homemade butterball but with lots of that flavourful, halitosis-expanding garlic.

Tie the legs together with string. Tie another string under the wings and across the back of the bird. I also tie another string between those two strings, so that they don't slide off during the big flip.

Spread remaining garlic butter over the skin of the chicken and sprinkle seasoning salt (or **Fired-Up Spice**, page 200), herbs of your choice and, finally, paprika over top.

Bake the bird on a greased rack in a roaster, uncovered, for 25 minutes. Turn the oven down to 350 degrees. With oven mitts and paper towel, flip the bird and bake breast-side down. Really! It keeps the breasts so juicy! Bake covered for 1½ hours or until done.

Flip again, baste and broil until skin is crisp and lightly browned. Keep an eye on that bird while you broil it, unless you want it Cajun style!

BEER CAN CHICKEN

(Desolate wilderness background with lone whistle intro)
ANNOUNCER: *"Today, Hinterland's Who's Who looks at the Beer Can Chicken. A migratory species, the Beer Can Chicken is best known for the wondrous flight it makes in anticipation of the best-before-date season, travelling from the cool, hostile environment of the butcher-shop window to the balmy confines of the smoke-filled barbecue. Perched high upon its aluminum nest, the Beer Can Chicken maintains incubation until its internal temperature reaches 180 degrees. Instinctively sensing its doneness, the Beer Can Chicken completes its journey by arriving at the dinner table, bringing joy and sustenance to the food-chain-abiding carnivores. For more information on the Beer Can Chicken and other recipes, contact your local poultry producer."*
(Desolate wilderness background with lone whistle out)

NOW BACK TO OUR REGULARLY SCEDULED RECIPE
Imagine roasting a chicken on your barbecue standing up! The secret is a beer can strategically placed in its (ahem) cavity! It looks hilarious, but it makes a great barbecued chicken! You can soak the chicken in the **Beer Chick Marinade** *first, or if time is tight, just rub it up!*

HERE ARE THE REQUIREMENTS

- **Beer Chick Marinade** (page 111)
- 1 can of good old beer—okay 2, one
- for you, one for the chicken
- 4- to 5-pound roasting chicken— a 3-pound fryer will also work
- Approximately 4 cups mesquite or hickory wood chips
- 2 tablespoons **Fired-Up Santa Fe Spice** (page 200)

HERE'S THE PLAN, LISTEN CAREFULLY

Mix up those marinade ingredients with a whisk. Hey! Wait a second! Hang on to that empty beer can; you're going to need it.

Place the chicken and marinade in a plastic bag and refrigerate overnight, and even for as long as 48 hours. Flip it over every 8 hours or so to distribute the marinade fairly.

Soak the wood chips in water for at least 1 hour for smoke-ability!

Remove the bird from the marinade—don't toss the marinade! Pat dry with paper towel and sprinkle with **Fired-Up Santa Fe Spice**.

Remember that empty beer can I told you to hang on to? Well, take it down from the display case and pour the marinade filling in until it's about ⅔ full. This will provide a little bird-steaming on the barbecue. With a can opener, make 3 more openings in the top.

Place the beer can in the chicken's cavity. Imagine a tripod, with the bird standing on 2 legs, the beer can acting as the 3rd leg. Now tuck his wings behind his back. Look, the bird's dancing; this is going to work!

Place the wood chips in 2 aluminum foil pouches; fold them up, poke a few holes in them to vent and place them on one side of the barbecue.

Fire up the barbecue! If you're at the firehouse, don full SCBA (air mask). When the smoke gets heavy, turn off the pouch-less side.

Place a disposable aluminum tray—those small lasagna dishes work well—on the unlit side of the barbecue, to catch the juices.

Stand our little buddy up on the unlit side, with the breast away from the heat. This will promote even cooking, and will help eliminate the dreaded Dry White Meat Syndrome.

Check it out. That chick has a beer gut!

Close the lid, turn down to medium–high, and let it smoke! If a meat thermometer in the thigh says 170–180—or juices run clear—it's ready. Another way to know that the chick's done is by wiggling its legs. If the legs move easily, the thigh meat is cooked, and chances are the bird is in a state of culinary completion.

Play it safe taking it off the barbecue; the hot liquid in the can will burn! Let stand 10 minutes and this Beer Chick is ready to party!

So can I make this recipe without the marinade, Jeff? Well, sure you can, but then it won't be this recipe, will it? Rest assured, you can make a Beer Chick happen by substituting a loving rubdown for the soaking-up-the-sauce routine. Here's how:

Mix up 2 tablespoons **Fired-Up Santa Fe Spice** with 4 tablespoons brown sugar. Toss a healthy helping of the fired-up sugary rub on the bird, drink about a third of the beer. I said a third! Slow down! You need the rest of that barley sandwich for steaming!

Punch a few extra holes in the lid of the beer, insert in the before-mentioned (ahem) cavity, and off to the barbecue you go!

Vampire-Free
CHICKEN

Keep Dracula at bay with this terrific version of the popular Chicken with 40 Cloves of Garlic. Now, I know 40 cloves sounds like a lot of garlic, but cooked in the sauce for half an hour, it's mellow, smooth and tasty!

GARLIC IS AN ANTI-OXIDANT
—it's good for you!

- 4 large boneless skinless chicken breasts
- Seasoned flour—3 parts flour to 1 part **Fired-Up Spice** (page 200)
- 3 tablespoons olive oil
- 2 tablespoons fresh herbs— try the poultry seasoning mix
- ¼ cup onions—finely chopped
- 1½–2 heads of garlic—yes heads— separated into cloves, ends cut off, and each clove cut in half to speed up the cooking process
- 1 cup dry white wine
- 1 10-ounce can chicken broth
- 1 tablespoon Dijon mustard
- ½ cup whipping cream

STICK A STAKE IN IT—it's done!

Mix up a batch of seasoned flour and coat the chicken breasts.

In a large, non-stick frying pan over medium heat, add the olive oil and brown one side of the chicken breasts.

When it's time to flip the breasts, add half the herbs, onions and garlic cloves, moving them around to brown them as well.

When breast side two is browned, add the white wine, reduce for 1 minute and add the chicken broth combined with mustard to the pan.

Cover and simmer for about 20 minutes, depending on the size of the breasts. Don't overcook or the breasts will become tough.

Remove the breasts to a plate and cover. Turn up the heat and reduce the cooking liquid at a boil to about half.

Let's move the cooking liquid into a blender, cloves and all, plus remaining herbs. Cover the blender tightly and pulse very carefully as hot liquid is known to explode. Blend until smooth.

Return sauce to the pan, add the cream and combine, then place the breasts in the sauce. Do a final season with salt and pepper.

Serve over egg noodles, rice or smashed potatoes, with sautéed mushrooms, and freshly chopped parsley sprinkled over top.

Mike's
LEMON GARLIC CHICKEN

Here's another of firefighter Mike Dowhayko's specialties. It's one of those recipes that you'll find yourself craving and cooking over and over.

SO GO OUT AND GRAB

- 8–10 bone-in chicken thighs, or 6 breasts—I'm a thigh man myself
- Paprika, seasoning salt and pepper
- 2 tablespoons butter
- 4 or 5 cloves garlic—minced or pressed
- Juice of 1 large lemon
- 1 large onion—cut into slices
- 1 10-ounce can consommé
- 1 10-ounce can cream of chicken soup
- 1 10-ounce can cream of mushroom soup
- 1 small can mushrooms or ¼ pound of the fresh sliced variety

AND LET'S PUT IT TOGETHER, SHALL WE?

Dust the chicken lightly with paprika, seasoning salt and pepper.

Warm up a frying pan over medium heat, toss in butter and 2 cloves garlic. Bring on half the chicken to brown.

Repeat the procedure, as you'll need to do two batches of chicken.

Preheat your oven to 350 degrees.

Remove the chicken, place in a 9- x 13-inch lasagna pan or roaster and sprinkle each piece with fresh lemon juice. Don't toss the drippings!

Why? It's time to fry the onion in the pan drippings, that's why!

Stir the soups and mushrooms—drained—together in a bowl.

Add the onion and pan drippings to the soup mixture.

Pour the soup mixture over the chicken pieces, coating evenly.

Bake, covered with foil, for 45–50 minutes.

Remove the cover, give your creation a wee baste and bake for an additional 15 minutes or until the chicken is cooked through.

Serve this dish over pasta or with **Rustic Garlic Smashed Potatoes** (page 179). The gravy will tempt you to lick your plate, but please, have some couth and use dipping bread instead.

A **Great Greek Salad** (page 44) always goes nicely on the side. Definitely one of my favourites. Thanks, Mike!

Orange
SEAFOOD-SAUCE CHICKEN

*Okay, I admit it; I pried this recipe out of my wife, Lori. She insisted that I marry her before she would release it to me. Now that it's mine, it's my most-requested recipe. Sweet, sure, but with a nice bite! You'll **love** it!*

WHAT YOU NEED IS

- A 1963 mint-condition, split-window coupe Corvette … No that's what I need. Where is my mind here? Okay, how about …

- 1½ pounds large chicken breasts for a main course or 3 pounds of wings or wing-drumettes for an appetizer

- 2 eggs beaten up—relax, they won't press assault charges

- 20 or so crushed-up Breton crackers

- 1 jar seafood sauce

- Equal part orange juice—use the empty seafood-sauce bottle

- Equal part sugar—use the empty bottle again. Reduce, reuse, recycle!

- 1 teaspoon kosher salt

HEY, THIS SHOULD BE EASY ENOUGH

Turn that oven dial to 400 degrees.

Dip the chicken in the eggs and then roll it around in the beat-up crackers. Place the chicken in a lasagna dish or roaster.

Bake for 15–20 minutes, uncovered.

Mix the heavenly sauce ingredients together—the seafood sauce, the orange juice, the sugar and salt.

Pour the sauce over the chicken and bake for 15–20 minutes more or until the chicken is cooked through—i.e., salmonella free.

Let the chicken stand 5 minutes and serve over rice.

HERE'S A NICE TOUCH

Why not top the chicken with pre-cooked shrimp before layin' on the sauce? Just excellent!

Sure, this recipe is easy, but it's also very different and decadent. When your guests, family or family of firefighters start handing out the praise, suppress the desire to admit how trouble-free this unique dish actually was to prepare. Oh, and let them do the clean-up!

LOUISIANA CHICKEN

I watched a firefighter make this on Food-TV, and I thought, "Man, that's got to be spicy!" He didn't give exact measurements, so I was forced to wing the recipe—pardon the pun. Surprisingly, though, it isn't that hot, as the brown sugar and butter really mellow and balance the hot sauce. Delicious!

HERE'S ALL YOU NEED

- Garlic butter
- Chicken thighs, wings or legs—I'm a thigh man myself—oh, sorry, I've already said that, haven't I?
- **Fired-Up Spice** (page 200)
- Louisiana hot sauce
- Brown sugar
- Melted butter

HERE'S ALL YOU NEED TO DO

Crank the oven to 425 degrees.

Prepare the garlic butter by simply adding pressed garlic to butter or margarine and including a sprinkling of Italian seasoning.

Take about a teaspoon and place it under the skin of each chicken piece. Ensure that the skin closes over top. Dust with **Fired-Up Spice**.

If using thighs—did I mention? Never mind—place them directly in a roaster or ovenproof casserole. If using legs or wings then rack 'em!

Bake for 25 minutes—about 15 for wings.

Blend the hot sauce with brown sugar and melted butter. Try a ratio of 3 parts hot sauce to 1 part each brown sugar and butter.

Give the sauce the good old taste test. The spiciness and sweetness should be about equal. *What's that biting the back of my throat? I thought you said this wasn't that hot, Jeff! FIRE! FIRE! 911!!*

If you're using wings or legs, turn and baste them with sauce. For thighs just baste them as they stand, skin side up.

Bake an additional 25 minutes or so until done. Or, if the weather is right, why not fire up the barbecue to finish them off?

My kids—well, 3 of the 5 anyway, the carnivores—love this recipe, and they're fussy farts. Of course, I blame my wife's side for their picky nature. I like to experiment with food and the kids hate it when I deviate. It's my curse. So, I end up cooking two meals. *Doh!*

Taste-Like-Fried
BARBECUED HOT WINGS

If you love restaurant-style Buffalo Hot Wings, well, I have a secret to share. You can make those crispy wings on the barbecue without any oil. Believe it! The great part is they're just so easy. Thanks to firefighter-chef Chris Blasko for another terrific recipe.

NOT MUCH TO GRAB

· Seasoned flour

· Chicken wings, drumettes or drumsticks

· Louisiana hot sauce

· Butter—melted

· Brown sugar

NOT MUCH TO DO EITHER

Prepare the seasoned flour. If you don't have a recipe, just combine 3 parts flour to 1 part **Fired-Up Spice** (page 200) or seasoning salt.

Toss the chicken in flour. No need to pat dry beforehand.

Get to the grill. Fire up one burner to about medium to medium–high. When the barbecue is heated up, spray the opposite side with non-stick coating.

Place the chicken on that opposite side—the so-called dark side—close the lid, and let the wings cook for about half an hour.

Flip the wings over, and cook until done, about another ½ hour. They'll actually look like fried

chicken when they are done, light brown on top and crispy.

Prepare the sauce by combining 3 parts Louisiana hot sauce to 1 part melted butter and brown sugar. Or if you prefer, be a man—a man with heartburn—do like Blasko and go for Louisiana straight up.

Get the wings off the barbecue and toss them in the sauce while they're still warm. Serve immediately.

Chili-Garlic Chicken Sauce Option. For an Asian twist, try dipping the chicken in purchased sweet chili-garlic sauce.

Other Sauces to Try. How about **Carolina Mustard Sauce** (page 204) or barbecue sauce, or visit the Golden Arches and snaffle a mittful of those little dipping sauces.

DERRAUGH MARINARA

If you love Greek salad then you're in for a treat, because many of its elements are here in a tangy pasta sauce. For maximum presentation, use a variety of peppers for colour. Get this dish fired up and before you know it, you'll be able to taste the Mediterranean!

YOU'RE GOING TO HAVE TO LOCATE

- 4 boneless, skinless chicken breasts—marinated in **Lemon Garlic Marinade** (page 111)

- 1 tablespoon olive oil

- 3 cloves garlic—run through the press, or mince 'em up

- 1 red and 1 green pepper—cut in strips

- 1 small red onion—also cut in strips

- 2 celery stalks—diced

- ½ pound mushrooms—sliced into Ts

- 1 28-ounce can diced tomatoes

- ½ cup crumbled feta cheese—or more to taste

- Basil, salt and pepper to taste

- ⅔ pound fresh pasta or 1 pound dry

- Olives—if desired

- ¼ head fresh parsley—chopped fine

YOU'RE ONLY A FEW STEPS AWAY NOW

Marinate the chicken in the Lemon Garlic Marinade and barbecue or broil until done—done being cooked through but still juicy.

Heat olive oil in a deep skillet. Toss in crushed garlic and the veggies. Stir-fry until tender crisp.

Add the tomatoes with juice to the veggies. Heat it up for 8 minutes on medium heat. Remove from the heat and add the feta cheese.

If you find the sauce is too dry or thick, you can always add a little dry sherry, white wine or tomato sauce to thin it out.

Give the dish a shot of basil, salt and pepper to taste.

Cut the chicken into strips and add them to the sauce.

Throw in your favourite olives if the desire strikes.

Toss the sauce with the pasta and let it stand for 5 minutes.

Plate each portion and garnish with parsley.

CHICKEN CORDON BLEU

Okay, I'll admit it, this one can be a bit of a challenge to make. If you're a klutz in the kitchen like me, then you'll probably resort to toothpicks to hold these babies together. This takes some effort but it's worth it. I just hope your guests are grateful!

SO WHAT YOU NEED IS

- Large boneless, skinless, meatless— kidding—chicken breasts
- Dijon mustard—that's French for "more expensive"
- Ham slices—try honey ham or Black Forest
- Swiss cheese—grated, about 2 tablespoons per breast
- Seasoned flour—3 parts flour to 1 part **Fired-Up Spice** (page 200)
- 2 eggs—beaten in a bowl
- Breadcrumbs—how about using the Italian variety?
- Olive oil
- ½ pound mushrooms—sliced
- Parsley for garnish—chopped fine

AND FOR THE SAUCE YOU'LL NEED

- 1 10-ounce can cream of chicken soup
- ½ cup sour cream
- ¼ cup white wine
- 1 teaspoon mild curry paste or powder— add to taste

THIS MAY REQUIRE A LITTLE PATIENCE, BUT YOU CAN DO IT!

Place the chicken between 2 sheets of wax paper. You may need to remove the small tenderloin piece, as it will interfere with the foldability of the breast. Freeze it and save for a stir-fry.

With an anvil, sledgehammer, frost-free-fridge or heavy frying pan, pound the breast to about ¼-inch thickness without mulching it.

Spread a thin layer of Dijon mustard on the upside of the breast.

Before we stuff it, do yourself a favour: resist the urge to overstuff the breast. This is especially tempting for ravenous firefighters. The key is the less filling you use, the easier it is to stuff.

Cut ham slice to a size smaller than the breast and place on top.

Spread a little grated cheese in the middle of the ham.

You may have your own, better style for doing the big roll, but here we go with mine. Hey, it works for me—sometimes! Unless you've pounded out a perfectly round breast, you'll have a rectangular breast featuring a short side and a long side. Fold in the short sides a bit, enough to cover just the edge of the stuffing.

Now take the tip of the long side and roll the breast up jellyroll style.

If you're lucky, the breast will seal itself. If you're a no-talent low roller such as myself, then you may have to get out the toothpicks. So admit defeat if you must and place a toothpick through each of the 4 corners of the breast to hold that baby together.

The breast will stay together better if you place it in the fridge for an hour or so. After the frustration of folding the breasts, you may want to go for a walk to blow off some steam. Slow down your breathing. In ... out ... in ... out. That's good.

Now that you've calmed down, roll the breast in seasoned flour, pass it through the handy egg-wash station and finally toss it into the breadcrumbs, covering well.

After all that hard work it's time to relax in the hot tub. Not you, the breasts! Place olive oil in a heavy frying pan to a depth of about 1 inch and place over medium–low heat. Carefully add 2 breasts.

When the breasts have a nice tan on their backside, flip them over and give them the same treatment on the other side.

Remove them with a slotted spatula to drain the oil off and place in a casserole or lasagna dish.

Fire up your oven to 350 degrees.

Blend the sauce ingredients and pour over the breasts.

Bake, uncovered, for 20 minutes, or until the chicken's no longer pink inside. Wait a second here— it is pink inside! Relax, that's the ham you're looking at! What I mean is that the chicken itself— the so-called white meat—should no longer be pink.

Sauté the mushrooms in butter over medium–high heat, toss some over each breast and garnish with parsley.

That wasn't so bad, was it? Okay, I admit it was, but the next time it'll be that much easier. You didn't resort to the medicine cabinet, did you?

Try an Italian version of this recipe by using prosciutto instead of ham, Italian-style breadcrumbs and topping it with the tomato sauce from the **Red Wine Spaghetti Sauce** recipe (page 162).

CHICKEN AMANDINE
with Creamy Tarragon Sauce

This recipe is big on both flavour and presentation.

GET IT TOGETHER!

- Oil for deep frying

- 4 large chicken breasts

- Seasoned flour—3 parts flour to 1 part **Fired-Up Spice** (page 200)

- 2 eggs—beaten in a bowl

- ½ pound shaved natural almonds— the flat ones. Not the slivers; they'll puncture the roof of your guests' mouths!

GET THE PRODUCTION LINE GOING!

Preheat oil in a deep fryer, deep pan, or wok to 350 degrees F— 180 degrees C (C for "comfortably cozy").

Dip the chicken in flour, then through the egg wash and finally into the almonds, coating well.

While trying to keep the almonds on the chicken, get them in the oil. You'll want to cook them about 5 minutes—one at a time— until each is a light golden brown.

Preheat your oven to 375 degrees F (F for "fired up").

Place chicken pieces on greased baking sheet, and bake for 15–20 minutes until cooked through.

WHILE YOU'RE WAITING, GET THE TARRAGON SAUCE TOGETHER!

- 2 tablespoons dry white wine

- 2 cups chicken broth with garlic and herbs

- 2 tablespoons Dijon mustard

- 2 tablespoons melted butter combined with 2 tablespoons flour

- 1 cup whipping cream—or half and half

- ½ teaspoon dried tarragon— or more to taste

NOW FOR THE BIG FINISH!

Bring a medium saucepan to a medium temperature. How moderate!

Pour white wine into the saucepan, and reduce to about ⅔.

Add the chicken broth and mustard and bring to a boil. Meanwhile, mix the butter and flour and add it to the sauce.

Cook over medium heat, whisking constantly, until nicely thickened.

Add the cream, tarragon, and salt and pepper to taste. Whisk it and heat through. Pour the sauce over each breast, and it's game time!

Two Great
CHICKEN MARINADES

BEER CHICK MARINADE

This is a must for **Beer Can Chicken** *(page 100), but it can also be used to marinate chicken pieces before you toss them on the barbecue.*

HERE'S WHAT IT TAKES

- 1 bottle beer
- ¼ cup Dijon mustard
- ¼ cup canola oil
- 2 tablespoon each soy sauce and brown sugar
- 1 tablespoon coarse salt

Combine all ingredients. Place the marinade and chicken in a plastic bag for 2–4 hours for chicken pieces or overnight to 48 hours for a whole chicken.

LEMON GARLIC MARINADE

This is my favourite chicken marinade, and you'll notice it is used numerous times in other recipes. Yes, it's another great recipe from firefighter Glen Godri.

HERE'S THE ALL-IMPORTANT RATIO
—basically 3 to 1 lemon to oil

- Juice of 1 lemon or 1 lime
- 1 tablespoon cooking oil—canola, motor or, even better, olive oil
- ½ teaspoon lemon pepper—use straight pepper if using lime juice
- ⅛ teaspoon dried oregano
- A pinch of cayenne or a dash of Louisiana hot sauce
- Good old garlic to taste—about 3 cloves, pressed

HERE'S THE LOWDOWN
Combine the above ingredients. Place the chicken breasts and marinade in a plastic bag. Ensure that there's enough to completely coat the chicken. Place in the fridge and let 'em soak for 1–4 hours.

This recipe is perfect for making pork or chicken souvlaki. Just cut into bite-sized pieces, marinate, skewer, and barbecue or broil.

COOKING YOUR (MON)GOOSE

A tempting contraption that made its way around our fire halls was a wooden animal cage the shape of a shoebox and about four times the size, with a divider in the middle. One side had a wire mesh cover which showed a little dish half full of food scraps and a furry tail sticking out through a cubby hole that led to the cage's mysterious dark side. That was covered by a solid wooden lid, hinged at the divider and held down by a catch pin.

Many a firefighter was scammed by this prank but the joke wasn't limited to our firefighting brethren; anyone was fair game. One day, a woman knocked on the door of the fire station and asked, "My car's just broken down. Could I use your phone?"

As she stood chatting with the firefighters she spotted the cage and asked, "What's that?"

"Oh, you don't want anything to do with that thing!" one of the firefighters explained. "There's a mongoose in there, and the last time it got loose it ran around biting people."

"What does it look like?" she asked. "I've never seen a mongoose."

"It's this little furry thing," the firefighter continued. "One of the guys here is taking it in to the vet later to be put down."

"Could I have a little peek at it?" she inquired.

"It's pretty vicious. Let me have a look to see if it's asleep," the firefighter said as he walked over to the cage, the woman following at a safe distance. "Be very quiet—we don't want to startle him. Well, I don't hear anything. He must be asleep," he said as he gently pulled on an invisible fishing wire on the outside of the cage to subtly move the tail. "I'll just crack the lid and you have a quick look before I close it. You can come a little closer, ma'am. I'll just open the lid and ..." BOOIIINNGG!!

The lid sprang open, the powerful springs hurled a stuffed animal into the air and it flew by the terrified woman's face. She jumped onto a nearby chair, dancing wildly on the seat, before realizing that she'd been had. Yes, complimentary cardio-stress tests are our way of giving a little something back to the community.

PIGS TO THE TROUGH

When it's time to break free of the beef-and-potatoes ritual at the fire hall, we throw caution to the winds and—cook up pork and potatoes instead! I love pork, and find it even easier than beef to prepare because—depending on the cut—it has more marbling; therefore it maintains its moisture content better and will turn out tender and juicy, unless it's quite overcooked. Remember what the pork producers say—and it's true—we're not in the Stone Age anymore: pork is best served with just a hint of pink.

Try a boneless pork butt roast; it's reasonably priced and so good. Or how about a butt roast cut into ¾-inch slabs, popularly known as pork steaks. To my mind, cooked on the barbecue, it's every bit as good as a sirloin steak. Cover the pork steak with a mound of sautéed onions, peppers and mushrooms and, oh man, now we're talking! The pork steak is also good in slow-cooked dishes such as the **Sweet-and-Sour Pork Steak** (page 122) recipe.

One recipe you have to try is the **Blazin' Barbecued Pork Roast** (page 115). It features the before-mentioned boneless pork butt roast and makes a fabulous juicy offering popular among the barbecue fraternity in the American South. Best of all are the leftovers cooked as **Hot Pig Sandwiches** (page 37) the next day. Delicious!

My favourite cut of pork has to be pork tenderloin. Sure, it can be a little pricey, but really, the meat is so dense yet tender that you honestly don't need to follow the pound-per-firefighter rule; it's more like 8 ounces per. Pork tenderloin is a versatile cut—as you'll see from the recipes in this section—and can take as little as half an hour to cook. Or if you're really impatient, cut the tenderloin into medallions to speed things up even more.

Oh, and I'd be remiss if I didn't mention our family fave, pork ribs. I've included recipes for baby back and the thriftier-priced side rib, as well as a couple of barbecue sauces for you to paint on the ribs for the big finish.

So what are you waiting for? Fire up one of the following recipes, and make the call, "Pigs to the Trough!"

PORK ROAST
a Surefire Winner

Although I love both, I do prefer a pork roast to beef. Not only is it more reasonably priced—which is always a concern for us thrifty firefighters—but it's also a little lighter, yet still bursting with flavour.

BUTT ROASTS

Get your oven going at 425 degrees.

Cut garlic into matchsticks, cut slits in the roast with a paring knife and stuff sticks of garlic into the roast.

Rub the roast with pepper, onion and garlic powders and basil. Place it on a bed of thick onion slices.

Cook the roast for 20 minutes, uncovered.

Turn down the oven to 325 degrees, cover, and roast for approximately 25–30 minutes a pound.

LOIN ROASTS

Same as above except leave roast either uncovered or—preferred method—loosely covered with aluminum foil. Check roast with meat thermometer when close. A loin will dry out much more easily than a butt. A loin will taste best with just a hint of pink in the middle. Relax, there's no such thing as Mad Sow disease.

METHOD

Try marinating a pork roast for 8 hours or more in Jamaican jerk marinade (see **Jamaican Jerk Pork Chops**, page 120) and bake as you would a butt or loin roast.

EASY GRAVY

Drain some of the fat from the drippings. Add one 10-ounce can of consommé. Deglaze the pan over medium heat. Mix 2 heaping tablespoons of flour with ¼ cup water. Add it slowly to the gravy until you reach the desired consistency. Add salt and pepper to taste. For a treat, add some sliced mushrooms.

SWEET-AND-SOUR GLAZE FOR PORK LOINS OR HAM

- 1 tablespoon dry mustard
- 1 teaspoon garlic powder
- ¼ cup brown sugar
- ¼ cup white vinegar
- 1 tablespoon soy sauce

Spread it on the meat for the final half-hour of cooking time.

Blazin'
BARBECUED PORK ROAST

Pork butt roasts are always reasonably priced, and their generous marbling keeps the roast moist while you slow-cook it on the barbecue. This recipe from firefighter Chris Blasko is amazing. It's a staple at our house in the summer.

YOU NEED

- To check the propane in your barbecue—you may need 6 hours worth
- 5 tablespoons brown sugar
- 2½ tablespoons **Fired-Up Santa Fe Spice** (page 200)
- 5- to 6-pound boneless pork butt roast
- Hickory or mesquite wood chips

AND FOR THE BASTING SAUCE

- 1 cup cider vinegar
- ½ cup water
- 1 small red onion—thinly sliced
- 1 tablespoon each coarse salt and brown sugar
- 1 teaspoon each black pepper and hot pepper flakes

HERE'S THE RUB

Combine the brown sugar and **Fired-Up Santa Fe Spice**. Rub all over the roast. Cover with plastic wrap and cure overnight.

Soak the wood chips in water for 1 hour. Drain, place in a sheet of aluminum foil and fold into a packet. Cut a few holes in the top of the pouch with a knife for ventilation.

Place the pouches over lava rocks on one side of the barbecue. Put a foil pan over the rocks on the other side. Fire up the barbecue to high heat. When the pouches start to smoke, turn off the pouch-less side and turn the heat on the pouch side down to medium high.

Place the roast on the side of the grill opposite the pouches—let's call it the dark side. Cook for 15 minutes in the heavy smoke.

Turn the heat down to medium low. Brush the roast with basting sauce once an hour. Cook about 5½ more hours, or until the meat thermometer hits 170. Remove and let stand 15 minutes.

Everyone will be fighting over the outside pieces. Crispy and spicy—delicious! Serve with **Carolina Mustard Sauce** (page 204).

Do what you can to protect leftovers so that the following day, you can make **Hot Pig Sandwiches** (page 37)!

Citrus
HONEY-GLAZED HAM

I'm always amazed at how many recipe books recommend cooking a ham forever. A cooked (or smoked) ham is just that: cooked. All it really needs is to be warmed up and finished with a nice glaze. Why dry it out?

THE HAM AND THE GLAZE

- Whole cloves
- 8- to 10-pound bone-in smoked ham
- 1 10-ounce can of soft drink—lemon-lime flavour is good
- 1¼ cups brown sugar
- ⅓ cup orange juice
- ⅓ cup pineapple juice
- ⅓ cup honey
- Grated zest of 1 medium-sized orange
- 2 tablespoons Dijon mustard
- ¼ teaspoon ground cloves

THE EASY TO FOLLOW DIRECTIONS
—I trust!

Score the top half of the ham with a sharp knife, making 1-inch squares about 1 inch deep. Insert whole cloves.

Place the ham in a non-reactive dish. Pour the pop all over the ham. Cover with plastic wrap and allow it to marinate 8 hours or overnight. The ham is getting sweeeeter!

Now let's preheat that oven to 325 degrees. Take the ham and place it on a rack in a roaster. Pour the marinade over the ham again. How about we cover the ham loosely with aluminum foil and poke a couple of vent holes in the foil to let out the excess steam? This will keep our little buddy moist.

Off to the oven you go, little piggy, to bake for an hour.

Combine the remaining ingredients in a small saucepan over medium heat. Bring it up to a slow boil and simmer for 5 or 10 minutes to reduce and thicken.

Pull out the ham and dump off the marinade. Brush the glaze all over the ham, reserving some of the glaze for a second basting.

Back into the oven our uncovered ham goes for 15 minutes.

Baste the ham again and bake for about 15 minutes more.

Allow the ham to rest 10–15 minutes before carving.

Goes great with **Italian Scalloped Potatoes** (page 180).

PORK NORMANDY

The early incarnation of this recipe started in France, perhaps even on the beach during D-Day, given the name. Here's an easy way to serve up this beautiful dish at home. Pork and apples go so well together. This dish is one of firefighter Mike Dowhayko's specialties.

LET'S GO IN SEARCH OF

- 2 pork tenderloins
- Kosher salt and pepper
- ¼ cup butter
- 4 minced shallots or 1 medium onion
- 1 10-ounce can consommé
- ½ cup apple juice
- 1 cup table cream—the 18-percent variety
- 2 apples—cored and diced

LET'S PUT IT TOGETHER

Season the tenderloins with salt and pepper

Fire up the oven to 350 degrees.

Melt the butter in a frying pan and sauté the tenderloins over medium–high heat until they're lightly browned.

Remove the tenderloins, and place them in an ovenproof dish. Roast the loins, uncovered, for about 20–30 minutes, depending on size, or to 150°–160° on a meat thermometer.

While they're roasting, let's toss the shallots in the frying pan with the drippings. We'll sauté them for about 3–4 minutes.

Pour in the consommé, apple juice and cream. Bring to a slow boil, stirring up the browned bits from the bottom of the frying pan.

All right, let's get those apples in there.

Boil the apples gently, uncovered, stirring occasionally till sauce is thickened—about 20 minutes. Sprinkle in salt and pepper if needed.

Depending on the tartness of the apples, you may want to add a little sugar to the sauce.

Slice the tenderloin into ½-inch medallions against the grain.

Pour the Normandy sauce over the meat and serve.

Norm goes nicely over a bed of egg noodles. Oh, and a **Waldorf Salad** (page 50) is a great accompaniment.

PORK TENDERLOIN
with Blueberry Mushroom Sauce

I don't know why people don't cook pork tenderloin more often. Oh sure, there's the price, but really, they're fast and easy to cook, and the meat is so dense and fat-free that you don't need a big serving. Unless of course you're in the fire hall, where there's no such thing as a reasonable portion.

HERE ARE YOUR INGREDIENTS

- 3 small (1-pound) or 2 large (1½-pound) pork tenderloins
- Seasoning salt, pepper, garlic powder and basil
- Butter
- ½ pound mushrooms—cut into Ts
- ⅔ cup port—a dry red wine would also do
- 1 10-ounce can consommé
- 2½ cups blueberries—fresh or frozen
- 1 tablespoon cornstarch combined with 2 tablespoons water

HERE'S YOUR METHOD OF OPERATION

Let's get the oven going at 350 degrees.

Dust the tenderloins with the seasonings. Basil and pork are a great combination.

Brown the tenderloins in a couple of tablespoons of butter in a large frying pan over medium–high heat.

Remove the loins but save the drippings. You're going to need the pork flavouring from those little browned bits in a second.

Place the tenderloins in an ovenproof dish or roaster and bake, uncovered, for about 20–30 minutes, depending on size. There should be just a hint of pink in the middle of the loins.

Introduce the mushrooms to those wonderful pan drippings, and brown them, tossing 'em around constantly over medium heat.

Deglaze the pan with the port or wine and allow it to reduce for about 5 minutes over medium heat.

Add the consommé and reduce for about another 10 minutes.

I think those blueberries want in! Let them have their way! Heat them through, check the sauce for taste and add salt if needed.

If you think you need to thicken your sauce a little, add the corn-starch-water mixture a bit at a time, until you're happy.

Slice the tenderloin against the grain into medallions and fan them out on the plate. Top with the decadent blueberry mushroom sauce.

Mom D's
STUFFED PORK TENDERLOIN

Yes, the first person who ever prepared a meal for me is the source of this great recipe. If you want to impress guests, here's one that'll do it. It looks incredible fanned out in slices on a plate, and the taste—it's top drawer!

SO WHAT DO WE NEED?

- 1 pork tenderloin for every 3-4 people you are serving—about 1½ pounds is a good size. The bigger it is, the easier it is to stuff.

- Garlic, onion, pepper, sage and basil

- Store-bought stuffing mix. Prepare as directed. Celery, mushrooms, onions and apples are a nice addition to the basic mix. Ensure that the stuffing is just moist enough to stay together, as the juice from the tenderloin will add to the moisture content.

- Water

HOW DO WE DO THIS AGAIN, MOM?

First off, crank that oven to 425 degrees.

Pound the tenderloin flat with a meat tenderizer, or the bottom of a heavy frying pan. Here's a good way to vent the day's frustrations!

When the loin is flattened, sprinkle it with the spices.

Place the stuffing over one half of the tenderloin.

Fold the other side over the stuffing. Cut pieces of string and tie the tenderloin together in 3 places, width-wise, and one lengthwise. Dust the top of the loin with same spices.

Get the loin in the roaster and bake for 10–15 minutes to brown it.

Pour about ¼ cup of water into the roaster and cover.

Turn the heat down and bake for about 40 minutes at 300 degrees. Keep in mind that this time will vary according to size: a small tenderloin may be done in about 20–30 minutes.

Serve with the Easy Gravy from the **Pork Roast** recipe (page 114) and make sure that you throw in lots of mushrooms.

Let the tenderloin stand 10 minutes before slicing into medallions.

Serve with **Rustic Garlic Smashed Potatoes** (page 179), **Asparagus Parmesan** (page 188) and a **Waldorf Salad** (page 50).

By the way, Mom D makes her own stuffing out of coarse breadcrumbs, butter, onions, a teaspoon of sage, and salt and pepper. I don't know the exact amounts; just be sure to keep the dressing fairly dry, as the juices from the loin will moisten the stuffing while it cooks.

JAMAICAN JERK PORK CHOPS
with Fresh Mango Salsa

This marinade is incredible not only on pork chops, but on pork steaks and pork roasts as well. There are many commercial brands of Jamaican jerk sauce to try. Just be careful, as many jerks are off-the-scale hot. To make the marinade milder, add more lime juice.

YOU CAN MAKE IT THROUGH THE EXPRESS LINE WITH

- Bottled Jamaican jerk sauce
- Lime juice
- Thick-cut pork cops for barbecuing, or pork steaks

IT WON'T TAKE MUCH TO MAKE THESE CHOPS HAPPY

Mix the jerk sauce and lime juice at a ratio of between 2:1 and 3:1, for spicy. Or go high octane, and simply eliminate the lime juice.

Marinate the pork chops in the jerk sauce—plastic bags are the easiest. About 4 hours seems to be about right. The longer you let it go the stronger the flavour, and this marinade is already bold!!

Barbecue the pork chops over medium–low heat till just cooked— they can be slightly pink near bones. This prevents them from drying out.

As a variation, try marinating the chops or pork steaks in **Cuban Lime Marinade** (page 174).

DON'T FORGET THAT DELICIOUS MANGO SALSA

- 1 ripe mango—diced
- 4 ripe Roma tomatoes—diced
- ½ small red onion—diced
- 2–3 jalapeño peppers—seeded out, and yes, diced fine
- 2 cloves garlic—minced or pressed
- ¼ cup cilantro—chopped fairly fine
- 1 tablespoon lime juice
- Kosher salt, and pepper to taste

Combine all ingredients, sprinkle the lime juice over top, and let your creation stand in the fridge for 1 hour. Serve over each pork chop.

Beer-Brined
PORK CHOPS

Here is a great recipe for lean pork chops. Brine them in a beer-salt marinade and they'll hold their moisture on the barbecue. Cook them to just about medium, and you know what? No more dried-out pork chops! Top the chops with fried onions and mushrooms. So good!

SO FIRST YOU HAVE TO GET

- 1 12-ounce beer
- 1½ cups water—what are we making, American beer? Kidding!
- 3 tablespoons kosher or sea salt or table salt in a pinch
- 2 tablespoons dark brown sugar
- 2 tablespoons mild fancy molasses
- ¾ cup ice cubes—beer on ice, not traditional but hey, it works
- 6 1- to 1¼-inch-thick bone-in pork chops—preferably centre cut—or boneless butterfly chops
- 8–10 large garlic cloves—minced or pressed
- 3 teaspoons coarsely ground pepper
- 2 teaspoons dried basil leaves

THEN YOU HAVE TO

Exercise extreme restraint—I'm watching you now—and pour all of the beer, water, salt, sugar and molasses into a bowl, and stir it up until the salt and sugar dissolve. Add the ice to the mix.

Place the pork chops and marinade in a plastic bag and seal it up. Allow all those wonderful flavours to marry in the serenity of the fridge for about 4 hours.

Remove the chops from the brew and pat dry with paper towels.

Combine the garlic, pepper and dried basil. Rub the spices all over the chops as evenly as possible.

Fire up the barbecue, and cook the chops over medium heat until they're just slightly pink on the inside.

Why not put the side burner on your barbecue—the one you've been neglecting—to work? Fry up some onions and mushrooms in a little butter. That'll make a nice topping on the chops.

Remove chops, tent with foil for 5 minutes. Mmm—Beer Chops!

Sweet-and-Sour
PORK STEAKS

Why not give your pork steaks a little Asian treatment? Liven them up with some sweet-and-sour sauce and pineapples, and serve them over rice. Yes, it's another of the many great recipes from firefighter Mike Dowhayko.

GET YOUR LIST TOGETHER AND GO TO THE STORE

- 4–6 pork steaks
- Salt and pepper
- Butter
- ¾ cup white or rice vinegar
- 1½ cups white sugar
- 2 tablespoons soy sauce
- ¼ cup ketchup
- 1 tablespoon ginger
- 2 cloves garlic—minced or pressed
- 1 14-ounce can pineapple chunks or tidbits
- 2 tablespoons cornstarch in ⅓ cup water

I HAVE THE GROCERIES, NOW WHAT DO I DO?

Lightly season steaks with salt and pepper, and brown these bad boys in a buttered frying pan. Place the steaks in a roaster or lasagna pan.

In a saucepan, combine the vinegar, sugar, soy sauce, ketchup, ginger, garlic and pineapple. Give it a whisking to bring it together.

Bring to a slow boil. Stir the water and cornstarch together until smooth. Add the thickening agent slowly to the sauce until the consistency you're after is attained.

Taste the sauce. If it's too tart add more sugar and/or ketchup; if it's too sweet add a little more vinegar. Keep in mind that the juices from the steaks will dilute the sauce as it cooks.

Pour the sauce over the steaks. The sauce should just cover them.

At this point you can either continue or, for more tender meat, marinate the steaks in the sauce overnight.

Bake in a preheated 350-degree oven for about 1–1½ hours, depending on the size and number of steaks. Remove steaks to a plate and keep warm.

If your sauce has thinned out, you can thicken it with another shot of the cornstarch-water mixture. Just move sauce to a smaller pan, fire up the heat, and add the mix a little at a time until you're happy—with the sauce, that is.

Barbecued
BABY BACK RIBS

Is this the ultimate barbecue food or what? I don't cook them entirely on the barbecue; I like to start them in the oven, keep them moist and then finish them on the barbecue smothered in sauce.

FIRST OFF YOU NEED

- A wallet with a clear conscience. Baby backs are expensive!
- **Just Like Bull's Eye Barbecue Sauce** (page 205)
- Let's make it 4 pounds of pork back ribs
- Liquid smoke—available in the condiment aisle of the supermarket
- **Fired-Up Spice** (page 200)
- 2 lemons and 2 medium onions—sliced

THESE RIBS WILL BE FALLING OFF THE BONE

Preheat the oven to 375 degrees.

Prepare the barbecue sauce by combining all of the ingredients in a large saucepan. Bring to bubbling and let simmer. Add more crushed chilis, hot sauce or cayenne pepper if you like it spicier.

With a paring knife, pull off the very thin layer of fat on the back of the ribs. Keep the ribs on their racks; only cut them into sections if they won't fit in the roaster.

Sprinkle the ribs with liquid smoke and season them with the **Fired-Up Spice**. Top with slices of lemons and onions.

Bake in a roaster, meaty side up, covered, for about 1 hour, 15 minutes. Let the ribs stand, undisturbed, for ½ hour, covered.

Drain the fat drippings and slather the barbecue sauce on the ribs. At this point you could refrigerate them and cook them the following day.

Fire up the barbecue, and show the ribs the heat for about 10 minutes. That should be enough time to coat the ribs with sauce on each side twice and caramelize. Don't let those ribs dry out!

Smokin'
SIDE RIBS

If you're like me—basically cheap—then you'll probably end up making side ribs more often than baby backs, because they're half the price, and hey, we're trying to feed a family here! Cook baby backs at the fire hall and the whining will start, "Supper's how much?" Prepare them this way, and even though they won't be quite as meaty as baby backs, they'll be just as tender.

GO TO YOUR BUTCHER FOR

- A full rack of side ribs, and have them cut right down the middle

OH, AND YOU'LL ALSO NEED

- 2 lemons and 2 medium cooking onions—quartered
- 8 or 10 cloves of garlic
- Peppercorns—a bunch of them
- Your favourite barbecue sauce—why not try the **Just Like Bull's Eye, Hawaiian Barbecue Sauce** (both page 205) or the sauce from **Five-Star Whiskey Brisket** (page 96).

SIMPLY BOIL, BAKE AND SERVE

Place the ribs, cut in large sections so that they'll fit, into a large soup pot and cover them with water.

Drop in the lemons and onions.

Toss in the garlic and a couple of tablespoons of peppercorns, or put in a good wrist workout on the pepper mill.

Bring the ribs to a slow boil. It's essential that you don't go for a full boil here, or they'll cook too quickly and become tough.

Simmer them for about 1 hour, 15 minutes, or until tender.

Get the oven preheating at 325 degrees.

Remove the ribs from the water and place in a roaster.

Slather on the barbecue sauce liberally—meaning the free-spending Trudeau Liberals, not the corner-cutting Martin Liberals.

Cover the roaster and bake for 20 minutes.

Remove the cover, baste 'em in the sauce and bake about 10 more minutes or until nicely caramelized. You could barbecue them instead at this point, but only long enough to set the sauce. Keep them moist, now!

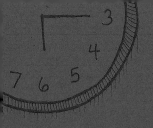

ROLLING, ROLLING, ROLLING!

At a downtown fire hall, one of the trucks carried Vetter Air Bags. These bags were designed to slide flat under an object, such as a car and, once inflated, would expand and thereby lift the car off, say, a trapped person. Of course, they had many other handy uses, which included acting as a valuable hi-jinks tool in the dorm. The operation involved a prankster sliding the Vetter bag under one side of a firefighter's bed: once the victim was safely off to the land of slumber, the assailant would inflate the bag. The dorm was very dark, so being a spectator for this joke was limited to listening to the air entering the Vetter bag, *psssttt*, followed by the thud of the firefighter hitting the floor, and the resulting, "What the ...?? What the heck's going on??"

JACK IN THE BOX

One day many years ago, the chief of the department—a.k.a. our boss—led a tour of our station for a group of city councillors—a.k.a. his bosses. The chief took great pride in explaining to the politicians, who determine our department's budget, the virtues of the equipment found on each fire truck. When he opened one truck's compartment, to everyone's shock a big cloud of smoke wafted from the confined space. As the smoke cleared, a firefighter who had hidden in the compartment popped out, greeting the VIPs with a cigarette dangling from his mouth and a cheery, "Hello dere!!"

The chief and councillors didn't see the humour in the gag and as you probably guessed, the prank earned the firefighter a suspension.

SOMETHING'S FISHY

As you make your way through this cookbook you may be wondering, "Why don't you feature recipes for meats other than beef, poultry or pork? What about wild meat or lamb?" Well, to quote my friend Rosie, "Sorry, but I don't cook Disney characters." So for deer, moose, bear, elk and all those other wildlife creatures, I'd rather allow them to die of natural causes in their native habitat. Yes, unlike many of my firefighting brethren—who will drag whatever animal happens to be in season into the fire hall for dinner—I just can't bring myself to hunt or prepare wild game.

Every year, Winnipeg Firefighters Game and Fish hosts a Firefighters Fishing Derby at scenic Great Whiteshell Lake, which I've yet to attend due to (a) my total lack of fishing ability and (b) my total lack of drinking ability. I know I'm missing out on staying up all night telling firefighting stories, which, believe me, can top any fishing story ever told and grow exponentially after each libation, but once again that's my choice.

Nonetheless I welcome anyone willing to bring fish for us to share for supper at the hall. That's filleted fish only, please; no head-still-on fish, thanks, as I don't feel the need to meet the fish I'm about to eat. That's probably why I'm not into hunting. I'd expect the animal in my sights to glare at me and say, "Now, you're not thinking of shooting me, are you, son?" Yes the cartoon-character voices are talking to me again.

Getting back to the fish topic here, pickerel (a.k.a. walleye) has to be the best catch in Manitoba; it's very tender and mild and absolutely delicious. I've included a few ways to prepare pickerel, but if it isn't easily accessible in your neck of the woods, sole, tilapia, or any other mild-tasting white fish is a suitable replacement.

If you love seafood the way I do, why not think about hosting a seafood-theme dinner? Try **Killer Crab Cakes** (page 132) as an appetizer, one of the clam chowder recipes for a soup, and one of the following fish recipes for the main course. Greet guests with a knife in your mouth, a patch on one eye and a parrot on your shoulder, and they'll be bowled over by your seaworthiness. However, expect a phone call the next morning when they wake up with gills!

TWO BATTERS
for Fire Hall Fish Fry

You choose the batter: light, fluffy, English-Style or Crispy Beer Batter.

ENGLISH-STYLE BATTER

Remember those English-style fish-and-chips places that used to wrap up your order in newspaper? You'd sprinkle in a little vinegar, and mm-mm—black ink! I mean, delicious battered fish. Here's my version.

SO DROP YOUR LURE IN THE LAKE FOR

- 3 eggs, separated
- 2 cups each milk and flour
- 3 teaspoons baking powder
- ½ teaspoon salt
- 3 pounds of your favourite fish —I recommend pickerel / walleye

So? Whip egg whites together; whip them well, now! Add milk and continue to whip, then add the egg yolks. Mix flour with baking powder and salt separately. Combine all ingredients with a mixer. Add more milk for a thinner batter. A third of this recipe is enough for 1 pound of fish.

CRISPY BEER BATTER
CAN YOU BELIEVE THIS IS ALL YOU NEED?

- 1 bottle light beer
- 1 cup all-purpose flour

Add the beer to the flour and whisk until smooth. Let the combo sit for 30 minutes to 1 hour. Season fish and dip them in dry flour before finishing with the beer batter. This recipe will batter at least 2 pounds of fish fillets.

NOW THAT YOU'VE PICKED A BATTER, FIRE UP THE DEEP FRYER

Heat the deep fryer to 350 degrees. If you don't have a deep fryer you can use a deep pot or even a wok. Just make sure that you fill it no higher than halfway with oil, and have a lid on hand in case tragedy strikes. Remember, never put water on a grease fire. *Okay, firefighter Jeff, slow down your breathing. This isn't a book on fire prevention.*

Dip fish in the batter and deep fry over medium heat till light brown.

CORNFLAKE-BATTERED FILLETS

Sure, it's a simple, traditional recipe, but it's the one that I keep coming back to. Serve it with **Carolina Tartar Sauce**, *or just squeeze some fresh lemon juice over the fillets.*

THIS IS ALL YOU NEED

- Your favourite fish fillets—pickerel / walleye or sole are mine

- Seasoned flour—3 parts flour to 1 part **Fired-Up Spice** (page 200)—or simply use seasoning salt

- 1 or more eggs—whisked or otherwise violated

- Cornflakes cereal—crushed up with a rolling pin

- Oil for frying

AND THIS IS ALL YOU NEED TO DO

Run your fingers along the centre of the fish fillets. If you feel a bone, cut it out lengthwise. Make the cut only as wide as the bone. Start at one end of the bone, and finish when you no longer feel any bone. You shouldn't need to cut the fillet completely in half.

Run the fillet through the seasoned flour first to absorb the moisture.

Dip the fillet in the egg wash, and coat it in cornflakes crumbs.

Ensure an even covering of crumbs. Don't put all of the crumbs out for dipping at once, as they'll become soggy.

Fry 'em up over medium to medium–low heat in a skillet, using a thin layer of vegetable oil in the bottom, until lightly browned on both sides. Place on a rack to drain off any oil.

Serve with **Glen's Non-Fries** (page 177) and some good old **Ralphie Slaw** (page 58) and **Carolina Tartar Sauce** (page 204).

THE ITALIAN JOB

Looking for a little variety? No, don't cheat on your spouse; that's going to cost you half your pension, not to mention the guilt and shame! No, I mean a little variety in the breading department. Try some seasoned Italian breadcrumbs instead of crushed-up cornflakes. They are readily available and just excellent on fish.

Prepare as above, except use plain flour rather than seasoned flour.

SWEET-AND-SOUR SOLE

Here's a recipe that would be equally at home in the Great Wall section. Whenever I mention Sweet-and-Sour Sole to newcomers, they wince. But once they try it, they're hooked. This is definitely one of my faves!

HERE'S YOUR GROCERY LIST

- 1 pound sole, pickerel or other mild-tasting white fish—or try shrimp

- **English-Style batter** (page 127). Use ⅓ of the recipe if you're preparing it for 1 pound of fish.

- 2 cloves garlic—minced or pressed

- 1 tablespoon ginger—chopped fine

- 2 green onions—chopped

- 5 tablespoons white vinegar —rice vinegar if authenticity is desired

- 5 tablespoons sugar

- 5 tablespoons water

- 1 tablespoon wine or sherry

- 1 tablespoon cornstarch

- ½ teaspoon sesame oil

- A little ketchup for colour

HERE'S YOUR GAME PLAN

Cut each fillet into about 3 chunks. Dip them in the English-style batter, and deep-fry them in a wok half full of peanut oil heated to 350 degrees. Fry in batches till light brown on all sides. Drain fish on a rack.

Remove the oil from the wok, leaving only 1 tablespoon of oil.

Add garlic, ginger and green onions to the wok, and stir-fry the flavour enhancers until fragrant.

Combine the sauce mix of vinegar, sugar, water, wine, cornstarch, sesame oil and ketchup. Toss it in the wok and stir until thickened.

Get the fish in there with the sauce and turn off the element. Toss it through very quickly to coat the fish and serve immediately.

Deluxe Asian Fried Rice (page 195) and **Asian Persuasion Coleslaw** (page 51) would be great accompaniments.

This one never fails to impress. Come on, get busy—you'll love it!

SHRIMP SCAMPI

The Viva Italiano section lobbied heavily to have this recipe included there, as Shrimp Scampi can be served over a bed of pasta or risotto for a main dish, or on its own as a side dish or appetizer. If you love seafood sautéed in garlic butter, this recipe is for you—maybe not for your hips, maybe not for your heart, but definitely for your taste buds.

I'M DROOLING JUST READING THE INGREDIENTS HERE

- 3 tablespoons olive oil
- ¼ cup butter
- 1 or 2 green onions—sliced
- 6 cloves garlic—minced or pressed
- 1 tablespoon fresh lemon juice
- ½ teaspoon kosher salt or sea salt
- 1 pound large shelled, deveined shrimp, with tails on
- ½ teaspoon grated lemon rind—a.k.a. zest
- ¼ cup fresh parsley—chopped fairly fine
- Dash hot pepper sauce, cayenne pepper or dried red pepper flakes—optional

OH MAN, THIS IS GOING TO BE GOOD

Place the oil and butter in a wok—*Wait a second! I thought you said this was an Italian recipe, Jeff?*—or a large frying pan, over medium heat.

When the butter is melted, add the onion, garlic, lemon juice and salt. The sauce is coming together quickly!

Turn the heat up to medium high and fry the shrimp till they turn pink all over. Don't overcook them, or they'll become rubbery.

Add the lemon zest, parsley and, if you're looking to fire this one up, go for the hot sauce, cayenne or dried pepper flakes to taste. Fire it up real good, and before you know it, this once-Italian dish will have been transformed into the New Orleans special, Creole Shrimp.

Looking for more ideas? Well, here's a great combo to try. Prepare the **Rip Roarin' Risotto** (page 192), **Asparagus Parmesan** (page 188) and Shrimp Scampi. Serve the risotto in the middle of the plate surrounded by the scampi, with the asparagus piled on top. Why, you clever chef, you've just created Seafood Risotto!

Lee's
SALMON FILLET

I just can't get enough fish, and often my choice is pickerel, or this simple dish, barbecued salmon. My good friend, firefighter Lee Harrison, made this for us, and oh, it is so good! Moist, flavourful and easy to make.

YOU'LL BE WRAPPING THIS UP IN ALUMINUM FOIL

- 1 salmon fillet—approximately 2-plus pounds
- Seasoning salt
- Lemon pepper
- Garlic powder
- Dill—chopped fresh is best, but dried will do
- 1 medium onion—cut in ¾-inch slices
- 1 or 2 lemons, depending on size—sliced thickly
- Pats of butter
- **Hall-a-Blaze** or **Lemon Dill** sauce (pages 206 and 203)

AND IN A MATTER OF MINUTES YOU'LL BE FIRING UP THE GRILL

Place the salmon fillet on a section of heavy aluminum foil—about twice the length of the fillet—lightly greased with non-stick spray.

Sprinkle the fillet with a light dusting of spices.

Place slices of onion on top of the salmon.

Now place slices of lemon on top of the onions.

If desired, place a few pats of butter on top of the salmon as well.

Fold up the aluminum foil to completely package the fish.

Place the salmon on the top rack of the barbecue on medium–low heat for about half an hour to 45 minutes, or until the salmon just begins to flake easily with a fork.

Or bake in a preheated 325-degree oven for 45 minutes to 1 hour.

Serves 4 to 6, depending on who they happen to be.

For side dishes, how about **Wild Rice Casserole** (page 197) and **Asparagus Parmesan** (page 188)? Now let's drizzle that **Hall-a-Blaze** or **Lemon Dill** sauce over the salmon and asparagus. Oh man, we're talking decadent!

Killer
CRAB CAKES

A definite Emeril influence here, although being landlocked in Winnipeg, and basically a thrifty firefighter, I use crab-flavoured pollock instead of the real thing, plus a few other substitutions. Call it a fault or an obsession if you will, but I just can't help but tinker with recipes.

OFF TO THE MARKET YOU GO FOR

- 2 tablespoons butter
- 1 cup sweet red or yellow onions— finely chopped
- ½ cup celery—finely chopped
- ½ cup red, yellow or orange pepper— finely chopped
- 1 pound crab-flavoured pollock. Of course, you could use the real thing if you're either closer to the sea than I am or not on my budget.
- 1½ cups Italian breadcrumbs
- ½ cup salad dressing or mayonnaise
- 1 tablespoon **Carolina Mustard Sauce**— (page 204) or prepared mustard
- 2 eggs
- Seasoned flour—3 parts flour to 1 part **Fired-Up Spice** (page 200)
- Olive oil for frying

LET'S GET THESE PATTIES TOGETHER

Heat the butter in a frying pan and sauté the onion, celery and pepper. Once they're softened, take them off the heat and let them chill out for a bit.

Place the pollock or crab in a food processor and pulse away until it is chopped fine.

Once the veggies are cool, place them in a mixing bowl and toss in the pollock or crabmeat, ¾ cup of the breadcrumbs, salad dressing or mayo and mustard. Get your hands in there! Come on, it's combining time—get sticky, get dirty—people are hungry here!

If the mixture doesn't hold together properly, simply add another touch of salad dressing or mayo and that fine-tasting **Carolina Mustard Sauce**.

Let's make the mix into patties, like hamburgers. Depending on the size you go for, you should be able to make 8–10.

If you have the time, place the patties on a plate or pan and toss them in the fridge for an hour. This will help keep them together.

Don't fire up the range quite yet; they still need to be coated! Whisk the eggs in a bowl, combine the flour and **Fired-Up Spice** in another bowl and—I hope someone else is doing the dishes here—in a third bowl drop in the remaining ¾ cup of breadcrumbs.

Pour about an inch of olive oil into a large frying pan and bring to medium heat. Have a lid nearby, just in case catastrophe strikes.

Meanwhile, get the assembly line going. Dip the patties in the seasoned flour, then the egg wash and finally the breadcrumbs.

Into the frying pan the tasty devils go. Cook until golden brown on the bottom, then flip and go for that golden sheen again.

These cakes could be used as an appetizer (make smaller patties), for lunch on a bun with coleslaw and fries or as a dinner entree.

How about making the **Broccoli-and-Cheese Casserole** (page 183), some **Twice-Baked Crab Cake Potatoes** (page 181) or **Wild Rice Casserole** (page 197) and a **Let the Sunshine Salad** (page 48) for accompaniments? I'm in!

Don't forget to whip up some of the **Carolina Tartar Sauce** (page 204)!

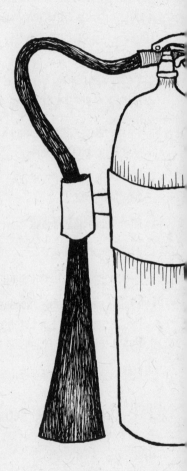

PESTO BASA

*Basa—not bass—is a farmed fish from Vietnam that has become quite popular and plentiful here in North America. Basa have large, firm, white fillets that are chock-full of flavour. But you know me, I'm always thinking that there's more flavour to be had, and that's why we're going to fire the basa up with a delicious pesto coating. But why stop there? Top these fat fillets with **Shrimp Scampi** (page 130) or Ranch-salsa dressing to fire the flavour scale into the red line.*

SET THE HOOK IN YOUR GROCER'S FISH SECTION FOR

- 4 basa fillets—they average 8 ounces each, enough for 1 diner
- **Fired-Up Spice** (page 200) or seasoning salt
- All-purpose unbleached flour
- 3 tablespoons olive oil
- 2 tablespoons butter or margarine
- 2 tablespoons pesto—choose **Mexican Pesto** (page 168) or **Lemon Garlic Pesto** (page 154) or purchased pesto
- Fresh lime or lemon juice

AND FIRE UP THE FRYING PAN

But first, fire up the oven to 400 degrees. While that's heating, pat the basa boys down with paper towels. Hey, I don't mean frisk them! Come on, use a paper towel to absorb the excess moisture.

Give each of the basas a little whack of **Fired-Up Spice**.

Dredge the basa through the flour and shake off the excess.

Heat a frying pan over medium heat and add the oil and butter.

Bring the pesto to the party, add to the pan and combine.

Fry the fillets for about 3 minutes each side until lightly browned.

Place on a baking pan and bake until the fish flakes easily. We're talking about 10 minutes at the most.

Top each Pesto Basa with lime juice for **Mexican Pesto**, or lemon juice for Italian, or even a fresh batch of **Shrimp Scampi** (page 130).

Salsa Basa Option. Give this a try. Use the **Mexi-Pesto** and before baking the fish uncovered as above, top it with a 50-50 mix of Ranch dressing and your favourite bottled salsa. The fish will melt in your mouth, as your mouth melts from the heat of the salsa. Delicious!

TROPICAL TILAPIA

Sure, those tiny tropical fish are tough to fillet, but they're well worth the trouble! Wait, I'm kidding. I'm talking tilapia with a tropical topping. Oh yah, mon— bananas, oranges, kiwis in dark Jamaican rum for a fruity drunken fish!

GO TO THE AQUARIUM —I MEAN GROCERY STORE—FOR

- 2 pounds of tilapia, red snapper or any mild, fleshy fish
- Lightly seasoned flour—3 parts flour to 1 part seasoning salt
- Olive oil for frying
- ½ cup chicken broth
- ½ cup dark rum
- ½ cup orange juice
- 2 tablespoons butter—yes, butter and rum, mon. Get the picture?
- 4 fresh basil leaves, chopped fine, or 1 teaspoon dried basil
- The old adage, salt and pepper, even sugar to taste
- 2 cups of diced fresh fruit—banana, orange, kiwi, mango, etc.

YOU KNOW THAT JAMAICAN RUM'S GOING TO TASTE GREAT!

Get the oven fired up to 350 degrees. We're not going to need it for long, but we are going to need it.

Let's get the dredging operation going here, and dip the fish through the seasoned flour, giving each fillet a light coating.

Fire up a frying pan to medium and place a few tablespoons of olive oil on the bottom. Get those fillets in there, and don't give up until both sides are lightly browned. Move them onto a cookie sheet, place them in the oven and keep the little fishies warm.

The olive oil will most likely be totally absorbed by now but if there's still some remaining, drain from the pan before continuing.

Add the chicken broth and the rum to the pan and reduce to about half, say about 2 minutes. Oh, does that ever smell good!

Okay, now that you're a little tipsy from the fumes, add the orange juice, butter and basil to the stock and rum, and blend together.

Test the sauce, add salt, pepper and sugar if needed. Add the fruit and place the frying pan in the oven for 5 minutes to finish cooking.

Divvy up the fish on plates, and top each with the delicious sauce.

FACE-OFF WITH FISH

As a rookie, I was sent to a different station on a temporary transfer. Our acting captain was a man well known for his eccentricities, especially when it came to food. He loved the outdoor life and, it was said, would eat absolutely anything. The word was, "Whatever he's cooking, just say no, because it could be something he spotted on the road coming to work."

"Boys!" our captain announced one day, "I saw some beautiful breaded fish today at Safeway. Our district chief retires in two weeks. How about if I pick some up and invite him over for supper tomorrow?"

We were sceptical, but we reasoned that if it's frozen fish from Safeway, we should be relatively safe.

The following night, our captain proudly entered the kitchen carrying the groceries: a couple of bags of coleslaw, potatoes and best of all, that beautiful fish—Generic Brand Fish Cakes! Despite our disappointment, we did our best to conjure up something edible before the chief arrived for dinner.

As usual, I was finished eating first and as I got up from the table I spotted a lonely fish cake on the counter. "There's another fish cake left. Does anybody want it?" I asked.

"Oh, I'll have that!" our captain replied without challenge.

Soon the guys were snickering under their breath, their shoulders bobbing up and down as they held back their laughter. I, meanwhile, was out of the loop as to what was so funny.

When it came time for our guests to leave, the chief walked over to me, shaking his head, and said, "Son, what you did made the evening. The food was the s#*ts, but you made it all worthwhile. That was a great prank!"

I laughed along, clueless as to what part I had played, and later, I asked one of the guys what was so hilarious.

"You know the fish cake you offered the cap?" a crewmember laughed. "Well, it fell on the floor when we took it out of the oven, so we played floor hockey with it for about 5 minutes. It was all covered in dirt, crumbs and hair—*disgusting!* Oh man, after picking up that ridiculously crappy fish, he deserved it."

FROM THE GREAT WALL TO THE TAJ MAFIRE HALL

Back in my late teens, when I started to fend for myself in the kitchen, I had a deep-seated desire to cook Chinese. My first attempts at Chinese culinary brilliance were those pre-fab, two-can dinners. Yes, stir-fry strips of meat, add the vegetables from the big can, and the sauce from the small can and mm-mm, not so good!

When I'd visit an Asian restaurant, I'd be intimidated by the amazing variety of vegetables cooked to tender-crisp perfection and the awesome use of colour. For years, I thought that Chinese was the ultimate cooking challenge.

What it took me the longest time to discover was how quick and easy a stir-fry can be. All you need to do is stir-fry bite-sized chunks of chicken or turkey thighs—I find them to be tastier than the breast meat—pork, beef or even seafood, in a hot wok with a little peanut oil, garlic and ginger. Remove the meat to a plate, add a little more oil, garlic and ginger, and stir-fry fresh chopped veggies—onions, carrots, celery, broccoli, peppers, etc.—with perhaps a little water to steam and keep the veggies from burning. Check the veggies with a fork, and when they gently give, return the meat to the wok and add a sauce. You can use a bottled stir-fry sauce or plum or hoisin sauce. If the sauce thins out on you, bring it to a boil and add cornstarch mixed with an equal part water a bit at a time to thicken it.

Yes, it really is that simple. Well, unless you take leave of your senses and attempt a stir-fry for 20 people, as I often did. Rather than a wok, we used an industrial-sized, flat-bottom grill, and I employed a fellow firefighter armed with two huge spatulas to mix like mad while I added ingredients, all the while praying to the Alarm Gods, "Please, hold back the calls. Now is *not* the time!" Unlike a stew or soup that gets better with time, a stir-fry left on a counter crashes as it sits.

Curry, I find, is a love-it-or-hate-it meal, and I *love* it! So I've included a few East Indian classics to tempt your palate and permeate your kitchen walls. The Far Eastern pleasures are here for you to enjoy, so fire up that wok and get at it!

Chickity China
THE CHINESE CHICKEN

Thanks to the Barenaked Ladies for the name of this recipe!

HERE'S WHAT YOU'LL NEED TO GET THIS CHICK ROCKIN'

- 1 pound boneless, skinless chicken thighs—sorry, no drumsticks—cut into 1-inch cubes
- ½ cup red onion—cut into 1-inch cubes
- 1 cup mixed peppers, green, yellow, red, they all work—cut into 1-inch cubes

FOR THE MARINADE

- 2 tablespoons sweet soy sauce, a.k.a. kecap manis, or regular soy sauce
- 2 tablespoons cornstarch
- 1 egg white

FOR THE SEASONING SAUCE

- ¼ cup each light soy sauce and water
- 2 teaspoons each sugar, dry sherry and cornstarch
- 1 teaspoon sesame seed oil

FOR THE PEANUT MIXTURE

- 2 tablespoons ground roasted peanuts
- 1 tablespoon ground roasted sesame seeds
- 1 tablespoon sugar

WOK DON'T RUN WITH THAT CLEAVER

Toss the cubes of chicken into the marinade. Let it mellow for about 30 minutes. Meanwhile, chop up the veggies and set aside.

Prepare the seasoning sauce and peanut mixtures, and set aside.

It's 30 minutes already? Better drain the marinade from the chicken.

Heat the oil in a wok to 350 degrees. Deep-fry the chicken, a handful at a time, for about 2 minutes. Remove the chicken to a rack to dry.

Heat about 2 tablespoons of oil in the wok to cook the red onion and peppers.

When the veggies are just getting tender crisp, add the seasoning sauce and let the mixture cook until the sauce starts to thicken.

Let's get the chicken back in there, and combine all of the ingredients, tossing them quickly to heat through.

Move your creation to a platter and serve with the ground-up nuts and seeds sprinkled on top. Look at the colours! It tastes as good as it looks!

ORANGE HOISIN CHICKEN

Here's an easy stir-fry if you're in a rush. The sweetness of hoisin blends nicely with the acidity of the oranges. Looks great on a plate, too!

LET'S SEE IF WE HAVE

- Peanut oil for frying
- 4 cloves garlic—minced or pressed
- 2 tablespoons finely diced ginger
- ½ jumbo onion—chopped into large pieces
- 3 stalks celery and 3 carrots—cut on the bias, get out the mitre saw
- ¼ pound mushrooms—cut into Ts
- 1 pound boneless, skinless chicken thighs
- The zest of 1 small orange—i.e., the finely grated rind
- Salt and pepper
- Small can of mandarin orange segments—drain and reserve juice
- Hoisin sauce—found in your grocer's Asian foods section
- ½ cup orange juice combined with 2 tablespoons cornstarch

WOK ON!

Let's get those veggies prepped!

Well, since your cleaver is warmed up, cut the chicken into cubes.

Get your wok rockin' and smokin', add 2 tablespoons peanut oil, and toss in the garlic and ginger. Cook briefly, not even 20 seconds.

Follow up with the chicken, and stir-fry till cooked through. Remove.

Add a couple more tablespoons of peanut oil to the wok and toss in the veggies and zest. Season with salt and pepper. Stir a few times, then add a splash of mandarin orange juice: just enough to create some steam to help cook the veggies. Cover and cook until tender crisp.

Re-add the chicken and enough hoisin sauce to coat your stir-fry.

Introduce the orange juice-cornstarch mixture a bit at a time, until the sauce reduces and clings to the meat and veggies.

Finish by adding mandarin orange segments and heat through quickly. The oranges will fall apart if you cook them for too long.

For variety, try using plum sauce in place of the hoisin sauce, add a little chili-garlic sauce to fire it up and eliminate the oranges.

Szechwan
PEANUT CHICKEN

Firefighter Michael Sparks is the source for this spicy chicken dish. I like the twist-from-traditional method of cooking the veggies in the sauce, rather than stir-frying the veggies first and then adding the sauce. Just excellent!

LET'S SEE WHAT WE NEED HERE

- 1 350-mL bottle Szechwan peanut sauce
- 1 10-ounce can chicken broth
- 2 tablespoons each honey and soy sauce
- 1 heaping tablespoon cornstarch
- 2 tablespoons peanut oil
- 4 cloves garlic—minced or pressed
- 2 tablespoons minced ginger
- 1½ pounds boneless, skinless chicken breasts or thighs—cubed
- 1 bunch green onions or half a purple onion—diced or sliced
- 1 red and 1 green pepper—diced into 1-inch squares
- ⅓ pound mushrooms—optional
- 1 can baby corn—buy them in cuts or cut them up yourself
- A healthy bunch of broccoli— cut into mini-trees
- Honey-roasted peanuts—chopped
- Chili-garlic sauce to taste—to fire this dish up!

IF I COULD WOK THAT WAY I WOULDN'T NEED THE PEANUT OIL

Mix up the sauce by combining the peanut sauce, chicken broth, honey, soy sauce and cornstarch. Cut up all the veggies and chicken.

Get your wok smokin' and add 1 tablespoon peanut oil. Toss in half the garlic and ginger, and cook briefly. Get the chicken in there and stir-fry until cooked through. Remove.

Place another tablespoon of oil in the hot wok with the remaining garlic, ginger and onions. Add the sauce and heat. Bring the veggies into the mix and continue cooking, stirring, until the veggies are tender crisp.

Re-add the chicken. Adjust the consistency by mixing 1 tablespoon cornstarch with 2 tablespoons water. Add a bit at a time until the sauce takes on a gravy-like consistency.

Top with a handful of peanuts, and you're good to go! Serve over rice or, my favourite way, over spaghetti. For pasta you may want to use a thinner sauce by lessening the cornstarch mixture. For more kick, add chili-garlic sauce to taste.

LEMON CHICKEN

This sauce recipe comes from fellow firefighter Ed Yuen. Ed's family owns the Peking Restaurant in Winnipeg, known for its incredible Chinese take-out, of which Lemon Chicken is a specialty. However, instead of deep-frying the chicken— the traditional way of cooking it—I gave this one a health-conscious twist by baking the breasts instead.

GET WHAT YOU NEED, WHICH IS

- Saltine crackers—breadcrumbs will also do
- 4–6 chicken breasts—depending on size, no silicone please!
- 1 or 2 eggs—beaten up
- 1 cup each water and white vinegar
- ½ cup plus 2 tablespoons white sugar
- ¼ cup packed brown sugar
- ¼ teaspoon soy sauce
- 1 tablespoon lemon juice
- 3 tablespoons cornstarch and ½ cup water
- Thin lemon slices

AND PUT THIS TASTY PLAN TO WORK

Start your oven up at 400 degrees.

Crush up the crackers with a rolling pin until they're fine, fine, FINE!

Dry each breast with a paper towel. Dip the chicken in egg, and then through the cracker crumbs, making sure that you coat them evenly.

Place the chicken in an oven-proof dish large enough to park the breasts and bake, uncovered, for 15–20 minutes depending on breast size. Yes, in this case, size does matter!

While the chicken is baking, combine the water, vinegar, both sugars, soy sauce and lemon juice in a saucepan. Bring to a boil. Mix up the cornstarch and water.

Blend the cornstarch mixture into the sauce to thicken it.

Pour the sauce over the chicken, top each breast with 1 or 2 lemon slices, and bake for about 15 more minutes, uncovered, or until the chicken is cooked through. Baste with sauce before plating.

Serve over a bed of stir-fried coleslaw—presentation is important! —with a side of **Deluxe Asian Fried Rice** (page 195) and a combo of your favourite stir-fried veggies to round it out.

KOREAN CHICKEN

I first tasted this dish at the Korean Pavilion at Folklorama in Winnipeg. Our friend Joanne Park said, "Oh, I can give you that recipe. Just take some soy sauce, ginger, sugar and garlic ..." No amounts were given, so I had to get to work in the kitchen to figure it out for myself. Here it is, my version, which has become a big favourite at my house and the firehouse. This recipe makes enough for a party. Halve the sauce if you are making a smaller amount.

A LITTLE OF THIS, A LITTLE OF THAT

- 6–9 pounds chicken legs (preferred) or thighs or both—with the skin on

- 1 cup soy sauce

- ½ cup Indonesian sweet soy sauce—a.k.a. kecap manis

- ½ cup white vinegar, or rice wine vinegar if you like it a little funkier

- 1¾ cups white sugar

- 6 cloves garlic—minced or pressed

- 2 1½-inch chunks of fresh ginger—minced

- 2–3 tablespoons hot sesame oil—depending on desired heat—or 3 tablespoons regular sesame oil and 2–3 teaspoons chili-garlic sauce

- 2 tablespoons cornstarch

- ¼ cup water

OH, THIS CHICKEN IS SOOO GOOD!

In a large saucepan ¾ full of water, cook the chicken at a very slow boil for about 20 minutes. This will rid the chicken of fat.

Meanwhile, mix all of the remaining ingredients together, with the exception of the cornstarch and water.

Remove the chicken from the water and place it in a roasting pan sprayed with non-stick coating. Top the chicken with lots of sauce, until those legs are almost swimming. (Kick, kick, kick ...)

At this point you could let the chicken cool, then cover with foil and refrigerate it until the next day. This will marinate the meat. Then follow the upcoming baking instructions, keeping in mind that the cooking time will be slightly longer, considering that the chicken is starting from cold.

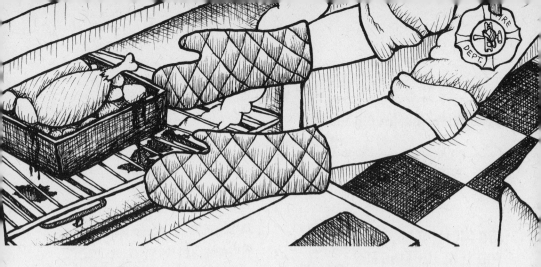

Bake, uncovered, in a preheated 375-degree oven for about 30 minutes, basting with sauce every 10 minutes, until the chicken is cooked through.

Remove the chicken from the sauce and set aside.

Transfer the sauce to a saucepan and bring it to a slow boil. Combine cornstarch and water, and add to the sauce to thicken it.

Place the chicken on a serving dish and toss with the thickened sauce.

Here's an idea. Sprinkle the chicken pieces with sesame seeds, either lightly browned in a dry frying pan, or uncooked. Hey, we're talking maximum presentation here!

Place the chicken and sauce over a bed of **Deluxe Asian Fried Rice** (page 195) or serve it for lunch with one of the Asian salads found in the Rabbit Food section.

Note to thrifty firefighters— the sauce can be saved and frozen after using. Then you've got your next batch of Korean Chicken half-cooked! Keep in mind that you should only re-use the sauce once.

BEEF TENDERLOIN
with Oyster Mushroom Sauce

No, it's not oyster mushrooms; it's an oyster mushroom soy sauce. Oh all right, if you insist, go exotic and try oyster mushrooms. The bottom line is, no matter what mushroom you choose, this is a deliciously decadent dish.

FOR THE MEAT MARINADE YOU'LL BE LOOKING FOR

- 2 tablespoons soy sauce
- 6 tablespoons water
- 2 teaspoons sugar
- 2 tablespoons cornstarch

AND YOU'LL NEED TENDER BEEF AND VEGGIES

- 1 pound beef tenderloin
- Peanut or canola oil for cooking
- ¼ cup fresh ginger—mince it up
- 1 green onion—cut to 1-inch lengths
- ½ pound button, brown or even oyster mushrooms—Td up
- 1 pound broccoli—cut into florets

OH, AND FOR THE OYSTER SAUCE YOU'LL REQUIRE

- ½ cup premium oyster sauce— in your store's Asian foods section
- ¼ cup dry sherry
- ½ cup water

- 2 tablespoons mushroom soy sauce or regular light soy sauce
- 2 tablespoons cornstarch
- 2 teaspoons sugar

INSERT YOUR OWN CLEVER WOK-ISM HERE

Let's marry those marinade ingredients to get things rolling.

Cut the beef into strips against the grain and toss them into the marinade. Add 3 tablespoons oil, mix and let sit for 30 minutes.

Combine the sauce ingredients and set them aside.

Heat 2 cups oil in a wok to 300 degrees—medium–low heat. Cook the beef in batches till browned. Drain oil, reserving 2 tablespoons.

Intro the ginger and green onions to the wok. Add the mushrooms and broccoli, and stir-fry till tender crisp. Then bring on the tender beef.

Introduce the sauce over high heat and reduce. Absolutely delicious!

Outrageous
EGG FOO YUNG

Here's a dish that looks much more complex to make than it actually is. Really, it's just a stack of four pancake omelettes topped with a simple sauce.

HERE'S WHAT YOU'LL NEED TO COLLECT

- 8 eggs
- 1 tablespoon soy sauce
- 1½ teaspoons dry sherry
- ¼ teaspoon each salt and pepper
- 2 cloves minced garlic—optional
- 1 cup cooked chicken, shrimp or crabmeat—diced or julienned
- 1½ cups of veggies—try half a cup each of sliced mushrooms, bean sprouts and red pepper, cut in strips or diced
- 4 teaspoons peanut oil

AND FOR THE SAUCE YOU'LL NEED

- 1 cup beef broth
- 2 tablespoons mushroom soy sauce or regular soy sauce
- 1 teaspoon sesame oil
- 3 teaspoons cornstarch combined with 2 tablespoons water
- 2 green onions—chopped

OKAY, BRAVE SOUL, HERE'S HOW WE DO IT

Beat the eggs together with the soy sauce, sherry, salt, pepper and garlic. Bring the meat and the veggies into the omelette mix.

Heat 1 teaspoon peanut oil in an 8-inch non-stick frying pan over medium heat. Add ¼ of the egg, meat and veggie mix.

Cook till the omelette's bottom is browned. Flip and cook through.

Repeat this procedure three more times. Stack omelettes on top of each other, tenting them with foil to keep warm after each addition.

Meanwhile, combine the beef broth, mushroom soy sauce and sesame oil. Bring this combo to a slow boil in a small saucepan.

Mix the cornstarch and water together and toss it in to thicken the sauce. Bring on the green onions and heat through.

Place the omelettes on a serving dish and top with sauce. You did it, my friend! The ancient Chinese secret is out!

What did you
SATAY?

Have you ever tried Indonesian soy sauce? Sample this sweet variation and you may never go back to the Chinese version. A wonderful blend of sweet and spicy, that's the Indonesian satay way. Get ready to fire up the barbecue!

INTRODUCING THE ESSENTIAL INGREDIENTS

- 1½ to 2 pounds pork tenderloin or chicken—cut in 1-inch cubes

- 2 tablespoons butter

- Grated rind of one good-sized lemon

- Oh, and you'll need to get the juice out of that lemon too

- 3 tablespoons onion—grated, oh my watering eyes!

- 2 tablespoons brown sugar— for a little sweetness

- 1 teaspoon dried coriander

- ½ teaspoon cumin—to give it that funky flavour

- ¼ teaspoon ground ginger or 1 tablespoon minced fresh ginger

- ½ cup Indonesian sweet soy sauce— a.k.a. kecap manis

- 2 teaspoons chili-garlic sauce— find it in the Chinese food section

- 6 good grinds of fresh pepper from the old pepper mill

MEAT MEETS MARINADE

Place the meat in a cooking dish. Melt the butter in a saucepan. Toss in the remaining ingredients, bring to a boil and simmer for 5 minutes.

Pour the marinade over the meat, allow to cool, cover and put in the fridge overnight to maximize that flavour infusion. Turn the meat a few times as you go. It's looking and smelling good already!

MEAT MEETS GRILL

Soak a number of wooden skewers in water for at least 1 hour.

Skewer up the meat and barbecue until done—for the pork, cook until pink in the middle. Don't overcook it, now; we want tender meat here!

Oh, I almost forgot, save the marinade. Boil it in a saucepan for 5 minutes and serve over the pork. I see **Deluxe Asian Fried Rice** (page 195) and **Lemon Poppyseed Salad** (page 47) served on the side!

THAI CHICKEN CURRY

This is a great, quick, easy, tasty and, believe it or not, low-cal, low-fat meal. Come on, what are you waiting for, more adjectives? Fire up the wok, and get those fantastically fragrant, fabulous, fired-up flavours happening!

FIRST OFF YOU'LL NEED TO

- Preheat the oven to 425 degrees.
- Spread frozen chicken fingers evenly on a greased baking sheet. (You didn't think the kids would be willing to try curry, did you? Kidding!)

OKAY THEN, HERE'S WHAT YOU REALLY NEED

- 4 good-sized chicken breasts —cut into bite-sized pieces
- 1 jumbo onion—coarsely chopped
- 1 red and 1 orange or yellow pepper— cut into strips
- 3 cups broccoli florets—optional
- 2 tablespoons grated rind of lemon or lime
- oil
- 2 tablespoons curry paste
- 2 cups regular plain yogurt
- 2 tablespoons lemon or lime juice
- ¼ cup premium oyster sauce
- ⅔ cup chopped cilantro

AND HERE'S ALL YOU NEED TO DO

Prepare the chicken, veggies and grated rind.

Add 2 tablespoons oil to a smokin' wok, and stir-fry the curry paste for 20 seconds. Stir-fry the chicken in that potent curry paste till cooked.

Toss in the onion and cook for 2 minutes, tossing continuously.

Add the pepper, broccoli and lemon rind to the wok and fry until tender crisp. If the wok starts burning, add just a touch of water.

Combine the yogurt with lemon juice and oyster sauce. Thai cooking generally calls for fish sauce, but I can't bring myself to use it. Have you ever smelled fish sauce? Go with the oyster sauce.

Stir in the yogurt mixture. Boil until the liquid is slightly reduced.

Toss in the cilantro. Stir through. Serve over rice, angel hair pasta or even some of that trendy but silly-sounding couscous.

CURRIED PASTA
Prima-Derraugh

Here's what you get when you put an East Indian and an Italian chef in the kitchen together. Goes great with **Tandoori Chicken** *(next page)! Very smooth.*

A BIT OF ITALY, A BIT OF INDIA

- 2 tablespoons olive oil
- 2 heaping tablespoons of mild curry paste—or kick it up with a Madras or hot paste. Go for it; turn your face into a flame-thrower!
- 1 jumbo onion—cut into 1-inch squares
- 1 red and 1 orange or yellow pepper—cut into strips
- 1 big bunch broccoli—cut into florets
- 2 cans premium coconut milk
- 2 chicken bouillon cubes or 2 teaspoons powdered bouillon
- ⅓ cup chopped cilantro—plus more for garnish
- Approximately 1 pound linguine

LET'S GET THINGS FIRED UP HERE!

Heat the olive oil over medium heat in a large frying pan. Add the heaping helping of curry paste and cook for 30 seconds, breaking it up as you go. I love that smell, but if you aren't too keen on it, well, that's what exhaust fans are for!

Introduce the onions to the pan, add just enough water so that they don't burn, and cook until the onions start to soften.

Let's add the peppers and broccoli to the mix, and toss them with the curry paste until well coated.

Open up the coconut milk. Chances are that there is a thick cream on top and thin water under it. Mix the cream of the crop with the water and pour it into the pan.

Toss in the bouillon cubes or powder, and half the chopped cilantro.

Simmer for 30–40 minutes to allow the flavours to build.

Uncover the pot for the last 10 minutes to allow the sauce to thicken. If you prefer a thicker sauce, combine a tablespoon of cornstarch with 2 tablespoons water and add this to the mixture over boiling heat a bit at a time, until it reaches the consistency you want.

Serve over linguine with the rest of the cilantro sprinkled over top. Don't forget that **Tandoori Chicken** (page 149)!

TANDOORI CHICKEN

Okay, so it makes your teeth and hands pink, not to mention your inner being. I'm serious. I cooked this for one of my training officers, Les Brown, and the next day he thought he had a gastrointestinal bleed. Men, don't let the rich pink colour threaten you. This wonderful spicy chicken is so good that you'll soon be hooked on it. You can bake it or barbecue it or both. Thanks to our friend Kathi Shay for the recipe. I confess—I'm addicted!

SO GO OUT AND HUNT DOWN

- 10-ounce bottle Tandoori paste, readily available in your friendly grocer's Indian foods section
- 3 cups plain yogurt
- ½ cup lemon juice
- 4 teaspoons garam masala, or Tandoori masala—also found in the Indian foods section
- Seasoning salt to taste—optional
- About 10 chicken legs with the thighs attached

MAKE UP THE MARINADE

Combine the Tandoori paste, yogurt, lemon juice, garam masala and seasoning salt. Sure, it tastes a little spicy, and a little salty, but believe me, it really mellows as it marinates.

Place the chicken and marinade in a plastic bag or glass dish, and allow it to marinate at least 24 hours—even up to 48 hours.

AND GET THAT CHICKEN FIRED UP!

Place the chicken, dripping in that wonderful marinade, on a rack in a roaster and slide it into a pre-heated 275-degree oven, uncovered. Bake for 2 hours.

Or if you're impatient try 375 degrees for 50–60 minutes.

Hey, if it just happens to be summertime, why not take the chicken out a little early and finish it up on the barbecue?

Try the Tandoori Chicken with **Coconut Curried Rice** (page 196) or **Curried Pasta Prima-Derraugh** (page 148) on the side.

"LIKE BUTTER" CHICKEN

I tried Butter Chicken at a local East Indian restaurant, and it was so good that I just had to come up with a clone. I saddled up to the trusty Internet, gathered all the info that I could find on the subject and married several recipes together. Here's the result of my quest for this "like butter" chicken in a creamy tomato sauce. If you want to fire up a 4-alarm blaze, add as much Indian chili powder to the final cooking sauce as you dare.

START WITH

- 2 pounds boneless, skinless chicken thighs in large, bite-sized pieces

AND MARINATE THE CHICKEN IN

- 1 cup plain yogurt
- 2 tablespoons olive oil
- 2 tablespoons butter—melted
- 1 teaspoon salt
- ½ tablespoon garam masala—found in the East Indian spice section
- ½ tablespoon East Indian chili powder—found in same section
- 3 tablespoons lime juice
- 2 tablespoons garlic paste—also hanging out in the East Indian section
- 1 tablespoon ginger paste—ditto

THEN BUILD THE FINAL COOKING SAUCE

- 2 tablespoons butter
- 1 tablespoon garam masala
- 1 tablespoon garlic paste
- 1 tablespoon ginger paste
- 2 cups canned tomato sauce
- ½ tablespoon East Indian chili powder—this yields a moderately spicy sauce. Start at ½ teaspoon and work your way up if unsure.
- 1 cup water
- 1 tablespoon honey
- 2 teaspoons dried fenugreek leaves—see East Indian specialty stores
- 1 cup whipping cream

SURE, I'LL TAKE A HIT OF THAT FIERY CHICKEN!

Place the chicken and marinade in a plastic bag and refrigerate overnight.

Preheat your oven to 250 degrees. Move the chicken and the marinade into an ovenproof dish, cover with foil and bake oven for 1½ hours.

While it bakes, let's build the final cooking sauce. We'll start by melting the butter in a medium saucepan over medium heat.

Stir in the garam masala until fragrant. That's fragrant, not flagrant.

Mix in the garlic and ginger pastes, and combine, stirring constantly for about 20 seconds. Smells great already!

Toss in the tomato sauce, chili powder and water. Bring to a boil.

Reduce the heat to low and stir in the honey and fenugreek leaves.

Remove the sauce from the heat and stir in the whipping cream.

When the chicken's time is up, strain it from the marinade. We're finished with the marinade so give it the toe. Put the chicken back in the dish and add the final cooking sauce.

Bake the chicken in its new sauce for another ½ hour, or until cooked through, and oh, so tender.

Serve over **Coconut Curried Rice** (page 196) with a **Let the Sunshine Salad** (page 48) on the side.

THE GONG SHOW

At the start of a night shift, our crew was asked by the day-shift captain to return a set of keys to the seniors complex across the street from the hall, as they had neglected do so after a recent alarm. Rather than get in the truck, Moe volunteered to simply run over with them.

Once Moe had reached the other side of the busy, four-lane street, we put our plan into action, ringing the alarm gong twice. Moe promptly looked over his shoulder to see us briskly walking toward the fire trucks. Suddenly a sense of panic overwhelmed him: "We've got a call!" Without checking traffic, he started to run blindly across the street when HONK! SCREECH!

Moe stood wide-eyed and Moe-tionless, inches from the hood of a car that had barely managed to stop before hitting him. His heart pounding, he then decided to look both ways before completing his journey, dodging through heavy traffic. He raced to his gear and as he began to get dressed, he clued into the gag as we all suffocated with laughter.

I can remember his reaction as if it were yesterday. "Oh for [bad word] sake, you guys. All I have is seven years to go. Seven years left to work on this job, and because of you guys I almost get run over by a car. Only seven years left, and I almost got killed by your stupid prank!"

VIVA ITALIANO!

When firefighters take a break from the meat-and-potatoes habit, you can count on many to go Italian with spaghetti and meat sauce, pizza or lasagna —all great meals which I prepare myself. But I never seem to follow the basic script very well, so I often stray into the more eclectic versions in this section. You'll find such hybrid recipes as **Thai**, **Pacific Rim** and **Tex-Mex Pizzas** (pages 156–158), **Coq Au Vin Cacciatore** (page 165) and **Scorchin' Lasagna** (page 159).

Many Italian dishes start with an excellent tomato sauce that you can certainly make from tomatoes, tomato sauce, tomato paste and spices—as in the **Fired-Up Bolognese Sauce** recipe (page 163). Or you can join me in cheaters' corner as I fire up prepared spaghetti sauce with a few additions. My buddy, firefighter Lee Harrison, definitely influenced the tomato sauce that I make, adding the tart and sweet elements of red wine and brown sugar. I also like to toss in a few dried red chili flakes or jalapeños to fire up the sauce a bit. If the sauce has too much kick, I'll add a bit more brown sugar, which not only balances the acidity of the tomatoes and wine but also counters the chilies.

Since I'm not a big proponent of white flour, I try to use the somewhat pricier but healthier whole-wheat pastas in recipes, as well as a 50-50 blend in the **Bread-Maker Pizza Dough** recipe (page 155).

Firefighters *love* pizza, and I'm reminded of a particularly great firehouse pizza chef at a downtown hall. An individual who was not in on the meal would often dive into the leftovers on the sly without paying. This ticked off the chef, so he laced a piece one night with a "burn a hole in the seat of your pants" hot sauce, sneaking it in between crust and topping.

Well, much to the chagrin of the chef, the pizza thief failed to strike that night, but an unsuspecting member of the relieving shift decided to try a slice for breakfast. One bite, and the poor guy's mouth was a 4-alarm fire as he scrambled for the bathroom to jettison the pizza. "Stop, drop and roll." Whoops!! Wrong guy.

So let's get into the Viva Italiano section, tour around the lush Italian countryside and find a recipe to fire up for you and yours tonight!

LEMON GARLIC PESTO CHICKEN

You can serve it as a main course or as a lunch salad. It's a great one-dish—eventually one-dish, anyway—dinner, with terrific colour and flavour.

IT'S TIME TO HUNT AND GATHER

- 4 chicken breasts in **Lemon Garlic Marinade** (page 111)

FOR THE LEMON GARLIC PESTO

- 1 cup fresh parsley—packed and ready to move

- ½ cup fresh basil—packed, as in volume

- 6 cloves garlic—pressed or minced

- 3 tablespoons pine nuts or almonds—optional, but a great addition

- 2 tablespoons lemon juice—fresh is best

- 1 teaspoon salt—kosher or sea salt is best

- ½ teaspoon pepper—grind it up fresh

- ⅓ cup each olive oil and Parmesan cheese

FOR THE REST

- 1 medium red onion—cut into strips

- 1 red, yellow or orange pepper—strip 'em down too

- ½ pound mushrooms—T 'em, or quarter 'em

- ½ pound fusilli pasta or tri-colour rotini

- 4 ripe Roma tomatoes, diced—optional

I KNEW I BOUGHT THAT FOOD PROCESSOR FOR SOMETHING

Marinate the chicken for 1–4 hours. Blend the parsley, basil, garlic, nuts, lemon juice, salt and pepper in a food processor, or in a pinch you can use a blender.

While the machine is running, slowly add the olive oil. Now that you're in the groove, do the same with the Parmesan cheese.

Barbecue or broil the chicken on medium heat, allow it to cool for 5 minutes and slice the chicken into strips against the grain.

In a frying pan or wok, stir-fry the onion and pepper until just tender.

Bring on the mushrooms and cook them briefly. Remove.

Cook the pasta according to the package directions and drain.

Add the blended pesto—at room temperature—to the hot pasta. Stir through, and then add the cooked veggies, tomatoes and chicken.

Serve your creation up immediately with Parmesan cheese on the side.

Bread-Maker
PIZZA DOUGH

I make this every week at home, and my kids don't even realize that the crust is loaded with healthy ingredients. They just love the texture and the taste. This makes enough for 2 to 3 large pizzas. Need a change from traditional toppings? Break free of the pepperoni-and-mushroom habit. Be brave, be innovative, with the diverse assortment of pizza recipes that follows.

LET'S LOAD UP THE MACHINE, IN ORDER OF APPEARANCE

- 1⅛ cups slightly warm water—about 80–90 degrees
- 1½ teaspoons salt
- 1½ tablespoons dry milk powder
- 2 tablespoons olive oil
- 2 tablespoons honey
- 1½ cups whole-wheat flour
- 1½ cups unbleached white flour
- 2 teaspoons fast-acting or bread-maker yeast
- Cornmeal—optional

YOUR CHRONOLOGICAL ORDERS

Add the ingredients to the bread-maker pan in the order listed.

Set the machine on the dough setting. Allow 2 hours for this cycle.

When the cycle is finito—that's Italian for "Espresso Time!"—take the dough out of the machine and separate it into 2 equal amounts.

Form into rounds and place on a cookie sheet. Cover with a tea towel and allow them to rise for 20 minutes then roll them out. I find that a floured rolling pin on a floured surface works well.

Hey, if you want to be a show-off, toss it into the air a few times. I don't think it actually does anything, but it will look like you know what you're doing. Unless, of course, it sticks to the stipple ceiling.

Preheat the oven to 425 degrees. Spray the pizza pans—I find that a baking stone or pizza pans with small holes in the bottom work best. If you're so inclined, dust the bottom of each pizza pan with cornmeal for a nice touch.

Place the dough on the pan and spread to the edges.

Cut off the excess dough around the edges with a knife.

Cover with spaghetti sauce, your favourite toppings and cheese.

Bake in the centre of the oven for about 20 minutes.

PESTO PIZZA
with Greek Pesto Option

GET TOGETHER

- 6 boneless, skinless chicken or turkey thighs marinated in **Lemon Garlic Marinade** (page 111)

- Store-bought pesto sauce or make your own—see **Lemon Garlic Pesto Chicken** (page 154)

- The prepared pizza dough—see **Bread-Maker Pizza Dough** (page 155)

- Grape or cherry tomatoes—sliced in half

- Red onion and a red or green pepper—sliced into slivers

- Mushrooms—cut in Ts, not tease

- Mozzarella cheese—grated, of course

- Italian seasoning

PUT TOGETHER

Grill the chicken, allow it to cool and cut it into bite-sized pieces.

Fire up your oven to 425 degrees.

Spread a light coating of pesto sauce on the pizza crust. Add the rest of the toppings, finishing up with the cheese.

Sprinkle the top with Italian seasoning.

Bake on the middle rack for about 20 minutes.

HEY, HOW ABOUT MAKING THIS A GREEK PIZZA?

Good idea. Here's how. Add oh, about ½ cup of feta cheese after the chicken. Top with the veggies, sliced olives and mozzarella cheese.

Despite the Greek theme, keep the Italian seasoning in there as well. It really gives the pizza a nice flavour.

Instead of pesto sauce, you could also use a half-and-half mixture of finely diced roasted red peppers—packaged in a jar and found in the deli department—combined with purchased spaghetti sauce.

Thai
CHICKEN PIZZA

Firefighter Marcel Gauthier suggested that I try this one at Boston Pizza. I loved it! So I did what I always do when I like something in a restaurant: I picked apart the ingredients to see how they made it. Here's my version.

LET'S WANDER OFF THE TRADITIONAL PIZZA HIGHWAY

- **Bread-Maker Pizza Dough** (page 155) or a store-bought shell
- 1 teaspoon each garlic and ginger—minced
- 6 chicken thighs—sliced into small bite-sized pieces
- Bottled Thai or Szechwan peanut sauce
- Red peppers—sliced in thin strips
- Mozzarella cheese—you grate on me
- Bean sprouts—washed and dried
- Green onions—chopped

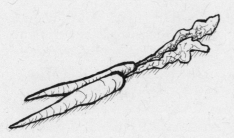

BETTER BRING ALONG A WOK AND A PIZZA PAN

Fire up the wok over medium–high heat, add 2 tablespoons peanut oil and then the garlic and ginger for a 30-second blast.

Toss the chicken in the wok and stir-fry, moving it around frequently until no longer pink inside. Remove the chicken and allow it to cool on a paper-towel-lined plate that will absorb any oil.

Preheat the oven to 425 degrees.

Spread a light coating of Thai peanut dressing on a pizza crust.

Spread the cooled chicken and peppers on the pizza.

Top it off with cheese and finally a sprinkling of bean sprouts and green onions for bonus presentation points.

As I recall, Boston Pizza also puts some grated carrots on top. I exclude them, but if you're of that persuasion, go for it.

Bake for about 20 minutes on the middle rack of the oven or until lightly browned all around.

TEX-MEX PIZZA

Yes, it's a little-known fact that the Southwest has its own Little Italy!

Mix your favourite salsa with enough tomato paste to give it a nice thick consistency. Spread it over the pizza crust.

Top with browned and drained ground beef, cooked chorizo or Italian sausage (optional), pepperoni, mushrooms, peppers, jalapeño peppers and onions.

Then top it off with your favourite cheese. I like to mix marble with Monterey jack. Sprinkle the top with chili powder to finish.

PACIFIC RIM PIZZA

Apparently they have a Little Italy somewhere in the Far East as well.

Mix a funky pizza sauce by combining a ratio of ¼ cup hoisin sauce to 1 tablespoon black bean and garlic sauce.

Cut boneless, skinless chicken thighs into bite-sized pieces, then stir-fry in a wok with a bit of minced ginger and garlic.

Spread a thin layer of sauce on the pizza crust.

Top with the chicken, plus cooked shrimp or shrimp meat, red or green onion, red pepper, sprouts, mushrooms and a light topping of mozzarella cheese.

SCORCHIN' LASAGNA

A touch of salsa and a spicy pepperoni pizza topping add a nice zip to this once-traditional recipe. It's lasagna with a hint of Mexico. Mexagna?

HMMM, WHAT CAN WE THROW IN THERE?

- ⅔ pound lasagna noodles
- 1 pound each lean ground beef and chorizo sausage—removed from casing
- 1 package frozen spinach
- 1 medium onion—diced
- ½ red or green pepper—diced
- 1 cup mushrooms—sliced
- Spaghetti sauce—say about half a small jar
- Salsa—about a quarter of a similar-sized jar
- About half to three-quarters of a 5.5-ounce can tomato paste
- Brown sugar
- 1 pound cottage cheese
- ⅔-½ pound pepperoni
- Mozzarella cheese—show it the grater

AND HOW WERE WE GOING TO DO THIS?

Cook and drain the noodles, rinse, dry and set them aside.

Fry the meat until browned and drain off the fat.

Boil the spinach briefly. Strain and squeeze out all the water.

In a frying pan with a dab of olive oil, fry the veggies until just softened.

Mix the spaghetti sauce and salsa in a 2 to 1 ratio. Add tomato paste to thicken. I like to add at least 1 tablespoon brown sugar. Taste test!

Add the meat and veggies and heat through. The sauce should be thick!

Preheat the oven to 350 degrees.

Put down a thin layer of plain spaghetti sauce on the bottom of a lasagna dish.

Lay down a layer of noodles and half the meat and veggies.

Add another layer of noodles. Cover with cottage cheese and spinach.

Then more noodles and the rest of the meat-veggie sauce.

Cover with the remaining noodles, a thin layer of plain spaghetti sauce, then the pepperoni and finally the mozzarella cheese.

Oh, one more thing: dust the top with chili powder.

Bake for 45 minutes or until lightly browned and bubbling.

FETTUCCINE ALFREDO

I found this one in a Heart Smart cookbook. Ha, ha, ha, he jested! Okay, so there may be some guilt involved in this dish, but it's truly delicious and hey, it's a snap to prepare. So come on, indulge a little!

FILL YOUR GROCERY CART WITH

- 1½ cups finely chopped green onions
- 3 cups mushrooms—chopped into Ts
- ½ cup butter
- ⅔ cup half-and-half cream—as in light cream. Wait a second, maybe this recipe is Heart Smart!
- ⅓ cup parsley—chop, chop
- 1 cup Parmesan cheese
- A dash or 2 of nutmeg—if desired
- Fettuccine or linguine noodles

GET READY FOR DECADENCE

Sauté the green onions and mushrooms in butter over medium heat. Be careful not to burn or brown the butter.

Add the cream, parsley, Parmesan cheese and nutmeg if desired. Stir until the cheese melts and the sauce thickens.

If you find that the sauce is too thick, don't start throwing utensils; simply add a bit more cream. Salt and pepper to taste.

Toss with hot fettuccine or linguine noodles. Decorate the dish with a bit more parsley if you'd like.

Call a friend and makes plans to go to the gym tomorrow.

WHAT ABOUT MAKING THIS CHICKEN ALFREDO?

Let's go for it! Marinate 4 chicken breasts in the **Lemon Garlic Marinade** (page 111) and barbecue them over medium heat. Cut the chicken into strips and toss with finished pasta.

Other great additions to the mix are pieces of **Asparagus Parmesan** (page 188) and stir-fried or barbecued red pepper strips.

LINGUINE
of the Sea

When guests are coming over I'll often ask, "Do you like seafood?" I'm hoping they'll say, "Yes! I love seafood! Are you kidding? It's my favourite!" so that I can make this wonderful pasta dish.

A VARIETY OF SEAFOOD AND VEGGIES IN A CREAMY SAUCE

- 2 cloves garlic—minced or pressed
- 2 teaspoons olive oil
- 1 medium onion—chopped fine
- 1 red pepper—slivered
- 2 stalks celery—diced
- 1 teaspoon Italian seasoning
- 2 tablespoons flour
- ½ cup dry white wine
- 2 cups chicken broth
- 2 5-ounce cans baby clams—be sure to reserve the juice; don't toss it!
- 6 ounces cream cheese—at room temperature, cut into small pieces
- ⅓–½ pound each of baby scallops, crab-flavoured pollock and shrimp
- Sea salt, pepper, cayenne pepper or chili-garlic sauce
- 1 pound linguine noodles
- Chopped fresh parsley
- Parmesan cheese

I CAN'T WAIT UNTIL THIS DISH HITS THE TABLE

In a 4-quart saucepan on medium heat, sauté the garlic in the olive oil.

Toss in the onions and sauté—don't brown, just soften them up.

Intro the other veggies, plus the Italian seasoning. Sauté the veggies until fork tender, and dust them with the flour.

Add the wine, chicken broth and clam juice. Simmer for 30 minutes.

Drop in the cream cheese in small pieces. Whisk until well blended.

Bring on the seafood and heat through. There's a fine balance here. The fish takes little time to cook, and if you overcook it, it will toughen. But the longer you leave it, the more the flavours build. What I usually do is cook the seafood in the sauce, then turn off the element for 30 minutes. Then I simply reheat it just before serving.

Salt, pepper and cayenne pepper or chili-garlic sauce to taste.

Cook the linguine. Combine it with the sauce. Let stand 3–4 minutes.

Toss with fresh chopped parsley and serve with Parmesan cheese.

RED WINE SPAGHETTI SAUCE
with Barbecued Meatballs

Hey, if you love hamburgers on the barbecue, why not cook meatballs that way as well? I know it sounds a little different, but the results are incredible.

SO HERE'S THE SUPPLY LIST

- 2 tablespoons olive oil
- 2 medium onions—diced
- 3 stalks celery—diced
- 3 cloves garlic—minced or pressed
- 1 red, yellow or orange pepper—diced
- Kosher salt
- 5 ounces mushrooms—quartered
- ⅔ cup dry red wine—try a Merlot
- 2 cups prepared spaghetti sauce
- 2 tablespoons brown sugar
- 2 teaspoons red chili flakes
- 1 teaspoon Italian seasoning
- 1 teaspoon seasoning salt
- 1 pound each lean ground beef and ground pork or 2 pounds beef
- 1 pound of spaghetti

AND HERE'S HOW WE'RE GOING TO MAKE IT HAPPEN

Heat the olive oil in a deep frying pan or medium saucepan over medium–high heat.

Add the onions, celery, garlic and pepper. Sprinkle 1 teaspoon kosher salt over veggies. When softened, add mushrooms briefly.

Pour wine in the pan to deglaze. Allow it to cook down for 1 minute.

Bring on the spaghetti sauce, brown sugar, chili flakes and Italian seasoning. Cook over low heat, stirring occasionally.

Preheat the barbecue. Add the seasoning salt to the ground meat, work though without handling it too much and form it into meatballs. Use your favourite meatball recipe if you like, but I keep it simple.

Spray the grill with non-stick coating and get the meatballs on there. Cook on medium. Allow the meatballs to set up and brown before attempting to turn them. Use a metal spatula, and they'll stay together for you.

When the meatballs are cooked through, take them off the grill.

Boil the spaghetti and top with meatballs and the red wine sauce. A little stinky cheese wouldn't hurt either.

Fired-Up
BOLOGNESE SAUCE

Here's another delicious deviation from the standard firehouse favourite, spaghetti with meat sauce. Ground poultry, chicken broth, red wine and a touch of milk make for a wonderfully rich tomato sauce.

HMM, WHAT DO I NEED FROM THE PANTRY?

- 2 tablespoons olive oil
- 1½ cups onions—chopped
- 1 cup each celery and carrots—chopped
- 2 cloves or more garlic—minced
- 2 pounds of ground turkey, chicken or even beef
- ½ tablespoon fresh thyme or 1 teaspoon dried thyme
- ½ tablespoon **Fired-Up Spice** (page 200)
- ½ tablespoon Italian seasoning
- 1 teaspoon kosher salt—approximate measure—add a bit to start
- 1 28-ounce can diced tomatoes
- 1 24-ounce jar tomato sauce
- ½ to ¾ of a 5½-ounce can tomato paste— start with ½
- 2 10-ounce cans garlic and herb chicken broth
- ½ cup dry red wine—I like a Merlot
- ¼ cup of milk—the creamier the better
- mushrooms—sliced and sautéed in butter
- fresh parsley—chopped

PUT THIS ONE TOGETHER AND LET IT SIMMER ON THE STOVE

In a large stockpot or Dutch oven, heat the olive oil over medium heat. Toss in the onions and sauté until soft, about 3 minutes.

Introduce the celery, carrots and garlic, and cook another 3 minutes.

In goes the poultry. Stir to break up the meat and cook until browned.

It's seasoning time, so if you have the thyme (groan) toss it in with the **Fired-Up Spice**, Italian seasoning and kosher salt.

Bring on the remaining ingredients, saving the milk, mushrooms and parsley for later.

Here's the most important part. Lower the heat, and simmer, uncovered, stirring occasionally, for 2½ hours. This is how you get a flavourful, thick Bolognese. Do a final seasoning with salt and pepper.

Just before serving, add the milk and stir through. Serve over your favourite pasta. Top each serving with the mushrooms and parsley.

MOZZASAURUS CHICKEN

You may know it as Chicken Parmesan, but really there's more Mozza involved than Parma, so let's call a chick a chick. Make it monstrous!

SNOOP AROUND THE PANTRY FOR

- 4 boneless, skinless chicken breasts
- 1 cup Italian seasoned breadcrumbs or fine breadcrumbs
- ½ cup Parmesan cheese
- 3 tablespoons flour mixed with 1 tablespoon **Fired-Up Spice** (page 200)
- 2 eggs
- Olive oil—for frying Italian style, olive oil is a must!
- Your favourite spaghetti sauce
- Generous slices of mozzarella cheese

OH MAN, THIS IS GOING TO BE GOOD

If the chicken breasts are rounded, flatten them just a bit so that the cheese won't melt off the side. Place the boob—excuse my slang—between sheets of waxed paper and give it a few whacks with a heavy pan or the broad side of a shovel. You're looking for uniform thickness here.

Combine the breadcrumbs and Parmesan cheese.

Dredge the—sorry if I offended you earlier—breast with the flour-spice blend to coat it.

Now over to the egg-wash station. Dip the breast through. Good!

Breadcrumbs Parmesan is the next stop, so coat the breast evenly.

Heat about an inch of olive oil in a pan over medium–low heat. Introduce the chicken, and when the breast is lightly browned on the bottom, flip it over and repeat.

Preheat the oven to 350 degrees.

Place the completed breasts in a casserole dish. Cover each breast in sauce, and top with thick slices of mozzarella cheese. Bake for about 15 minutes or until no longer pink inside.

Push this one over the top by taking Italian or chorizo sausage out of its casing, crumbling it up and frying it until browned. Add the sausage to the spaghetti sauce to give this bronco more kick.

Looking for side dishes? Well, there's always the **Red Wine Spaghetti Sauce** (page 162)—omit the meatballs—or some **Lemon Garlic Pesto** (page 154) tossed with rotini noodles.

COQ AU VIN CACCIATORE

France meets Italy head on in World Cup Culinary Competition with this hybrid dish. Oh my word! Look over there! There's a brawl breaking out in the stands, and this recipe hasn't even started yet!

THIS CHICKEN WILL NEVER PASS THE BREATHALYZER!

- 12 boneless chicken thighs—each cut in half
- Seasoned flour—3 parts flour to 1 part **Fired-Up Spice** (page 200)
- Olive oil
- 4-6 links hot Italian sausage—removed from casing
- 6 cloves garlic—pressed, minced or otherwise defaced
- 1 cup each onion and celery—diced
- 3-4 carrots—sliced
- ½ pound fresh mushrooms—let's T them up
- ½ 750-mL bottle dry red wine. Half a bottle? Yes, that's 375 mL.
- 1 14-ounce can diced tomatoes with juice
- 1⅔ cups spaghetti sauce
- ½ teaspoon each dried rosemary, basil, oregano and thyme
- Your favourite pasta

COQ AU VIN OVER PASTA? THAT'S WHY IT'S A CACCIATORE!

Dredge the chicken in flour. Heat oil 1 tablespoon at a time over medium heat in large Dutch oven. Brown the chicken on each side. It will probably take two batches unless you have a humungous frying pan.

Remove the chicken and add the Italian sausage. Brown the sausage and break it up into small bits with a spatula. Drain off the fat.

Heat 2 tablespoons of olive oil in a pan. Add the garlic, onion, celery and carrots. Cook till softened and add mushrooms to brown.

Pour in the wine to deglaze the pan. Let it reduce for 5 minutes.

Re-add the chicken plus tomatoes, spaghetti sauce and herbs.

Stir and simmer the works over low heat for about 25 minutes.

Season with salt and pepper. Cook until the chicken is happy— the wine will certainly help there— and no longer pink inside.

Remove the pan from the heat and allow it to sit, covered, for 10 minutes, so that the flavours can blend—that dreaded set-up time!

Salt and pepper to taste. Serve over pasta with a garlicky **Sensational Caesar Salad** (page 46).

BEHIND THE FRIDGE DOOR

Let's take a peek inside the typical fire hall fridge. There's the usual assortment of condiments, plus a little bottle of that ridiculous, "Help, my butt's on fire" hot sauce. Depending on which day of the week it is, there will also be a variety of leftovers on plates or in bowls, some covered, others not. Every Sunday the crew on duty cleans out the fridge, signalling the start of a new collection of leftovers. Keep in mind that there is no "best before" date on leftovers, so it's often a mystery as to which shift even cooked them. The fire hall fridge truly is eater beware.

What's worse, cooks are exempt from meal clean-up, so those with food-care knowledge are not involved in the surplus-food packaging. That's why you'll find plates of uncovered food in the fridge. Some firefighters are oblivious to the fact that air contact affects food preservation.

I should also mention that food has been known to sit on the counter before it finally makes its way into the fridge. It could be the morning after a 14-hour shift when someone finally decides to put it in the fridge. Does he warn a comrade when he sees him pull that piece of counter chicken out to snack on? Of course not. This is an opportunity for a firehouse pool to see how long the grazer makes it into his shift without having to book off. Food biologists would have a heyday with the bacteria count in the firehouse fridge.

Oh, and when I say leftovers, I don't necessarily mean *good* leftovers. Often the carnivores will eat up all the meat, leaving only bowls of potatoes, mixed veggies and soggy salads. Remember, firefighters are a thrifty breed and have a hard time throwing food out. Until the following "clean the fridge out" Sunday anyway.

Here's a hint for fire hall chefs who want to see the leftovers eaten up. If you have, say, two whole chicken breasts sitting out on a plate, they may go untouched for hours. However, if you cut them into small pieces and stick toothpicks in them, chances are that every time a firefighter enters the kitchen he'll grab one, and the chicken will be gone before you know it.

SOUTHERN SIZZLERS

Ah yes, the infamous Four-Alarm Chili, a legendary concoction that simmers on the stove of many a firehouse in North America, warming the hearts of weary, famished firefighters. To me, chili should have some bite, but there's no need to make it a great white shark attack. I've had chili that I can't even taste, let alone eat because it's so hot. Since everyone has different tolerance levels when it comes to spice, I prefer to make chili mild to medium, and simply put the hot sauce on the table for those who want to peel the lining off their digestive tracts. Actually the **Funky Fire Hall Chili** (page 170) has a hint of sweetness, which complements the heat nicely and, like any chili, the longer it simmers, the better it gets.

If you like pesto the way I love Pesto, give the Mexican version a go. Pesto is very easy to make at home, and it tastes so much better than the bottled stuff. Put it together with the **Tequila Lime Chicken** (page 169) and you'll be climbing the ladder at work faster than—hey, wait a second, you'll be climbing the ladder at work anyway, if you're a firefighter!

Oh, and give the **Cuban Lime Marinade** (page 174) a try, not only on pork chops, but pork steaks and even chicken or beef fajitas. The same can be said for the **Jamaican Jerk Pork Chops** (page 120), a recipe that could arguably have been featured here in Southern Sizzlers. Two of my kids—the carnivores—actually love those spicy devils, and insist on Jamaican jerk by name.

Speaking of the picky wee people, they're one of the reasons I enjoy cooking at the fire hall so much. The appreciation level is bipolar between my two families: the firefighters and my five children. I have two carnivores, a vegetarian, a pasta-rice carbo-man and, the fussiest of all, my youngest, who has spent his short life researching his upcoming book, *Pepperoni Pizza and Chicken Fingers Only, For Fun and Variety at Mealtime*. Argh!!

If you're going Mexican at home, and you fear that your children won't be into it, try **Kick A** Quesadillas** (page 171). My kids—except for Pizza Man and Veggie Girl—nag me incessantly to make them. They're fast and easy, and they also double as a great firehouse lunch. So, what do you say we get fired up down south, and bring on the heat?

MEXICAN PESTO PASTA

Say what? Before you roll your eyes at me, try it. It goes great with **Tequila Lime Chicken** *(next page) or* **Cuban Lime-Marinated Pork Chops** *(page 174). Or make up some Cuban Lime chicken and toss it into the pasta for a great main course.*

FOR THE MEXICAN PESTO

- 1 cup cilantro—a.k.a. Mexican parsley
- ½ cup fresh spinach
- 2 tablespoons lime juice—fresh is best
- 5 cloves garlic—smashed or chopped
- 2 tablespoons pine nuts or almonds
- 1 teaspoon coarse kosher salt
- ½ teaspoon fresh ground pepper
- ⅓ cup extra virgin olive oil
- ⅓ cup Parmesan cheese
- 1 medium red onion—cut in strips
- 2 tablespoons olive oil

FOR THE REST

- 1 medium red, yellow or orange pepper—cut in strips
- ½ pound mushrooms—Td up
- ½ zucchini—coarsely chopped
- ½ pound rotini

NO TIME FOR A SIESTA, SEÑOR OR SEÑORITA

Into a food processor—or blender if you don't have a processor—toss the cilantro, spinach, lime juice, garlic, pine nuts, salt and pepper.

Hit the power button and away you go. When it's combined, slowly pour in the olive oil. Fancy cooks with degrees from culinary institutes will try to impress you by calling this "emulsifying."

Now add the Parmesan for some Parmesanification—Spell Check isn't very happy with that one, but the cooks all seem impressed.

Stir-fry the vegetables in 2 tablespoons olive oil over medium–high heat until cooked through.

Boil the pasta just the way— uh-huh, uh-huh—you like it.

Now all you have to do is combine the pesto—at room temperature—with the pasta. Toss it through and add the sautéed vegetables.

Yes, it's another one of those hybrid dishes. What should we call it, Mexalian or Itexican?

Tequila Lime
CHICKEN

Presentation is everything, because sight is the first sense that appreciates food. Serve up a beautiful dish like this one and you're sure to hear, "Oh, man! Does this ever look good!" Presentation makes a great first impression.

FOR THE EXCITING MARINADE INGREDIENTS

- 1 cup water
- ½ cup **Teriyaki Marinade** (page 203) ... *Er, Jeff, isn't this a Mexican dish?*
- 4 cloves garlic—minced or pressed
- 1 teaspoon liquid smoke
- ½ teaspoon salt
- ¼ teaspoon ground ginger
- ½ teaspoon tequila—that's all you need, believe me!
- 2 tablespoons lime juice—you know, a shot of tequila, a bite of lime

AND THE REST

- 4 boneless, skinless chicken breasts
- ¾–1 cup medium or hot salsa— hey, it's your system
- ¾ cup pesto Ranch, preferred, or regular Ranch dressing
- 3 tablespoons cilantro—chopped fine
- Monterey Jack or marble cheese— get it grated
- Nacho or tortilla chips—to nibble on and spoil your supper

WHAT ARE YOU DOING?

Stop taking shots of tequila while you're cooking here!

Composed? Okay, now mix the marinade and pour it into a plastic bag. Add the chicken and toss it into the fridge for 4 hours.

Barbecue the chicken over medium heat till juices run clear.

Place the chicken in a baking dish. Mix the salsa, Ranch dressing and cilantro, and pour it over the chicken.

Top the chicken with grated cheese. Broil until the cheese is melted and lightly browned.

Serve over a bed of tortilla chips with the **Mexican Pesto Pasta** (previous page) and an extra shot of cilantro garnish over the top.

Funky
FIRE HALL CHILI

This is a favourite of mine. It's a mild chili, with a sweet-and-sour twist. You can determine how many alarms you want to put in for this chili by adding jalapeño peppers, and/or good old mouth-numbing cayenne pepper. Olé!

HMMM, WHAT DO I NEED HERE?

- 2 pounds lean ground beef
- 1 each jumbo onion and red pepper—coarsely chopped
- 3–4 stalks celery—diced
- 1 28-ounce can diced tomatoes
- ½ cup white vinegar
- 3 tablespoons molasses
- 3 tablespoons brown sugar
- 2 tablespoons chili powder
- 2 teaspoons ground cumin
- ½ tablespoon Worcestershire sauce
- 1 19-ounce can kidney beans—washed and drained
- 1 28-ounce can brown beans
- 5 ounces mushrooms—coarsely sliced
- ½ of a 5½-ounce can tomato paste—optional

OH, WHAT TO DO, WHAT TO DO?

Brown up the ground beef and drain the fat.

Stir-fry the onion, pepper and celery till slightly softened.

Combine the tomatoes, vinegar, molasses, brown sugar, chili powder, cumin and Worcestershire sauce. Pour the lot into a large saucepan or Dutch oven and bring to a slow boil.

Toss in the browned beef, veggies, beans and mushrooms. Reduce to a simmer, and cook for about 2 hours, giving it an occasional stir.

Time for a taste test. Add brown sugar if it's too spicy; add chili powder or cayenne if it's too sweet or not spicy enough. If the sauce is too thin for your liking, simply add the tomato paste to thicken it.

Try cooking the chili for 8 hours in a slow cooker. Be sure to brown and drain the beef before adding it, and add the red peppers in the last hour or so of cooking so they keep a bit of crunch.

To dress the Funky Fire Hall Chili up (just like on the front cover), rim the inside of each serving bowl with taco chips and garnish with grated nacho cheese and chopped green onions.

Kick A**
QUESADILLAS

It's an appetizer, it's a lunch, or it's a main course. Dress it up and toss in your favourite ingredients. It's chicken, cheese, tortillas and whatever!

I KNOW WHAT I WANT IN MINE

- 4 chicken breasts—marinated with **Cuban Lime Marinade** (page 174)
- ½ cup butter
- 1½ tablespoons chili powder
- 2 teaspoons oregano
- 4 cloves garlic—minced or pressed
- 1 medium red pepper—sliced into strips
- 1½ cups red onion—sliced into strips as well
- 1 cup mushrooms—sliced into Ts
- 4-6 tortillas—depending on size and aggressive stuffing methods
- Monterey Jack or marble cheese—grated
- ⅔ cup cilantro—coarsely chopped

YOU KNOW, THIS IS LIKE A MEXICAN STUFFED PIZZA

Marinate the chicken in the previously mentioned—so why mention it again, Jeff?—**Cuban Lime Marinade** or store-bought fajita marinade.

Grill the breasts over medium heat until just cooked through.

Melt the butter in a sauté pan and add the chili and oregano. Man, is it ever smelling good in here!

Toss in the garlic, pepper and onion, and fry to tender crisp. Bring on the mushrooms and fry 'em until they're just starting to brown.

When the chicken has cooled off a bit, cut it into thin strips.

Brush one side of each tortilla with a thin coat of olive oil.

Flip it over, and spread some cheese on one half. Add the chicken, veggies and cilantro—not too much now, or it won't hold together. I'm speaking to firefighters in particular! You know who you are.

Let's add some more cheese on top, because this will be the binder. As in a grilled cheese sandwich, when it melts it pulls everything together.

Let's go out to our barbecue and place the tortillas over medium–low heat. When those wonderful grill marks happen and the cheese has melted, give them a very careful flip. You can also cook them in a frying pan if need be.

Slice each tortilla into 3 triangular slices. Serve with sour cream, and how about some of that **Simple Tomato Salsa** (page 201)?

Hot Chick
ENCHILADAS

This recipe brings together a number of individual recipes with great results. If you compare it to some enchilada recipes, I think you'll find this one to be a little lighter than most, yet still bursting with flavour.

GOT A PEN? LET'S MAKE UP YOUR GROCERY LIST

- 4 boneless, skinless chicken breasts
- **Cuban Lime Marinade** (page 174)
- 3 tablespoons olive oil
- 1 small red onion—diced
- 1 red pepper—dice it up too
- Sliced jalapeños—in a jar or bottle or even fresh
- 3 cloves garlic—minced or pressed
- 1 cup thawed frozen corn— (said the big dumb oxymoron)
- 1 28-ounce can diced tomatoes—drained
- 8 large whole-wheat tortillas— whole-wheat because I care
- 2 cups marble or Monterey Jack cheese— grated
- 3 tablespoons cilantro—coarsely chopped

OH, AND FOR THE ENCHILADA SAUCE

- 3 tablespoons olive oil
- 1 tablespoon flour
- ¼ cup chili powder
- 2 cups chicken broth with garlic and herbs
- 10 ounces Italian tomato paste
- 1 teaspoon each dried oregano and ground cumin

SO WHAT'S THE DEAL HERE?

Marinate the chicken in a plastic bag with the **Cuban Lime Marinade** and refrigerate for 4–6 hours.

Make the enchilada sauce by heating the olive oil in a saucepan over low heat. Add the flour to make a roux. Cook until well combined and then add the chili powder. Heat until fragrant, about 30 seconds.

Toss in the chicken broth, tomato paste, oregano and cumin.

Bring to a slow boil for about 15 minutes to thicken the sauce.

Barbecue the chicken over medium heat until no longer pink.

Allow the chicken to cool and then cut or pull into strips.

Heat a large saucepan and add about 3 tablespoons of olive oil. Add the onion and red pepper and fry until softened. Toss in the jalapeños if using—I use about 6–8 slices, more if you like it hotter. Bring in the garlic, corn and tomatoes, and fry for a minute or two to heat through.

Let's add the chicken, and if the mixture seems too loose, simply dust it with a bit of flour so that it will set up.

Hey, I think we're ready to make these bad boys. Preheat the oven to 350 degrees. With a spoon spread a thin layer of enchilada sauce over both sides of each tortilla.

Spread equal amounts of chicken-veggie filling over each tortilla and fold the tortilla over, rolling it so that the seam is down. Place them in a 9- x 13-inch lasagna dish. You'll be able to make 2 trays of 4 jumbo enchiladas.

Top the enchiladas with whatever enchilada sauce happens to be left over, and make the grated cheese the grand topping.

Bake until cheese is melted and set.

Allow 5 minutes of that dreaded standing time before serving.

When you serve them up, top with dollops of sour cream, a little **Fresh Tomato Salsa** (page 201) and how about another shot of that Mexican parsley—a.k.a. cilantro, a.k.a. fresh coriander leaves!

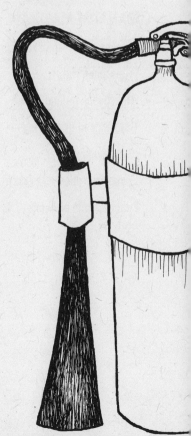

Cuban Lime-Marinated
PORK CHOPS

Did you know that a recent poll suggests that 97 percent of Canadians find fire-fighters trustworthy? That's a humbling statistic; it's great to know that the public is behind us and a far cry from the—stifled laugh—14 percent that politicians pulled down. So trust me—and chances are that you will—when I say that once you start marinating meat before barbecuing it, you'll never look back. Marinating simply adds character. Speak of the devil—who also performed better in this poll than politicians—here's a great tangy mix that doubles as an excellent chicken or beef fajita marinade.

ALONE, THEY'RE NOTHING

- 4–6 pork chops or pork steaks—depending on size

CUBAN LIME MARINADE

- 6 cloves garlic—minced or pressed
- ¾ teaspoon salt
- 2 teaspoons ground cumin
- 1 tablespoon dried oregano
- ½ teaspoon pepper
- ½ cup lime juice—fresh is best
- 2 tablespoons olive oil

BUT TOGETHER …

Mash the garlic and salt together in a bowl, work in the cumin, oregano and pepper, and whisk in the lime juice and olive oil.

Marinate the meat for at least 6 hours—plastic bags work great.

Crack a tall cool one to avoid life-threatening dehydration.

Have you grown tired of my flippant style? Let's continue anyway.

Barbecue the chops or steaks over medium heat until slightly pink inside. Hey, this isn't the Industrial Revolution; it's quite all right to eat pork with a hint of pink. Top with **Simple Tomato Salsa** (page 201).

WHAT CAN I SAY, WE LOVE TO EAT … TO A POINT

One night, a member of our crew brought in moosemeat for a stir-fry that our captain was going to prepare. The captain took one look and said, "Oh, that's too much. We only need about half of that."

"Well, I took the meat out of the freezer," the firefighter replied. "This is our last night shift and I can't refreeze it, so just cook it all up."

So he did. The cap was right; there was too much food, but it tasted so good that the six of us ate it all anyway! No sooner had we finished than the cap reached into the oven and produced two size-XXL apple pies. We couldn't believe our eyes as he cut the pies into thirds, yes, one third each, and topped each slice with a healthy whack of ice cream.

Our lieutenant was dumbfounded. "Oh, no, thanks. I couldn't eat another crumb."

"Come on!" the cap insisted. "Be one of the boys. That's your portion, now shut up and eat!"

The lieutenant rolled his eyes, realizing that the cap meant what he said and, as he was simply too stuffed to fight, he tied into his "pie and cream."

Soon afterwards an alarm came in for another fire hall which, back then, required that someone get up and acknowledge the call. The lieutenant—who was in need of any excuse to pull away—said, "I'll get it," and waddled off to the floor-watch area.

While his back was turned I plunged the scoop as deeply as I could into the 4-liter pail, producing a Himalayan-sized mountain of ice cream, which I deposited on the lieutenant's plate. I expected him to sit down, look at it and laugh at the ridiculous sight before scraping the ice cream back into the container. Instead, he resumed eating without noticing a thing.

The rest of us had finished and were up doing the dishes while he sat alone, struggling. "Oh man [big breath]," he uttered as he picked away. "It's like the food, [breath] is multiplying on my plate!"

It took all our willpower not to laugh out loud. Obedient to his captain's demands, our lieutenant managed to poke every morsel through his pie-hole, retiring his fork for the night with a heavy gasp of despair before saying, "Ohh—I think I'm going to explode!"

SPUDS AND HIS BUDS

I've heard several unfortunate tales of rookie firefighters suckered into cooking at the fire hall and, with only home life to compare, they'll ask their mom for a recipe and directions. She'll ask how many are eating, and they'll do the math—not factoring the to-the-second-power ravenous firefighter appetites into the equation—only to discover that they didn't even come close to making enough food. The still-famished firefighters will roll their eyes, utter disparaging comments about the cook and then, the ultimate insult, order pizza. The trick is, if you're unsure of quantity, just make lots, or at least have tons of potatoes and bread for them to fill up on.

Although I have broken the "meat-and-potatoes" law of the fire hall many times, I've also kept the peace and gone with tradition. I have found ways, though, to fire up the bland old spud with garlic, onions, parsley, cheese, pesto and even crabmeat to bring those firefighter taste buds to life.

A popular fire hall staple that goes along with the "m-and-p" routine is the classic frozen mixed vegetables. It's no favourite of mine, however, and that's why I offer several vegetable suggestions, including a variation on another old standby, the cooked carrot.

I—perhaps like you—grew up believing that the only way to cook vegetables was to boil them. Well, there are better, more flavourful options. All you need is a little butter or vegetable oil in a frying pan and some spices, and before long, tender-crisp stir-fried vegetables are yours to enjoy. Or toss the veggies in some olive oil, sprinkle them with kosher salt, pepper or other spices, and bake them on a cookie sheet. If it's summertime, treat the vegetables to olive oil and spice, and grill them on the barbecue.

I know that it may be impossible to convert some die-hard meat-and-potato types; I've had to stickhandle around some picky eaters in my time, but it's worth a try. Of course, there are those who just can't have certain vegetables, like a particular firefighter—not the most beloved member of the crew—who got wicked heartburn from green peppers. So for fun and frolic, the cook grated peppers into the stew and later that night the victim had a gall bladder attack. Yes, always keep the infamous firefighter adage in mind: "Whatever you do, don't tick off the cook!"

GLEN'S NON-FRIES

Why deep-fry when you can make these deliciously seasoned crisp fries in the oven? I haven't deep-fried potatoes since firefighter Glen Godri made these for us at the fire hall. Save a few calories, and add a ton of flavour.

SPUDS AND SPICES

- Russet potatoes—Yukon Golds also work well
- Vegetable oil—olive oil is my fave here, followed by canola
- Seasoning salt
- Garlic powder
- Onion powder
- Chili powder
- Parmesan cheese—optional

SIMPLY TOSS AND BAKE

Ladies and gentlemen, start your ovens—400 degrees please.

Cut the potatoes into either French-fry-sized pieces, or wedgies—not the "uncomfortable-feeling" variety, the big wedge tater type. Leave the skins on if you like. I usually do. Well, except when I cook them for my finicky "What's that on the fries" kids.

Toss the potatoes with vegetable oil until lightly covered. There should be very little oil in the bottom of the mixing bowl when you're done. If there's lots of oil, then you've gone and overdone it, haven't you?

Spice the potatoes with seasoning salt, garlic powder, onion powder and chili powder or paprika. Sorry, I don't have exact amounts. I've made them many times, never measured and they've always turned out. Experiment with your favourite spices. Toss well to coat.

Sprinkle with Parmesan cheese if desired. Toss until lightly coated.

Bake on a greased baking pan for about 40 minutes, or until lightly browned on the outside, and cooked through.

Turn every 10 minutes to ensure even cooking.

You can also make Roasted Potatoes the same way; it all comes down to how you slice up the taters. While we're at it, why not mix up some garlic butter, melt it in the microwave and toss the roasted potatoes in the garlic butter just before serving. Add a little fresh chopped parsley, and oh man! Now we're talking fired-up spuds!

Mom D's
GREEK POTATOES

I'll give my mom credit here, even though I know she snagged the recipe off a Greek friend. This is a great accompaniment to **Mike's Lemon Garlic Chicken** (page 103) *or* **Chicken Souvlaki Pitas** (page 34). *Again, they're baked instead of fried. Sounds healthy to me!*

SPUDS, LEMONS, SPICES, ETC.

- 5 russet or white potatoes—peeled and cut into quarters lengthwise
- ¾ cup water
- ½ teaspoon each kosher salt and pepper
- 2 teaspoons oregano
- 2 lemons—a short zap in the micro before juicing yields max juice
- Butter or margarine

INTO THE DRINK
AND INTO THE OVEN THE TATERS GO

Parboil the potatoes in salted water for 5 minutes. Drain.

Get the oven heating to 450 degrees.

In a lasagna dish or roaster, combine the water and spices.

Lay the potatoes down in the water mixture.

Juice the lemon and drizzle the nectar over the potatoes.

Put a dab of butter or margarine on each potato wedge.

Bake for 30 minutes. Turn once or twice.

Don't forget a **Great Greek Salad** (page 44) on the side.

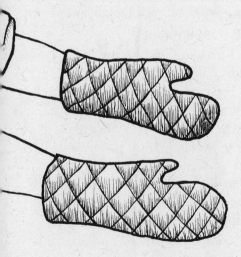

Rustic
GARLIC SMASHED POTATOES

The amounts are left vague, because everybody's taste is different. You can do it!

SPUDS AND HIS FOUL-MOUTHED FRIEND

- Potatoes—cut into quarters
- 1–2 peeled garlic cloves for each potato, or a head of garlic
- Butter
- Buttermilk or sour cream

BOIL THEM OR ROAST THEM
—your choice

Place potatoes in a pot of salted boiling water with garlic cloves.

When the potatoes are soft, drain and mash the potatoes and garlic.

If you like your garlic roasted instead, then wrap a head of garlic—take papery outer layer off but leave skin on—in foil and bake at 400 degrees till soft—about 30 minutes. Open foil, allow to cool and squeeze cloves into potatoes.

Add butter and buttermilk or sour cream and smash until smooth with an electric mixer. Taste the potatoes and add salt if needed.

Other great smashed potato additions include chopped green onions, parsley, pesto and grated cheddar cheese. So long, bland potato!

Italian
SCALLOPED POTATOES

*The next time you bake a ham (see **Citrus Honey-Glazed Ham**, page 116), try this unique take on the traditional scalloped potato recipe. The Italian seasonings and Parmesan cheese add a nice twist to this old classic. Oh, and if you're serving this to the "I told you I don't like onions" children, grate the onions up fine and—unless they have access to an electron microscope—they'll never know the difference! Advantage cook!*

TIME TO SEE YOUR GROCER FOR

- 4 medium red potatoes—sliced fine
- 1 medium onion—also sliced fine
- 1 cup mozzarella or marble cheddar cheese—grated
- ¼ cup Parmesan cheese
- 1 10-ounce can cream of mushroom soup
- ¼ cup milk
- ½ teaspoon Italian seasoning
- 2 cloves garlic—minced or pressed

HEY, LET'S BAKE THIS BABY

First, get the oven going. That's right, 400 degrees.

In a greased 6-cup casserole arrange half the potatoes, half the onions and half the mozzarella and Parmesan cheeses.

Once complete, simply déjà vu, simply déjà vu—repeat the layer again.

In a small bowl combine the soup, milk, Italian seasoning and garlic.

Spoon the mixture over the potatoes. No problem!

Bake, covered, for 1 hour, or until the potatoes are just cooked through.

Remove the cover and bake 10 minutes more, or until the potatoes are lightly browned on top and tender.

By the way, if you're thinking about making this dish for the masses, don't make the mistake of stacking layer upon layer in a big roaster. If you do—and I've made this mistake myself—you'll find that the potatoes on the bottom will burn before the potatoes in the middle are cooked through. Instead, make additional casseroles as required.

Twice-Baked
CRAB CAKE POTATOES

You could just skip by with good old once-baked potatoes or you could scoop out the spuds, add your favourite ingredients and pop them back in the oven. The result is incredible flavour and, of course, great presentation.

YOU'RE IN? THEN WE'LL BEGIN

- 1 head garlic
- 2 extra-large baker or 4 medium russet potatoes
- 2 tablespoons butter
- Sour cream or buttermilk
- Half a head of green onions— green ends only
- ¾ cup marble cheese—grated
- 1 4-ounce can of crabmeat— optional if you're not a fish fan
- Salt and pepper
- Paprika

IT'S ALL HERE IN FRONT OF ME: NOW WHAT?

Peel the paper-like cover off the garlic head. Place the head on a piece of aluminum foil and pour 1 tablespoon olive oil in the centre.

Bake in a preheated 400-degree oven for about 30 minutes, or until very soft.

Meanwhile, rub the potatoes lightly with olive oil, and either wrap in foil and bake for 1 hour at 400 degrees, or poke the skin a few times with a fork and microwave until cooked. Allow the spuds and garlic to cool to a point where you can handle them without screaming.

Cool? Okay, now cut the potatoes in half lengthwise and carefully scoop them out, allowing some flesh to remain to keep the skin intact.

Place the potato innards in a bowl and smash 'em up with butter. Squeeze in the cloves of garlic from the head and smash 'em again.

Add a few dollops of sour cream, chopped green onions, cheese, crabmeat and salt and pepper to taste. Stir the stuffing together. If the mixture is too dry, toss in more sour cream or buttermilk.

Fill the potato skins with the new potato blend. Give the tater tops a little sprinkle of sweet paprika.

Bake at 425 for 30 minutes or until light brown on top.

Feel free to substitute broccoli, bacon bits, or any fave ingredient in the potato mix. Take liberties with this recipe; have fun with it!

HURRY CURRY POTATOES

You can make these with either raw or leftover potatoes.

THESE POTATOES DEMAND MORE FLAVOUR!

- 3 medium red potatoes
- 3 tablespoons plain yogurt
- 2 teaspoons mild curry paste—or go high octane and try the hot
- 1 teaspoon lime juice—fresh is best
- 1 tablespoon cilantro or parsley—chopped
- 1 green onion—chopped

SO LET'S MAKE THEM HAPPY

Quarter the potatoes and place them in salted boiling water. Cook until they're just starting to soften. Rinse and cool. (You can also use leftover boiled or baked potatoes.)

Combine the yogurt, curry paste, lime juice and cilantro.

Place the potatoes in a skillet with 2 tablespoons butter, and brown.

Add the green onion and curry mixture and simply warm through.

SOUTHWEST SWEET POTATO FRIES

Tired of French fries? Looking for something different? Try these babies.

ALL YOU NEED IS

- 1 or more sweet potatoes
- Canola oil
- **Fired-Up Santa Fe Spice** (page 200)

AND ALL YOU NEED TO DO IS

Preheat the oven to 400 degrees.

Cut the sweet potatoes into wedges or French-fry-sized pieces.

Place the potatoes in a large bowl and toss with a bit of oil.

Sprinkle and toss fries with **Fired-Up Santa Fe Spice** until evenly coated.

Bake for about 40 minutes, tossing every 10 minutes.

Fries will be limp, not crisp like traditional fries, but still delicious!

BROCCOLI-AND-CHEESE CASSEROLE

This is one of those dishes that, whenever you bring it to a potluck dinner or serve it for friends, people will invariably ask you for the recipe. Hey, not to worry! Suck up the praise, accept their flattery and simply tell them, "Oh well, you know, it's just a little something that I threw together."

THERE'S A FEW GROCERIES TO PICK UP

- ¼ cup diced onions
- 1 cup diced celery
- Butter
- 1½ cups sliced mushrooms
- 1 10-ounce can cream of mushroom soup
- ½ cup salad dressing or mayonnaise
- 1½ cups grated cheddar or marble cheese
- 2 eggs
- 2 tablespoons sour cream
- 1 pound broccoli—cut into florets
- 2 tablespoons melted margarine
- Crumbled cheese crackers

HERE'S HOW THIS CASSEROLE COMES TOGETHER

Fire up a frying pan over medium heat, and sauté the onions and celery in a couple tablespoons of butter until tender crisp.

Bring the mushrooms to the fry-pan party, and sauté briefly.

Bring the soup, mayo, cheese, eggs and sour cream together in a mixing bowl, stirring until just combined.

The warm front is about to meet the cold front. Scattered recipe storms are in the forecast. So bring on the sautéed vegetables plus the broccoli, and blend everything with the mayo mix.

It's time to preheat that oven; let's go with 350 degrees.

Pour your creation into a 9- x 13-inch lasagna dish.

Melt the margarine in the microwave. Using a bowl would be smart.

Crumble the crackers over the top of the casserole.

Drizzle the margarine over the crackers.

Get that casserolin' in the oven for 40 minutes.

Don't expect any leftovers. Well, unless you happen to be dining alone and you possess the elusive willpower!

Lemon-Spritzed
ROASTED BROCCOLI

Broccoli doesn't have to be soggy and bland, you know!

SO GO AND FIND

- 1 pound broccoli—cut into florets
- 2 tablespoons olive oil
- Kosher salt and pepper
- 2 tablespoons butter
- 2 cloves garlic—minced or pressed
- Grated rind of 1 lemon—grate it before you juice it
- 2 tablespoons fresh lemon juice

THEN GET BUSY AND

Preheat the oven to 450 degrees.

Toss the broccoli with olive oil, salt and pepper in a bowl.

Cook the broccoli on a baking pan until tender crisp.

Melt the butter in a saucepan. Add the garlic and lemon rind.

Remove the butter from the heat and add the lemon juice.

Sprinkle it over the broccoli, toss through and serve *toute suite*—which is French for "My, that baguette is long and slender!"

ORANGE BEETS

But I thought beets were red? Hey, we're not talking colour here: we're talking flavour—a little tangy taste of orange in a smooth buttery sauce. It's a combination that can't be "beet!"

THE GOOD STUFF

- 3 medium-sized beets
- 1 tablespoon grated orange rind
- 1 tablespoon lemon juice
- ⅛ teaspoon salt
- 1 tablespoon water
- 2 tablespoons melted butter
- ¼ tablespoon cornstarch
- ¼ cup orange juice

THE STUFF ON THE GOODS

Peel the beets and slice or dice them, depending on how you want to present them.

Now that your hands are stained bright red, run from the kitchen screaming, *"Help me, I'm bleeding!! For the love of god, someone help me, please!!"*

Return to kitchen chuckling and shaking head over hilarious prank. Note: If you try this one at the fire hall, expect zero sympathy.

Place the beets in a saucepan and add enough water to cover. Boil until just softened, drain off water and cover to keep warm.

In a small pan, toss in the orange rind, lemon juice, salt and water, and reduce while boiling for a couple of minutes.

Add the melted butter and cornstarch to the orange juice, and heat until thickened. Taste, and if it's too tart, add 1 tablespoon sugar.

Let's bring those beet-red beets back into the picture and introduce them to the sauce, toss them together and heat through.

A word of caution: If you're unfamiliar with beets, keep the following equation in mind—what enters red, exits red. You'll be fine, believe me; there's no need to consult a trained medical professional.

RUTABAGAS AND CARROTS

Those root vegetables love to be together, so who are we to deny them!

YOU'LL NEED ROUGHLY

- Equal parts carrots and rutabagas. I tend to go with at least 1 large carrot per diner. Carrots and rutabagas are cheap; why go hungry?

- Butter up!

- Brown sugar or honey—your choice, both work well

- Dried basil

LET'S SWEETEN THESE GUYS UP!

Slice the carrots and dice the rutabagas. Boil until very soft.

Remove the veggies, drain them and smash 'em up.

Add a good dab of butter and work it through.

Introduce brown sugar or honey to taste.

Sprinkle with basil, taste test again and adjust the seasonings.

Zucchini and Tomato
PARMESAN

Here's one that takes just a couple of minutes to cook. It's excellent!

YOU ONLY NEED A FEW THINGS

- 2 tablespoons butter

- 1 medium zucchini—sliced into thin pieces

- 1 medium tomato—sliced and cut in half

- Kosher salt and pepper

- Parmesan cheese

AND IT'S SO EASY

Melt the butter in a medium saucepan over medium heat. Bring in the zucchini and cook until light brown and tender crisp.

Add the tomato and salt and pepper to taste. Cook 1 minute. Toss in the Parmesan cheese, toss again and serve immediately.

ASPARAGUS PARMESAN

Your boiled asparagus is soggy and limp? You say all the Viagra in your medicine cabinet couldn't bring it back to life? I've got the recipe for you.

ASPARAGUS AND LITTLE ELSE

- 1 bunch of asparagus—about 1 pound
- 1 tablespoon butter
- Kosher salt and pepper
- 1½ tablespoons Parmesan cheese—even this is optional

OH, THIS WON'T TAKE LONG

Break and toss out the woody end—no jokes, please—of the asparagus and cut the good end into 3 pieces. You can also keep the asparagus in one piece, providing you have a large enough frying pan.

Heat the butter in a frying pan on medium and add the asparagus.

Add salt and pepper to taste. Stir-fry the tasty fellows until tender crisp, about 3–4 minutes. Test for doneness by piercing the asparagus with a fork. If it goes in with a bit of resistance, it's done.

Remove from the heat and toss with Parmesan cheese.

CUMIN-SPICED CAULIFLOWER

You don't have to boil or steam cauliflower either. Instead, bake it with a touch of spice and you just might abandon your veggie steamer altogether.

THAT'S ALL, FOLKS

- Cauliflower—cut into florets
- Olive oil
- Ground cumin
- Kosher salt and pepper

QUITE SIMPLY THEN

Preheat the oven to 400 degrees.

Toss the cauliflower in just enough olive oil to lightly coat.

Dust with cumin and salt, and even a little pepper if you wish.

Place on a greased cookie sheet, and bake until tender crisp; we're talking about oh, 10 minutes or so.

Top with **Cheddar Cheese Sauce** (page 202).

BROWNED BEANS
Go Great with a Barbecue

Serve as the perfect complement to barbecued beef or pork. Hey, and why not add a **Mighty Caesar Barbecued Potato Salad** *(page 54) for a sizzling "boys of summer" triple play? The commercial beans pale in comparison.*

ROUND UP

- Half a pound of bacon—cut into small, bite-sized pieces
- 1 medium sweet onion—cut into small- to medium-sized pieces
- 2 jalapeño and 1 red pepper—diced fine
- ¼ cup each brown sugar and molasses
- ¼ cup maple syrup or maple-flavoured pancake syrup
- ¼ cup barbecue sauce—try **Just Like Bull's Eye** (page 205)
- 2 tablespoons **Carolina Mustard Sauce** (page 204) or prepared mustard
- 2 tablespoons each Worcestershire sauce and cider vinegar
- 1 teaspoon liquid smoke
- 2 19-ounce cans romano or white beans
- Salt, pepper and even red chili flakes to taste—if you dare!

FIRE UP

A medium-sized saucepan over medium heat, and cook the bacon until crisp. Remove the bacon to a paper-towel-lined plate.

Fry the onion and peppers in the bacon drippings, and expect to hear the following comment, "Oh man, is it ever smelling good in here!"

Whisk all of the sauce ingredients together in a bowl.

Add the beans and remaining ingredients to the onions in the saucepan, bring the bacon back in, and simmer for 10 minutes or so to reduce the sauce. Oh, and give it the odd stir to coat the beans and blend flavours.

Season the beans with salt and pepper to taste. If you really want to fire them up, toss in a few chili flakes or even a little cayenne pepper.

The beans are ready to serve, but if you want to maximize the flavours, turn the beans off and let them sit for an hour or so. Then reheat or bake them just before you're ready to eat.

THE UPSIDE OF BEING A FIRE HALL CHEF

1. Cooking gets you out of numerous fire hall duties. Oh, we cooks try to help out, but more often than not we're told, "Look, drop the mop. You just take care of the groceries and we'll take care of the rest."

2. The Golden Firehouse Rule: If you do the cooking, you don't do the dishes. So as a chef, feel free to use any and all pots, pans and plates you deem necessary or even unnecessary. I can't tell you how many times I've heard, "Jeff, is there a pot in the kitchen that you *didn't* use?"

3. It's your chance to showcase ad-lib recipe talents, when the guy you asked to pick up groceries failed to buy one or more crucial ingredients.

4. Uniform shirts boast prestigious, hard-earned perma-grease stains.

5. Groupies! I can't overstate this point enough!

6. Opinion on hotly debated issues becomes clearer as you jiggle a pocket full of coins from thrifty firefighters who choose to pay for their meals with piles of loose change they found in their lockers, pockets and under the cushions of chairs and sofas in the fire hall.

7. You shop, you get the air miles!

8. If the meal is good, there's no shortage of compliments from grateful firefighters. Here are a few examples: "Are you married?" "Your cooking sure makes it hard for me to choke down and compliment the stuff my wife serves at home." "If I were a captain, you're the kind of guy I could build a hall around." And (apologies to anyone offended, but this is a true, albeit borderline compliment), "You know, if you had breasts I'd marry you!"

One of my best customers, in terms of eating ability and level of appreciation, loved to go on and on about how much he enjoyed the meal. He was that dog in the Hanna-Barbera cartoon that ate the dog treat and bounced up in the air hugging himself: "Mmm—ohh—mmm—ohh—this is *decadent!*" His reaction to the meal made all the work well worth the effort.

Coming up later: The Downside of Being a Fire Hall Chef.

PLAIN WHITE RICE? ARE YOU CRAZY?

Yes, it's the other white side dish! Although not as popular as the good old potato, rice does make its way into firehouse cuisine. I've grown tired of plain white rice, and have found ways not only to fire up rice, but to make it complement the rest of the meal. For example, the **Rip Roarin' Risotto** (page 192) goes nicely with many meat dishes, especially those with an Italian flavour. The **Asian**, **Mediterranean**, and **Mexi(can) Rice** dishes (pages 195, 193 and 194) are self-explanatory, while **Coconut Curry Rice** (page 196) snuggles up beside an East Indian dish and **Wild Rice Casserole** (page 197) is a natural with seafood.

With the exception of the risotto recipe, I use parboiled rice in my recipes, brown parboiled if I can locate it. Parboiled—also known as converted—isn't instant; it's long-grain rice that has been partially boiled to remove much of its starch. Unlike regular long-grain rice, which you have to refrigerate overnight in order to re-fry it, parboiled rice can be re-fried soon after boiling. Also, while standard rice needs to be cooked uninterruptedly without lifting the lid, you can play with parboiled rice. Go ahead, lift the lid, check it often and, best of all, turn it off and resume cooking without goofing it up. This is especially important in a fire hall where cooking time can be interrupted by an alarm.

That reminds me of a day I was cooking lunch and a firefighter visiting from Chicago was talking to me when the gong went. I quickly shut off the elements and removed the food from the stove. As I scrambled, he asked, "What are you doing?"

"I'm driving the ladder truck," I replied. "I have to go on a call."

"Yeah but you're the cook," he said shaking his head. "In Chicago the cook stays with the meal until it's finished, and he doesn't go on calls until everyone's eaten."

Wow, and I thought the guys treated the cook with respect in *our* department! Lake Michigan must part for the firehouse cooks in Chicago.

Oh, and one more tip: instead of measuring, simply add water to a level one inch above the rice in the pot. For me, that level lines up with the first knuckle on my (historical reference coming up) Trudeau finger. Yes, you too can prepare perfect rice, but don't leave it plain. Try the following recipes and fire it up!

Rip Roarin'
RISOTTO

I can't get enough of this delicious dish. Toss out your tried-and-true traditional method of cooking rice, and get out the wooden spoon. Oh, it requires a little patience and some babysitting, but the results are amazing!

THERE'S A LOT GOING IN

- 3 tablespoons each olive oil and butter
- 1 small red onion—diced
- 1 red or orange pepper—diced
- 3 stalks of celery—diced
- 3 cloves garlic—minced
- 2 teaspoons lemon zest— the finely grated rind
- 3 tablespoons fresh parsley—chopped
- 4 tablespoons fresh herbs—try a poultry mix or 2 teaspoons Italian seasoning
- 1½ cups uncooked arborio rice— insist on it by name
- ½ teaspoon ground cumin or coriander
- ½ cup white wine
- 3½ cups chicken broth
- 2 tablespoons fresh-squeezed lemon juice
- ⅓ cup grated Parmesan cheese

BUT IT'S NOT HARD TO MAKE

Let's get the oil and butter fired up to medium in a Dutch oven or saucepan.

Get the onion, pepper, celery and garlic going. It smells great!

Stir the lemon zest and chopped herbs together and add half to the veggies.

Sauté away, my friend, until the veggies are slightly softened.

Get the rice and cumin in there, and stir until well coated.

The wine is rarin' to go to the party, so toss it into the mix as well.

Okay, let's turn the heat down to a slow boil, and stir until reduced.

Add 1 cup of the broth, and— hey, get back here! You're chained to the stove until you're done now, so get dedicated!

Stir and reduce, then add another cup of broth, and keep with the program until all the broth is gone and the rice is tender. This could take up to 40 minutes. Add a little water if it's not quite cooked.

Add the lemon juice, remaining herb mix and Parmesan cheese.

Adjust seasonings, and let stand loosely covered for 5 minutes.

Stir in a batch of **Shrimp Scampi** *(page 130) and it's Seafood Risotto!*

Mediterranean
RICE

*When you fire up **Mike's Lemon Garlic Chicken** (page 103) on the barbecue, try making a batch of this rice to saddle up beside your creation. It's also great with a pork or beef souvlaki.*

OLIVES, LEMONS, PEPPERS, THE USUAL SUSPECTS

- 1 19-ounce can Italian-style tomatoes
- 1 cup chicken broth
- 3 tablespoons olive oil
- 1¼ cups parboiled rice—brown is best
- 4 cloves garlic—minced or pressed
- 1 medium red onion—diced
- 1 red or green pepper—diced
- ¼ pound mushrooms—sliced
- The zest—a.k.a. the grated rind— of a lemon
- 1 small can sliced olives—optional

A TASTE OF THE MEDITERRANEAN IS ON ITS WAY

Drain the tomatoes, reserving the juice. Then add the juice to the chicken broth. You'll need about 2½ cups of total liquid.

Dice up the tomatoes, unless you pulled a fast one—why, you lazy slug, I'm disappointed in you—and bought diced tomatoes instead.

Combine the tomato juice, chicken broth, 1 tablespoon of the olive oil and rice. Cover and boil gently till liquid is absorbed, about 20 minutes, perhaps longer for brown rice. Remember, you can have a look at and stir parboiled rice during cooking. Let the rice stand for 15 minutes.

Meanwhile, heat the remaining olive oil in a pan, and stir-fry the garlic till fragrant. If you're wondering what fragrant garlic smells like, just drop by any firehouse around mealtime.

Add the onion and pepper and cook until they are just about soft, then add the mushrooms to the mix. When they're browned, remove the veggies from the heat.

Preheat the oven to 275 degrees.

Combine the rice, vegetables, tomatoes, lemon zest and olives. Taste and add a dash of oregano if desired. Pile into an ovenproof dish.

Bake, covered, for about 30 minutes to heat through.

MEXI RICE

Here's a perfect complement to the **Tequila Lime Chicken** *(page 169). It also goes nicely with fajitas, tacos, burritos and many other Mexican delights.*

YOU WON'T HAVE TO GO SOUTH TO FIND

- 1 19-ounce can tomatoes
- 1 cup chicken broth
- 1¼ cups parboiled rice—brown is still best
- 1 tablespoon vegetable oil
- 2 tablespoons butter
- 4 cloves garlic—minced or pressed
- 1 medium onion—diced
- 2 stalks celery—diced
- ½ red pepper—diced
- ½ tablespoon chili powder
- 1 teaspoon ground cumin

IT WON'T TAKE YOU LONG TO

Drain the tomatoes, reserving the juice. Dice up the tomatoes.

Add the tomato juice to the chicken broth until you reach about 2½ cups of total liquid.

Combine the liquid, rice and vegetable oil in a medium-sized saucepan. Cover and boil gently till moisture is absorbed, about 20 minutes, a little longer for brown rice.

Remember—unlike traditional long-grain rice—you can feel free to sneak a peek and stir the parboiled rice. Let rice stand 15 minutes.

While the rice is cooking away, let's heat the butter in a sauté pan, and stir-fry the garlic till fragrant.

Add the onion, celery and pepper to the garlic and fry till softened.

Preheat the oven to 275 degrees.

Combine the rice, vegetables, reserved tomatoes, chili powder and cumin. Taste the rice for the proper balance of spice. Fire it up with more chili powder and cumin if you like, and toss it all into an ovenproof dish.

Bake the rice casserole 30 minutes, covered, to heat through, ensuring that all liquid is fully absorbed.

Deluxe
ASIAN FRIED RICE

This is similar to a deluxe fried-rice dish found in Asian restaurants. But you don't have to serve it only with Asian food. This side dish also goes great with steak, chicken or just about anything!

CONFUCIUS SAYS YOU NEED

- 1 cup parboiled long-grain rice—brown rice rocks!
- 2 cups chicken broth
- 4 tablespoons peanut oil
- 4 cloves garlic—finely minced
- 1 tablespoon finely diced fresh ginger
- 1 medium onion—chopped coarse
- 1 cup frozen peas
- ¼ pound mushrooms—T 'em up
- Light soy sauce, added to taste
- 4-5 pork sausages boiled and cut into small pieces—optional
- 3 eggs—scrambled, cooked and diced—attendance is optional

NO NEED TO BE CONFUCIUSED, IT'S SIMPLE!

Combine the rice, chicken broth and 2 tablespoons of the peanut oil in a saucepan. (Canola or corn oil are acceptable substitutes.)

Bring the rice to a boil and simmer, covered, for 20 minutes, or until all of the moisture is absorbed. Let the rice stand 15 minutes, or even overnight in the fridge. Give the rice a fluff through with a fork.

You can also use any leftover rice, as long as you've allowed it to cool and dry out. Just break it up and you're ready to wok!

So come on, get your wok rocking. Heat it up, add the remaining peanut oil and toss in the garlic and ginger. Smells great already!

Toss in the onion, followed by the peas and mushrooms. Get stirring. Give the veggies a little shot of soy sauce if the wok is getting too dry, and cook through.

Bring on the cooked rice and sausages and work them into the mix.

As you stir the rice, simply add more soy sauce to taste.

Stir until the rice is reheated and even slightly browned in places.

Add the diced-up eggs to the mix and serve it up hot.

Coconut
CURRIED RICE

Here's one that I serve not only with East Indian dishes, but also with Asian food, chicken or pork. It's versatile and delicious!

SO YOU'LL HAVE TO FIND

- 1 cup parboiled rice—I still prefer brown
- 1 cup chicken broth
- 1 cup plus 2 tablespoons coconut milk
- 2 tablespoons vegetable oil
- 4 cloves garlic—minced or pressed
- 1 tablespoon—or more for fired up— curry paste
- 1 medium onion—chopped coarsely
- 1 cup frozen peas
- ¼ pound mushrooms—sliced

AND THEN YOU'LL HAVE TO

Combine the rice, chicken broth, coconut milk and 1 tablespoon of the oil in a saucepan.

Bring to a boil and simmer, covered, for about 20 minutes, or until all of the moisture is absorbed. Remember, you can peek at and stir parboiled rice. I know parboiled is a cheat, but hey, it works!

Allow the rice to stand 15 minutes, or even overnight if you planned ahead. The rice should be fairly dry and flake easily.

Add the remaining 1 tablespoon oil to a hot wok or frying pan. Cook garlic till fragrant.

Add curry paste and stir for 15 seconds. Talk about your fragrant!

Let's bring in the onion, and cook for 1 minute.

The peas and mushrooms are on deck, so toss them in as well, stir them up and cook them through.

The rice is revved up and ready so bring it to the party and stir through. If you find that the rice is drying out too quickly, simply add a bit of water or chicken broth.

Okay, let's give the rice a taste test. If you feel as though your rice is a little shy on the Bombay side, add a little more curry paste, and work it through the rice until everyone is completely satisfied.

This is my favourite! The heat of the curry is balanced out nicely by the smoothness of the coconut milk. Fire up a batch today!

wild
RICE CASSEROLE

When I make **Lee's Salmon Fillet** *(page 131) on the barbecue, it absolutely, positively, has to be accompanied by this casserole. It's a natural with fish, but it's also excellent with many chicken dishes.*

YOUR GROCERY LIST

- ⅔ cup wild rice—soaked in water overnight
- ¾ cup parboiled rice
- 2 10-ounce cans consommé
- 6 tablespoons butter or margarine
- 1 medium onion—diced
- ½ cup celery—diced
- ½ green pepper—diced
- 1 cup mushrooms—sliced

AND YOUR HELPFUL SET OF DIRECTIONS

Drain the wild rice and place it in a small saucepan along with 1 of the cans of consommé and 1 tablespoon of the butter or margarine. Cook the rice, covered, at a slow boil for 45 minutes. Wild rice is cooked when it pops open.

Cook the parboiled rice in the other can of consommé plus ¼ cup water. Toss in 1 tablespoon of butter or margarine to help it keep from sticking.

When both rice—or is that rices?—are finished cooking, allow them to stand for about 30 minutes, covered but away from the heat.

Stir-fry the onion, celery and green pepper in 2 tablespoons butter or margarine. Don't add the mushrooms yet!

Get the oven firing at 275 degrees.

Place the wild and parboiled rice, veggies, raw mushrooms and pats of remaining 2 tablespoons of butter in a covered casserole.

Bake for 30 minutes or until heated through.

THE DOWNSIDE OF BEING A FIRE HALL CHEF

1. The Shopping. If done off shift—which is how I do mine—it can be time consuming and momentarily expensive; well, until you shake the guys down for their share of the bill. When I cook for 16 to 20, it means pushing two shopping carts—one for work and one for my family at home. We're talking $100-plus in groceries for just one firehouse meal.

Some guys will offer to pick up groceries, while others will find excuses not to help you out. Then there are guys who offer to pick up for your next tour, and when you return to work, you discover that they're on holidays.

2. They gain the weight, you get the blame.

3. That sickening feeling in the pit of your stomach when you arrive at an alarm and a late-breaking news flash suddenly crosses your mind, *"The food!!* I forgot to turn off the stove!! Our meal is going to be ruined!"

Let's just say that it's not an accepted practice to go on the fire department frequency—monitored not only by firefighters, but by news agencies and even the general public—and say, "Control, could you get a crew to drop by number 18 station to take our food off the stove, wrap it up in foil and turn the oven off, please?" Minutes feel like hours at the call, and when you finally return to the station, there's tragic irony for all to see as smoke billows out the kitchen window. Don't laugh; this has happened to many a fire hall cook.

If this happens to you, just tell your crew, "Of course it's burnt. It's Cajun cuisine!"

4. Picky eaters. Enough said.

5. Q: What's the difference between a hungry firefighter and a terrorist?

A: There's a chance you may be able to negotiate with a terrorist.

Night shifts begin at 5:30 P.M. in our department. We work until 7:30 the following morning but we don't generally eat until 8:00 P.M. As you can imagine, the boys are hovering, and the pressure is on as the magical time approaches. One firefighter was known to say in a pathetic, weak voice, "Can't—talk. Must—conserve—energy—fading." That's why you should always buy a loaf of bread as a sacrificial pre-meal offering, pacifying the ravenous masses that are just going to pace and hang around the kitchen, asking, "Is it ready yet? Man, I'm *starving!*"

6. Zero tolerance toward "bad meal policy" heavily enforced in firehouse. Yes, you're only as good as your last goof-up. Oh, and being busy and interrupted by alarms during meal preparation is *no excuse!*

7. Zero tolerance toward "not enough to eat policy" also heavily enforced in firehouse. When in doubt, make lots! I made two huge roasters full of **Funky Fire Hall Chili** (page 170) for lunch one day, an amount that I thought was more than enough food for 16 to 20 guys. Just before lunch, my ladder crew of two was called to the repair shop to have work done on our aerial ladder. As we waited for the mechanics to finish up, we received a phone call: "You guys better stop for burgers on the way home. The chili's all gone!"

We thought, "Yeah, right, they're kidding." Well, they weren't. It was true. Here I'd picked up the food, spent the morning preparing it, and I didn't even get to try it! Apparently the gannets wolfed it down, and all went for seconds and thirds, not considering the absent ladder crew.

The only pleasure I got from the meal happened the next day when the chief—who, I understand, led the multiple-portions charge—said, "Oh, I cursed you last night, Jeff. I was at league bowling, and when I threw my ball I dropped a silent one. I was so embarrassed—I cleared 3 lanes."

WELL?

The verdict is in and it's Ups 8, Downs 7. Bottom line, "If you can't stand the heat get out of the kitchen." Yes, the job of the fire hall chef has its pressures, but it's a team game, and you'll be an MVP if you can carve a niche for yourself in the land of the pots and pans. A firehouse crew is just like a family and, just like at home, food is what brings us together. Sitting down for a meal as a crew is a chance to share a few laughs, whether it be discussing current hot topics, telling a story from home or spinning a tale drawn from our many experiences as firefighters. A great meal brightens moods and sparks spirited conversation, and it all starts with the efforts of the fire hall—or family—chef.

SPICE IT UP, GET SAUCED!

The following pages feature two Fired-Up Spice rubs, as well as a couple of tasty homemade salsas, and a number of sauces to dress up your next meal. If you tour around the cookbook you'll notice that there are a few other sauces. For example, the **Just Like Bull's Eye** and **Hawaiian Barbecue** sauces (page 205) are included in this section, but you'll also find the great **Five-Star Whiskey Brisket Sauce** (page 96) in the Hay, What's Moo section. Yes, there's more to this book than meets the spice rack!

FIRED-UP SPICE

- 3 tablespoons kosher salt—it's less bitter than iodized salt
- 2 tablespoons Spanish sweet paprika—go for quality
- 2 tablespoons roasted granulated garlic or regular granulated garlic
- 1 tablespoon fresh-ground or restaurant-style black pepper
- 1 tablespoon onion powder
- 1 tablespoon dried basil
- 1 tablespoon dried oregano
- 1 tablespoon, or more if you dare, cayenne pepper

FIRED-UP SANTA FE SPICE

- 2 tablespoons Spanish sweet paprika
- 2 tablespoons good-quality chili powder
- 2 tablespoons kosher salt
- 1 tablespoon roasted granulated garlic or regular granulated garlic
- 1 tablespoon ground coriander
- 1 tablespoon cayenne pepper
- 1 tablespoon dried oregano
- 2 teaspoons ground cumin
- 2 teaspoons fresh-ground or restaurant-style black pepper
- 2 teaspoons onion powder

For either seasoning, place the spices in a small bowl and use a whisk to combine them. Place the mix in a spice jar with a tight-fitting lid, and store in a cool, dark place. Spice generally keeps for about 6 months before losing its effectiveness, so label your next batch with a best-before date. If you're like me, though, you'll find that it never lasts that long anyway.

Simple
TOMATO SALSA

Fresh salsa makes a wonderful topping for barbecued meats. This one was inspired by firefighter Chris Blasko. Give it a try on steak, pork, chicken or even fish!

BROTHER, CAN YOU SPARE

- 6–8 ripe Roma tomatoes—diced
- ½ small red onion—diced
- 2 jalapeño peppers—seeded and diced fine
- 2 cloves garlic—minced or pressed
- ⅓ cup cilantro—coarsely chopped
- Ground cumin, kosher salt and pepper to taste
- 1 tablespoon lime juice—fresh is best

BROTHER, LEND ME A HAND

Chop what you need to chop and combine all of the ingredients, sprinkling the lime juice over top, and let the salsa stand in the fridge for 1 hour to blend the flavours.

To use as a tortilla chip dip, simply add canned crushed tomatoes.

Do a little experimenting. Try this recipe with diced mango, peach, avocado, blueberries or other favourite fruits.

Scandalous
STRAWBERRY-ORANGE SALSA

Here's a fired-up salsa that goes especially well on barbecued fish and chicken.

SO YOU SAY WE NEED

- 3 tablespoons Cantonese or regular plum sauce
- 3 tablespoons lime juice—fresh is best
- Pint of strawberries—sliced into small segments
- 2 seedless oranges—chopped into segments
- Half a small red onion—diced fine
- ⅓ bunch cilantro—chopped
- 3 jalapeño peppers—seeded and diced very fine
- The usual—you know, kosher salt and pepper to taste

AND WE NEED TO

Combine above and toss in a bowl. Refrigerate for 30 minutes to 1 hour.

CHEDDAR CHEESE SAUCE

If you're cooking broccoli or cauliflower, then I think it's best that you make up a batch of cheese sauce to drizzle over top. This recipe makes lots!

YOU NEED TO LOCATE

- 3 tablespoons butter
- 2 tablespoons flour
- 1½ cups milk—could be a little more or less
- 1 cup cheddar or marble cheese—grated
- ½ teaspoon each salt and paprika
- Dash of cayenne

THEN YOU NEED TO BUILD YOUR SAUCE

Melt butter over medium heat in a frying pan. Add the flour and whisk.

Continue stirring, and slowly add the milk a bit at a time till smooth.

Add the cheese and allow it to melt in as you stir. If you find that the consistency is too thick, then simply add a little more milk.

Season to taste with salt, paprika and cayenne.

LEMON DILL SAUCE

This sauce is wonderful over fish or asparagus.

GET TOGETHER

- 2 tablespoons each butter and flour
- 1½ cups milk—approximately
- Juice of 1 lemon
- 1–2 teaspoons of fresh dill weed—chopped fine
- Salt and pepper to taste

ARE ROUX READY?

Melt butter in a frying pan over medium heat. Add the flour, and whisk into a roux. Add the milk slowly, whisking constantly to the desired consistency. Add lemon juice and dill, salt and pepper to taste. Warm through.

TERIYAKI MARINADE

Works great on steak or chicken!

THE GOODS

- ¾ cup teriyaki or soy sauce
- ¼ cup vegetable oil
- 3 tablespoons liquid honey—melt in the microwave if necessary
- 1 teaspoon ginger powder
- 1 teaspoon garlic powder
- 1 teaspoon or more chili-garlic sauce—to fire it up!
- 3 green onions—chopped small

THE DIRECTIONS

Combine all of the ingredients in a bowl.

Place the steak or chicken in a plastic bag, toss in the teriyaki and let it meld for 4 hours for chicken to overnight for a juicy steak. Makes a great **Stacked Steak Sandwich** (page 39).

Carolina
MUSTARD SAUCE

I love this sauce. It's fantastic with a barbecued pork roast or barbecued beef. You can also use it as a barbecue baste, or as a table sauce for ham or chicken. Or mix 2 parts commercial salad dressing or mayonnaise to 1 part Carolina Mustard Sauce as a spread for sandwiches. You'll find many uses for this sweet, tangy sauce.

THE PARTICIPANTS

- ¾ cup prepared mustard
- ¾ cup red wine or apple cider vinegar
- ¼ cup sugar
- 1½ tablespoons butter or margarine
- 1 tablespoon Worcestershire
- 1½ teaspoons white pepper
- 1 teaspoon Tabasco or hot pepper sauce
- 1–2 teaspoons kosher salt— depending on your taste

HOW TO BRING THEM TOGETHER IN A SUPER SAUCE

Combine all of the participants in a medium saucepan. Simmer for 30 minutes (yes, it's the vinegar causing that funky odour) and let stand 1 hour before using. If you prefer a thicker sauce, let it reduce for a little longer, until you get the consistency you like.

CAROLINA TARTAR SAUCE

RUMMAGE THROUGH THE FRIDGE FOR

- 6 tablespoons salad dressing or mayonnaise
- 3 tablespoons sour cream
- 2 tablespoons **Carolina Mustard Sauce** (above)
- 2 tablespoons relish
- 3 tablespoons lemon juice
- Chili-garlic sauce or cayenne pepper to taste—for kicks!

BLEND AND TASTE

Yeah, like I said, blend the participants together in a bowl, and give it the old taste test. Simply add more salad dressing or mayonnaise for sweetness and a little more lemon juice and/or chili-garlic for tang.

Bring on the fish dish!

Just Like Bull's Eye
BARBECUE SAUCE

Firefighter Ken Proulx parted with his secret recipe, and since then it's become a staple in my household as there's always a bottle made up in the fridge. It's incredible on ribs, barbecued chicken or just about anything!

SIMPLY COMBINE THE FOLLOWING IN A LARGE SAUCEPAN

- 6 cups ketchup
- 1½ cups icing sugar
- 1 cup each molasses and brown sugar
- ¼ cup each prepared mustard and liquid smoke
- 1 tablespoon each Worcestershire sauce, garlic powder and crushed dried red chili flakes

AND FIRE UP THE SAUCE WITH A LITTLE HEAT

Heat the sauce over medium heat, stirring often.

Let the sauce simmer, uncovered, for ½ hour, or even longer. The flavour will intensify the longer you cook it.

Give the sauce a taste. You can add hot sauce, cayenne or another whack of crushed chilies if you like it *bold!*

HAWAIIAN BARBECUE SAUCE

Fire up the fire pit at the luau!

LAY IT OUT AND LAY IT ON

- 1 tablespoon vegetable oil
- 1 small onion—chopped finely
- 3 cloves garlic—minced or pressed
- 1 cup ketchup
- ⅓ cup liquid honey
- ¼ cup seasoned rice vinegar
- ¼ cup hoisin sauce—in your grocer's Asian foods section
- 2 teaspoons liquid smoke— it's that familiar house-fire odour
- 1 teaspoon cayenne pepper—or more if you like it smokin'!

COMEONIWANNAMAKEYA

Heat the oil in a saucepan and fry up the onion and garlic. Blend in the remaining ingredients and you're ready to barbecue. This is a great funky sauce for ribs and chicken. Aloha!

HALL-A-BLAZE SAUCE—it's Hollandaise made easy!

You'll be using this sauce for several of the recipes in this book, including **Eggs Benny**, **Ham-and-Asparagus Omelette** *and* **Steak Neptune** *(pages 11, 7 and 86). But why stop there? It goes great on salmon, asparagus and your hips. Due to space restraints I'm unable to give a nutritional breakdown, so let's just say that this sauce is a treat. Oh, and it's a snap; you make it in a blender.*

THE AMAZINGLY FAT-FREE INGREDIENTS—are my fingers crossed?

- 1⅓ cups butter—Yikes! Oh relax, it's a natural product

- 6 egg yolks—those egg whites are just going to clog your arteries

- ½ teaspoon sugar

- ½ teaspoon Tabasco sauce—more if you want to fire it up!

- ½ teaspoon dry mustard

- 1 tablespoon fresh lemon juice

IN A BLENDER? WHAT, NO WHISK AND DOUBLE BOILER?

That's right. Why fuss with bowls, whisks and double boilers when you can make this sauce quickly, easily and without fail in a blender?

Well, there is one pan involved, but it's only making a cameo. Place that whack of butter in a saucepan and bring to medium heat. We want the butter rolling to a slow boil, but not to the point that it starts to brown. Give it a stir, even a whisk if you insist on tradition.

Combine the remaining ingredients in the blender. Put on the lid unless you're hoping to decorate the walls of your kitchen.

Hit warp speed 9 on the blender and while it's running at full tilt, slowly pour the boiling butter into the egg-yolk mix in a thin stream. Once blended, allow the sauce to stand for a couple of minutes. This will allow the blaze to thicken.

If you're making this for seafood, you may want to add another tablespoon of lemon juice to the sauce for added zzzzzzzzip!

This makes about 1½ cups of sauce, or roughly the same as one envelope of the powdered hollandaise sauce. I confess, I've been known to cheat on occasion.

THE BONDS THAT TIE

One afternoon, we decided to pull out the backboard and collars, and prac-
tise immobilization for our daily drill session, to simulate how we would
package a patient who had a suspected neck or back injury. Firefighter
Mike volunteered to be the victim—I mean patient—and lay on the backboard while we applied the cervical collar to his neck and tied the cotton
cravats across his shoulders, hips, thighs, head, ankles and hands, so that
he and the backboard became one, making any movement impossible. In
fact, once we had finished tying him in, we even stood the backboard up-
right, and Mike remained static, proof that we had done a perfect job of
immobilizing him.

Well, now that he was at our mercy and completely unable to move, we
decided to have some fun. It was a beautiful June day and we didn't want to
deny Mike the opportunity to enjoy the midday sun, so four of us carried
him across the busy street on the backboard stretcher and laid him down
on a bus bench in front of a Dairy Queen.

"Hey! What are you guys doing? Get back here," Mike yelled from his
incarcerated position, as we all ran back across the street to the firehouse.

It was like a scene from Candid Camera. We closed the overhead door
and watched through its windows as people walked or drove by, rubber-
necking with curiosity, wondering why on earth this seemingly critical-care
patient had been abandoned. Had he fallen out of the back of an ambu-
lance? Had he been dropped from a medevac helicopter in the sky? As you
can imagine, we were all in hysterics, as Bondage Man could do nothing
but look straight up at the sky from his imprisoned position.

BONG, BONG sounded the alarm!!

"Oh, shoot! We've got a call!" we yelled as we quickly opened the big
door and scrambled across the street in a panic to Mike, working madly to
undo the many straps that held him down, and spring him from his cocoon
so that he could attend the call with us.

Sure, I know, it's all fun and games—until you almost miss an alarm.

NO REALLY, I SHOULDN'T ... Desserts

DESSERTS

DESPERATELY SEEKING DECADENCE

What's the number-one dessert at the fire hall? Ice cream, ice cream, ice cream! Get at it early, though, or you'll find that your fellow workers have mined the butterscotch vein. But don't make the mistake of digging in to the other shift's leftover ice cream. This is a sore spot in platoon relations, and firefighter hit men have been known to infuse ice cream with laxatives in an attempt—successful, I might add—to dissuade others from stealing their treasured stock.

Sometimes, on a hot summer afternoon, we'll go out for ice cream cones. The danger is that many a prankster fire-truck driver will watch out of the corner of his eye and just as his passenger attempts to take a lick from his cone, he'll slam on the brakes, driving the cone into the victim's face. As he wipes his mug, the dupe—ranking as high as a district chief—will yell, "What are you doing?" The poker-faced driver will innocently claim, "A dog! A dog just ran out in front of us!"

I think back to working with Ralph Okrainec. Ralphie-boy loved making dessert, and soon the firefighters at the hall made it into a competition between Ralph and me to see who could come up with the best offering. They egged us on to go bigger and better. Being suckers, we fell victim to their praises, and just kept raising the bar on each other, creating more and more elaborate desserts. We knew we'd gone too far when we found that it was costing us $15 to construct a cheesecake. Ralph and I kept saying that it was time to cut back on desserts, but we never did, at least not until I got transferred. Since then, I've toned down my act.

Getting out of the house with something I'd worked on for two hours without my sweet-toothed wife noticing was a major challenge. I don't know how many times I heard her exclaim, "Don't tell me you're taking that to work!"

So, to keep the peace, I'd have to make my family a dessert in addition to the one I made for the hall. Work, work, work.

Here are my favourite dessert ideas, from the simple and cost effective to **That $15 Kahlua Cheesecake** (page 216). Just say no to plain ice cream, go for broke and fire up your dessert menu today!

HARD-TIMES PUDDING

A firefighter I worked with once asked, "What's the main ingredient in bread pudding?" (Insert eye roll here.) Although this isn't a true bread pudding, it is a tasty, sweet loaf in a delicious sauce. I snagged this one from firefighter Ken "Squeaky" Mills. Quick, simple, cheap and delicious! Let's call it the Anti-$15 Kahlua Cheesecake.

YOU PROBABLY HAVE THESE ITEMS ON HAND

- 1 cup flour
- 2 teaspoons baking powder
- ¼ teaspoon salt
- 2 tablespoons sugar
- 1 tablespoon ground cinnamon
- ½ cup milk—buttermilk is even better
- 1 cup raisins
- 1½ cups boiling water
- 1 cup brown sugar
- 2 tablespoons butter

YOU CAN MAKE THIS WITHOUT INCIDENT

Preheat the oven to 375 degrees

Whisk the flour, baking powder, salt, sugar and cinnamon together in a bowl. Do 4 sets of 30 push-ups to remove any feeling of guilt.

Toss in the milk and raisins, and work it into a ball. You may need to add a little more milk if it's too dry, or more flour if it's too moist.

Place the dough in the centre of a greased 6-quart baking dish.

Flatten the ball just enough so that there's some space on all sides for expansion—1½ inches or so should do it.

Get the water boiling and pour it into a separate bowl. Add the brown sugar and butter, and stir until the butter melts.

Pour the liquid over and around the flour batter.

Bake, covered, for 30 minutes or until golden brown. Allow the pudding to cool a few minutes so that the sauce can thicken.

Slice the pudding into portions and place each serving in a bowl.

It goes without saying that you need to place a firefighter-sized scoop of vanilla ice cream— 1½ quarts, approximately—on each slab.

ORANGE CARROT CAKE

This cake is very moist and delicious. It makes lots and requires no advanced culinary skills. Just mix it all together and bake.

RAID THE CUPBOARDS FOR THE GOODS

- 3 cups white flour—I go for the unbleached variety myself
- 2 cups sugar
- 2½ teaspoons baking soda
- 1 teaspoon salt
- 2½ teaspoons ground cinnamon
- 2 cups carrots—shredded, as in fired through the grater
- 1¼ cups canola oil
- 2 teaspoons vanilla
- 1 teaspoon orange peel—finely grated
- 3 eggs
- 1 11-ounce can mandarin oranges— with the juice
- 1 cup raisins

LOOK AT HOW LITTLE THERE IS TO DO

Preheat the oven to 350 degrees.

Combine all of the ingredients (except raisins) with an electric mixer at low speed until moistened. Then beat for 2 minutes at high speed.

Bring on the raisins and mix through with a spoon.

Pour the batter into two 9- x 9-inch cake pans, or a greased 9- x 13-inch baking dish.

Bake for 50–55 minutes. Insert a toothpick in the centre, and if it comes out dry, you're done, cake!

Allow the cake to cool before frosting. What frosting, you ask? Why ...

HERE'S A GREAT FROSTING

- 1 ½-pound package cream cheese
- 3 cups icing sugar
- 2 tablespoons melted butter or margarine
- 1 teaspoon vanilla

Combine all and beat till smooth. Frost the cooled cake, and refrigerate at least 1 hour before serving it to the salivating masses!

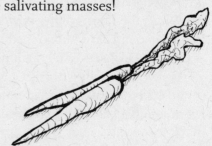

Mega Banana
COFFEE CAKE

Our friend Cathie Filyk passed along this sweet gem, and it's over-the-top decadent. In her original recipe, she uses chocolate chips in both layers rather than my "raisins-in-the-middle" deviation, but then she is a woman, and let's face it, chocolate is an essential component of their lifestyle!

ALL INGREDIENTS, OUT FOR ROLL CALL!

- 1 cup margarine or butter—softened
- 2 cups sugar
- 2 eggs—beaten
- 1 teaspoon vanilla
- 6 previously frozen bananas—mashed up
- 1½ cups each all-purpose and whole-wheat flour
- 2 teaspoons each baking powder and baking soda
- ½ teaspoon salt
- 1 cup low-fat sour cream— 14% fat if it makes you happy
- ¼ cup packed brown sugar mixed with 1 teaspoon cinnamon
- ½ cup raisins
- 5 ounces milk-chocolate chips

ROLL 'EM OUT!

Preheat the oven to 350 degrees.

It's manly power tool time as we fetch the electric mixer from the workshop, affix the beaters, and cream the butter and sugar.

Add the eggs and hit the throttle on the mixer again until smooth.

Here's a Cathie tip. Freeze your aging bananas, and thaw them when you find the time to bake. The mushy guys make the best banana bread.

Toss in the vanilla and bananas, and fire up the mixer once again.

Let's form our dry team. In a separate bowl, whisk the two flours, baking powder, baking soda and salt together. Add a third of the dry guys to the bananas and mix. Add half the sour cream, another third of the dry ingredients, the rest of the sour cream, and the remaining dries, mixing after each addition.

Batter up! Grease a 9- x 13-inch lasagna pan, and pour in half of the batter. Top with half the brown sugar-cinnamon mix and the raisins.

Top with the remaining batter, the rest of the sugar-cinnamon combo, and bring on the milk-chocolate chips to finish up.

Bake for 45–50 minutes or until cooked right through.

PEACHES 'N' CREAM PIE

This is a hybrid recipe—part fruit pie and part cheesecake. It's easy to make, and so good! Not as in "good for you" perhaps, but a great treat nonetheless! Thanks to our friend Liz Appleby for sharing this with us.

YOUR PANTRY WILL BE DEPLETED BY

- ¾ cup white flour
- 1 teaspoon baking powder
- ½ teaspoon salt
- 3 teaspoons margarine—softened
- 1 egg
- 1 5½-ounce package instant vanilla pudding and pie filling mix
- 1 28-ounce can sliced peaches—drain, but reserve some juice
- 1 ½-pound package cream cheese—at room temperature
- 1½ tablespoons reserved peach juice
- ¾ cup sugar
- Cinnamon "let me in"

YOU CAN MAKE THIS WITHOUT LOSING YOUR TEMPER!

Preheat the oven to 350 degrees.

Combine the flour, baking powder, salt, margarine, egg and pie filling with a mixer for 2 minutes. It should be crumbly. Not lousy crummy, texture crumby!

Spread out the crumbs evenly on a greased 9- or 10-inch pie plate. Compact the crumbs with your hand to make an even crust. Keep the crust going up the sides of the pie plate as well.

Fan the peaches in an even circle around the outer rim of the crust. Butt them all up against each other. Fall into line: Left, right, left, right. Fill centre with remaining peaches.

Get the electric mixer going on the cream cheese, peach juice and sugar, and blend till smooth. Whatever you do, refrain from sampling the topping or it'll never make it onto the pie. Remember, you can always lick the bowl after. You're the cook, so you get first dibs.

Spread the topping evenly over the peaches. Sprinkle with cinnamon.

Bake for 35 minutes. The cream cheese should be light golden brown on top. Refrigerate for at least 1 hour before serving.

FLAMING BANANAS

Or if you really want to impress your guests, call it Bananas Flambé. Firefighter Curt Cyr's our guest chef for this simple yet sensational dessert.

THERE ARE ONLY 5 INGREDIENTS

- ½ cup butter
- ½ cup brown sugar
- ¼ cup dark rum
- 4 large bananas—sliced
- Crushed walnuts

AND THERE ARE ONLY A FEW STEPS

Melt the butter in a frying pan over medium–low heat.

Add the brown sugar and mix through the butter. Heat to a slow boil. Once the foam from the butter has subsided, you're ready to ...

Bring rum to the mix. Man, that rum smells good. Maybe I'll just have a rum and Coke here while I'm ... Hey! Get back to work

You'll probably need to whisk the ingredients to keep them together. If it looks like one happy combination then ...

Turn down the heat and add the bananas. Heat until just warmed. Do NOT boil. If you cook the bananas too long they'll turn mushy and grey. Believe me, it's not a pretty sight.

Toss the walnuts over the top and serve over vanilla or, even better, butterscotch ice cream.

If you want to be fancy—and don't mind your smoke alarm going off—you can light the mixture on fire to burn off the alcohol.

I said you can light it up, but to be honest, I never have. I guess I just love the house I live in more than fancy culinary theatrics. As for trying it at the firehouse, well, as you can imagine, one goof-up there and I'd never be able to live it down for the rest of my career.

Coconut Bananas anyone? Let's try a Thai dessert! Warm a 14-ounce can of coconut milk in a pan, whisk in a dash of salt and up to 5 table-spoons sugar. Add 4 sliced bananas and warm. Thanks to Mary-Jane Feeke of Benjamin's in Selkirk, Manitoba, for that suggestion!

That $15
KAHLUA CHEESECAKE

It"s my favourite!

THE CRUST—is solid!

- 1½–2 cups Oreo cookie crumbs—depending on pan size
- ¼–⅓ cup melted butter—ditto

THE FILLING—is incredible!

- 1½ cups milk-chocolate chips
- 2 tablespoons butter
- ¼ cup Kahlua liqueur
- 2 ½-pound packs of low-fat cream cheese at room temp—low fat?
- 1 cup low-fat or non-fat sour cream—who am I kidding? Here, have a slice of low-fat cheesecake! Ha, ha!
- 2 large eggs
- ½ cup sugar
- ¼ teaspoon salt

THE TOPPING—should be illegal!

- 1 cup milk-chocolate chips
- ⅓ cup light corn syrup or regular corn syrup. How many calories is that?
- ¼ cup Kahlua liqueur
- 1 tablespoon milk

THE METHOD TO THE MADNESS
—is well worth your time!

Preheat the oven to 325 degrees.

Combine the crust ingredients and press them into a springform pan.

In a saucepan over low heat melt the chocolate chips with butter and Kahlua. If it starts to separate on you, just beat it with a whisk.

Beat the remaining filling ingredients with an electric mixer in a bowl. Add the melted chocolate mix and beat. Pour over the crust. Bake for 45 minutes to an hour or until just set up. Cool for 1 hour.

You're licking the bowl and beaters, aren't you? I knew it. I sensed it.

The cake should drop in height, leaving a ridge around the edge. Perfect. Now you've got a spot to put the decadent topping.

Melt the topping ingredients in a saucepan over low heat, and pour over the cake until it just reaches the lip. Don't overfill. Now, carefully move the cake off to the fridge for 4 hours to overnight.

For a finishing touch, you can combine ½ cup icing sugar with ⅛ teaspoon vanilla and 1 tablespoon milk, and drizzle some over each individual slice.

AMARETTO CHEESECAKE
with Kahlua Topping

Imagine two great liqueurs in one desperately decadent cheesecake. Hey, even dieters have "cheat days!" Come on, indulge: life is good, my friends!

THE CRUST

- 1 cup graham wafer crumbs
- 3 tablespoons butter, softened
- 2 teaspoons ground almonds

THE FILLING

- 3 ½-pound packages cream cheese— at room temperature
- ½ cup sugar
- 3 eggs
- ⅓ cup sour cream—low fat for sure!
- ⅔ cup whipping cream— the high octane, 35% stuff
- ½ cup Amaretto liqueur— speaking of high octane

THE TOPPING

- 6 tablespoons milk-chocolate chips
- 2 tablespoons corn syrup
- 2 tablespoons Kahlua liqueur

THE METHOD

In a bowl, blend the graham wafer crumbs, butter and almonds until the crumbs hold together. Pat flat onto bottom of pan. Chill. Not you, the crust! Come on, we just got started here.

Preheat the oven to 325 degrees.

In a new bowl, beat the cream cheese and sugar till smooth. Add the eggs one at a time, beating well after each addition. Beat in the sour cream. Stir in the whipping cream and Amaretto with a spoon. Pour into the crust. Bake for 1 hour. Allow it to cool 1 hour.

In a small saucepan, melt the chocolate chips and corn syrup over low heat. Add the Kahlua. Remove from the heat.

Drizzle the topping over the cake. Chill in the fridge for several hours. One small piece each will do it, unless you're carbo-loading for a marathon. In which case, go nuts!

You could also wait and add the topping after slicing and plating each piece. Then drizzle. Hey, you're going to have your own show on Food-TV!

NECTARINE COBBLER

This is a must-bake recipe when the nectarines are in season. For variety, you can also mix blueberries with the nectarines. It's a solid marriage.

THE FABULOUS FILLING

- 4 pounds of ripe nectarines, skin on, sliced into wedges—blueberries and/or strawberries can also be added without incident
- ¾ cup sugar
- ⅓ cup unbleached flour
- 2 tablespoons lemon juice

THE TANTALIZING TOPPING

- 1¼ cups unbleached white flour plus 1 cup whole-wheat flour
- 6 tablespoons white sugar
- 1 tablespoon baking powder
- ¾ teaspoon salt
- ½ cup margarine—softened
- 2 large eggs
- ¾ cup plus 2 tablespoons buttermilk

THE MOUTH-WATERING METHOD
—Oh stop it, you idiot!

Preheat the oven to 400 degrees.

Combine the filling ingredients, place them in a 9- x 13-inch lasagna dish, and bake at 400 degrees for 15 minutes, uncovered.

Meanwhile, whisk the flours, sugar, baking powder and salt together in a bowl. Cut in the margarine, dropping it in as small pieces. Fetch the power tool! Fire up the electric mixer and go to town till you get a uniform coarse consistency. Think tiny dough balls.

Combine the eggs and buttermilk. Make a well in the centre of the coarse dough and mix them in with a spoon until a batter forms.

When the filling is ready, remove from the oven, and drop spoonfuls of batter over top of the filling. Twelve evenly spaced blobs should do. Don't worry; when the batter rises, the biscuit topping will merge together.

Turn the oven down to 375 degrees and bake for about 30 minutes, until lightly browned.

Cool 15 minutes and serve with a mound of vanilla ice cream.

JOHNNY APPLE CRISP

This is a staple dessert at the fire hall. Thanks to firefighter John Senkowsky, who passed along this great version of Apple Crisp to us.

SEE IF YOU HAPPEN TO HAVE

- 6 large apples
- Lemon juice
- ⅔ cup white sugar
- Ground cinnamon
- 1¼ cups brown sugar
- 1¾ cups flour
- 1 cup melted margarine
- ¾ cup quick-cooking oats—that explains the crisp component

ACT 1

Preheat the oven to 350 degrees.

Slice up the apples, tossing as you go with just enough lemon juice to coat lightly—this keeps them from turning that ugly brown.

Toss with white sugar.

Grease a 9- x 13-inch lasagna dish and spread the apples over the bottom.

Sprinkle the apples with cinnamon.

ACT 2

Combine ½ cup of the brown sugar, 1 cup of the flour, and ½ cup of the melted margarine. The consistency will be dough-like. Spread it over the apples evenly and pack lightly on top.

EPILOGUE

Combine the remaining brown sugar, flour and margarine with the oats. Crumble the mixture and spread evenly over the apple crisp as the final topping.

Bake for 35–40 minutes or until heated through and light brown on top.

Oh, that smells so good! Now get out the vanilla ice cream!

ICE CREAM

OREO MUDSLIDE

Thanks to firefighter Ralph Okrainec for this excellent dessert. As I mentioned earlier, he was our go-to dessert guy when we were stationed together. Chocolate pudding, whipped cream, cream cheese and Oreo cookies. It sounds as good as it tastes. Top-drawer results, Ralphie!

HERE'S YOUR GROCERY LIST

- 1 1-pound package Oreo cookies

- ¼ cup butter—at room temperature

- 1 ½-pound package light cream cheese—also at room temperature

- 1 cup icing sugar

- 1 teaspoon vanilla

- 2 packages instant chocolate pudding

- 3 cups milk

- 4 cups whipped cream—you can cheat and use prepared whipped cream

HERE'S YOUR METHOD OF OPERATION

Crush the cookies and set them aside—get your hands out of there!

In a mixing bowl whip the butter, cream cheese, icing sugar and vanilla together—well, at least wash your hands first!

In a separate bowl combine pudding mix with 3 cups milk. I know, I know, the package instructions say 4 cups—2 each—but I'm telling you that you're going to want 3, for added sweetness.

Mix for 2 minutes. Let the pudding stand in the fridge until the proper consistency is obtained.

Blend the pudding and cream cheese mixture together.

Fold in the whipped cream until just combined.

Place ⅓ of the Oreos on the bottom of a 9- x 13-inch lasagna dish.

Cover with ½ of the pudding mix. Repeat the layering process.

Sprinkle the remaining ⅓ of the Oreos on top of the mudslide.

Put the slide in the fridge until serving time. It can even be overnight. Yeah, as if anything in the fridge makes it till morning in the firehouse.

Check to see if the coast is clear. No one around? Then proceed to …

Lick the bowl. Go on, get your head right in there—until it's sparkling clean and you're riddled with guilt.

Oreo Blizzard
ICE CREAM CAKE

Do you have kids coming over? I've yet to meet a little—or big—kid who doesn't love this quick and easy classic. And it's a great dessert for any confirmed choco-holic. It appears that the 12-step program is out the window—again!

THAT'S ALL I NEED?—If you're dieting, read that as a statement, not a question

- 2 quarts of your favourite vanilla ice cream
- 1 1-pound box Oreo cookies—more if you're unable to resist the temptation of snacking while you work
- ⅓ cup melted butter
- A springform pan—one of those cheesecake contraptions
- Several mini-Oreo cookies—for garnish

AND THAT'S ALL I NEED TO DO?

Allow the ice cream to soften on the counter while you get your butt going on the crust.

Crunch, munch, mangle—yes, totally destroy the entire bag of Oreo cookies with a rolling pin, food processor or under the wheels of your SUV—ensuring that the vehicle is in 4-wheel low for this operation. The consistency should be fairly fine.

Place 2 cups of the crunched-up cookies in a bowl, add the melted butter and mix it all together with a spoon.

Press the mixture onto the bottom of a lightly greased spring-form pan to form the crust. Depending on the size of the pan you're using, you may have to make up a little more crust. Crunch, crunch!

Take the remaining violated Oreos—minus 2 tablespoons—and blend them with a wooden spoon into the softened ice cream.

Pour the ice cream mixture over the cookie crust.

Sprinkle the reserved 2 table-spoons of mangled Oreos over top.

Place mini-Oreos over the top, in a circle around the edge or as desired. Hey, presentation is important!

Freeze for several hours until it's completely frozen and set.

Thanks to our friend Diane McNaughton for this recipe.

LADDER 649

"Lotto 649 is $10 million this week. Who's in for tickets?" is the common cry heard in many a fire hall. Some guys have even developed elaborate numerical systems and annual membership schemes involving a group of firefighters in hopes of hitting it big.

I'm not a lottery player unless I'm at the firehouse. The reason? I know that if I ever say, "I'm not in," the boys will hit pay dirt, and I'll be the only one still working.

One day at morning coffee one of the firefighters—we'll call him Pete—asked, "How did we do last night with our numbers?"

The guy whose job it was to buy them tossed the tickets on the table and replied, "I don't know. I haven't had a chance to check them."

"I'll check them," Pete offered, adding the often-heard line, "We might not even have to be at work today. We could already be rich."

Pete opened up the newspaper to the lottery number, and methodically worked his way through the tickets. All of a sudden a look of shock came across his face. He dropped the rest of the tickets and, with his jaw ajar, looked at the numbers, the ticket, the numbers, the ticket, the numbers, the ticket, the numbers and the ticket before taking a few hyperventilated breaths and announcing, "Guys ... g-g-guys! We ... we ... I think we WON! Ten million dollars! Here ... check the numbers, just to be sure!"

Another firefighter grabbed the ticket from his hand and asked one of the boys to read the numbers. "He's right! We did win!!"

With the numbers confirmed, they all jumped around celebrating like idiots, while Pete went to the phone to tell his wife the incredible news. When he came back to the kitchen, he asked, "Now what do we do? How do we claim our prize? I can't believe this! We're millionaires!"

"Well, first we should check our ticket again, just to be double sure. Here, Pete, I'll read the numbers to you again."

"That's them!" Pete screamed. "We got all six! We're millionaires!"

"Oh, and what's the date on the ticket?" the firefighter asked.

"Let's see here, the 18th ... wait a second ... that's *this* Saturday! You [bad word] guys! You bought last night's winning numbers this morning and put the ticket in with the others, didn't you!!"

METRIC CONVERSION CHART

Volume

¼ teaspoon	1.25 mL
½ teaspoon	2.5 mL
1 teaspoon	5 mL
2 teaspoons	10 mL
1 tablespoon	15 mL
⅛ cup	30 mL
¼ cup	60 mL
⅓ cup	80 mL
½ cup	120 mL
⅔ cup	160 mL
¾ cup	180 mL
1 cup	240 mL
1½ cups	350 mL
2 cups (1 pint)	475 mL
3 cups	700 mL
4 cups (1 quart)	950 mL

Weight

1 ounce	28 g
4 ounces (¼ pound)	113 g
⅓ pound	150 g
8 ounces (½ pound)	230 g
⅔ pound	300 g
12 ounces (¾ pound)	340 g
1 pound (16 ounces)	450 g

SECONDARY SEARCH and RESCUE

Please don full protective firefighting gear before entering

About the AUTHOR

Cookbook writing is just the latest in a long string of creative careers for Winnipeg firefighter Jeff Derraugh. After graduating from the University of Manitoba in 1981, Jeff began writing and voicing skits for morning-show radio. Soon landing his own show on Winnipeg's 92 CITI-FM, he hosted various time slots over the following seven years. Jeff's next stint was as a senior writer for Western Canada Lotteries, where he won a North American Batchy award for a radio commercial that he wrote and produced.

In 1990, Jeff switched to the related field of firefighting (radio station, fire station—what's the difference?) but kept his hand in radio as a free-lance voice-over performer. Jeff also moonlighted for three seasons as the writer/host of the nationally syndicated radio program *The Comedy Show*. As a firefighter, he volunteered his writing and character-voice skills to the non-profit stayingalive.ca website, for which he helped create an interactive fire-safety game and CD for children.

Although not professionally trained as a chef, Jeff has had a lifelong love of food and cooking. Finding his niche as a fire hall chef, he learned the art of cooking from the firefighters he's worked with, and he continues to take a keen interest in developing new recipes to satisfy the demands of his hungry families at work and at home.